WILDLIFE SANCTUARIES & THE AUDUBON SOCIETY

John M. "Frosty" Anderson

WILDLIFE SANCTUARIES &

THE AUDUBON SOCIETY

Places to Hide and Seek

University of Texas Press, Austin

LIBRARY OF CONGRESS
CATALOGING-IN-PUBLICATION DATA

Anderson, John M. (John Merrick)
    Wildlife sanctuaries and the Audubon Society :
places to hide and seek / John M. "Frosty" Anderson. — 1st ed.
        p.   cm.
    ISBN 0-292-70498-4 (cloth : alk. paper). —
ISBN 0-292-70499-2 (pbk. : alk. paper)
    1. Wildlife refuges—United States.
    2. National Audubon Society.   I. Title.
    II. Title: Places to hide and seek.
QL84.2.A53   2000
333.95'416'0973—dc21   99-44164

To my wife, Nancy Jane, and all the men and women

who managed those places to hide and seek.

CONTENTS

Foreword by Donal C. O'Brien Jr.   xi

Introduction: Places to Hide and Seek   xv

1. Paul J. Rainey Sanctuary, Abbeville, Louisiana   I

2. Green Island Sanctuary, Rio Hondo, Texas   25

3. Lillian Annette Rowe Sanctuary, Gibbon, Nebraska   34

4. Maine Coastal Islands Sanctuary, Medomak, Maine   51

5. Vingt-et-une Sanctuary, Smith Point, Texas   56

6. Emily Winthrop Miles Sanctuary, Sharon, Connecticut   68

7. Sydnes Island Sanctuary, Bridge City, Texas   95

8. Constitution Island Marsh Sanctuary, Garrison, New York   108

9. Corkscrew Swamp Sanctuary, Naples, Florida   134

10. Lake Okeechobee Sanctuary, Okeechobee, Florida   143

11. Sabal Palm Grove Sanctuary, Brownsville, Texas   146

12. Starr Ranch Sanctuary, Trabuco Canyon, California   153

13. Edward Brigham Alkali Lake Sanctuary,
Jamestown, North Dakota   175

14. Francis Beidler Forest Sanctuary,
Harleyville, South Carolina   197

15. Tampa Bay Sanctuaries, Tampa, Florida   225

Conclusion   243

Index   247

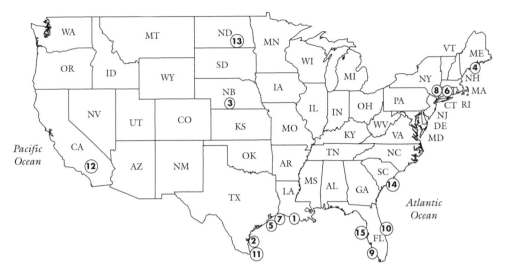

Map and short logistics description of the fifteen sanctuaries in the book.

1 Paul J. Rainey, LA: Ten miles off shore from Intracoastal City in Vermilion Bay.

2 Green Island, TX: South Texas, Lower Laguna Madre, near Rio Hondo.

3 Lillian Annette Rowe, NE: North of the Platte River, near Gibbon, east of Kearney.

4 Maine Coastal Islands, ME: Off the coast east of Medomek in Muscongus Bay.

5 Vingt-et-une, TX: Near Smith Point, at the mouth of Galveston Bay.

6 Miles Sanctuary, CT: Four miles east of Sharon, in the northwest corner of Connecticut.

7 Sydnes Island, TX: In Sabine Lake, near the mouth of the Sabine River.

8 Constitution Island, NY: East side of the Hudson River near Garrison, across the Hudson River east from West Point Academy.

9 Corkscrew Swamp, FL: Northeast of Naples, west of Immokalee.

10 Okeechobee, FL: Near north end of Lake Okeechobee.

11 Sabal Palm Grove, TX: Southmost Road, Brownsville, on the Rio Grande.

12 Starr Ranch, CA: South of Los Angeles, northeast of Mission Viejo, near Trabuco Canyon.

13 Alkali Lake, ND: North of Jamestown, near Spiritwood Lake.

14 Francis Beidler, SC: About 35 miles northwest of Charleston, near Summerville and Harleyville in Four Hole Swamp.

15 Tampa Bay, FL: Halfway down the State on the Gulf Coast (west) side.

FOREWORD

It is a great pleasure and a special honor to write this foreword to *Wildlife Sanctuaries and the Audubon Society*. John M. "Frosty" Anderson was one of the National Audubon Society's great "living legends." I had the privilege of knowing Frosty for over two decades and of working with him on behalf of birds and other wildlife and their habitat. No one has done more for wildlife than this modest man who had the best sense of humor of anyone I've known.

Frosty served as the manager of the nation's oldest duck club, the Winous Point Duck Club on the southwest corner of Lake Erie. It was here that the National Audubon Society found him and hired him away to serve as senior vice president for all of our sanctuaries—a position he held with great distinction until his retirement.

Frosty's experience, common sense, and good judgment combined to make him an exceptional conservation leader. One of the reasons for Frosty's success was his rare ability to take a strong position for what he knew to be right and still retain the respect of those who opposed him.

It is widely known that Guy Bradley was the first wildlife warden of the National Audubon Society to be murdered while trying to protect great and snowy egrets from plume hunters. It is less known that two other Audubon wardens met the same fate before protection of birds and other wildlife was taken seriously by the general public.

As Frosty so well documents in *Wildlife Sanctuaries and the Audubon Society*, each species of wildlife requires a unique combination of plants, climate, soil, and water to survive. Under Frosty's supervision, the Everglade kite population in Florida, faced with extinction in the 1960s, has been restored to safe levels. The brown pelican, completely extirpated in the Pelican State, Louisiana, and reduced to a few struggling pairs along the Texas coast in the 1960s, is now a common sight throughout the Gulf Coast wetlands. Audubon's protection of the reddish egret and roseate spoonbill has removed them from the endangered species category. The wild whooping crane population at last count was 182. While still an endangered species, 4 or 5 individuals stop in the spring at the Lillian Annette Rowe Sanctuary on the Platte River in Nebraska, along with about 110,000 sandhill cranes, approximately 25 percent of the North American population.

In 1953 the roar of chain saws was heard throughout the world's last remnant of virgin cypress swamp near Naples, Florida, in which the endangered wood stork nested. That the ancient trees and storks are still there is due to the establishment of National Audubon's Corkscrew Swamp Wildlife Sanctuary. Under wise management, Corkscrew Swamp has become one of our nation's most popular natural areas, as well as an outstanding educational facility.

Along with ecosystem preservation and restoration, education has played a dominant role in our sanctuary management program. To meet the requirements of what it takes to be an Audubon sanctuary manager, one must be an outstanding wildlife ecologist, an experienced wildlife enforcement agent, research scientist, and teacher.

Keeping suitable habitat available for birds and other wildlife, from Maine to California and from Texas to North Dakota, requires the right men and women in the right places at the right time. The plants and animals on Audubon Wildlife Sanctuaries speak well for the personnel in charge of them.

In *Wildlife Sanctuaries and the Audubon Society*, a rather intricate character is revealed. The author's casual tone does not disguise his profound love for wildlife. He can be playful in reference to "flat-faced fowl," "hootie owls," and "winged vermin," yet he is deeply penetrating in his plea for protection and management of predators. He manages to tease his readers while being very intense about his favorite subjects: wildlife and wildlife managers on National Audubon Society Sanctuaries.

I know you will enjoy *Wildlife Sanctuaries and the Audubon Society* and meeting Audubon's incomparable Frosty Anderson.

Donal C. O'Brien Jr.
Chairman of the Board
National Audubon Society

INTRODUCTION:

PLACES TO HIDE AND SEEK

At the beginning of the twentieth century, long before "endangered species" became a household term, the forerunners of the National Audubon Society were determined to set aside essential habitat for birds. Pioneers in wildlife conservation such as George Bird Grinnell, William Dutcher, T. Gilbert Pearson, Teddy Roosevelt, and Ludlow Griscom realized that, in order to survive, each species requires a unique combination of plants, animals, climate, soil, and water. In addition to these environmental factors, birds of value to the millinery trade or as food for the table had to be protected from market hunters.

Early in the twentieth century, the Florida Audubon Society, then in its infancy, was determined to set aside, as a sanctuary, an egret rookery at Cuthbert Lake in the Florida Everglades. At the time, an ounce of gold was worth thirty-two dollars, as were the plumes of a single egret. Since egret plumes were literally worth their weight in gold, it is not surprising that plume hunters looked upon any egret colony as a source of instant wealth.

Guy Bradley, a young man with an intense interest in wildlife and a native of Cape Sable, Florida, was thoroughly familiar with Cuthbert Lake. He readily accepted the Florida Audubon Society's offer to patrol and protect this rookery for the generous salary of thirty-five dollars per month. Kirk Munroe, of the Florida Audubon Society, wrote to Mrs. Kingsmill Marrs, president of Florida Audubon, about his young friend, describing him as "a thorough woodsman, a plume hunter by occupation before the passage of the present law, since which time, as I have ample testimony, he has not killed a bird . . . I know of no better man for game warden in the whole state."

On July 8, 1905, plume hunters murdered Guy Bradley. Later two other Audubon sanctuary wardens met the same fate.

In those early days, the Florida Audubon Society, like the Audubon Societies in Massachusetts and New Jersey, was reluctant to become an affiliate of the National Association of Audubon Societies. It took the diplomacy and organizational skill of Carl W. Buchheister to weld the reluctant state Audubon Societies into what is now the National Audubon Society.

Today the common egret is truly common; the snowy egret is likewise; and the reddish egret is out of danger. Egret plumes no longer appear on ladies' hats; egret breasts are nestled down on eggs or young in nests instead of roasting pans. Can we conclude that Guy Bradley did not die in vain?

In those days, state and federal wildlife agencies showed little or no concern for any wildlife species not ranked as "economically important." Hunters were willing to buy licenses to hunt waterfowl, doves, and gallinaceous birds such as turkeys, grouse, and quail, thus providing some income for the agencies. Consequently, some effort was put forth by federal wildlife enforcement agents to protect and manage migratory species such as waterfowl, woodcocks, and doves, while responsibility for nonmigrants such as quail, grouse, and turkeys was left up to the states. Over lengthy and determined opposition, state and federal laws were eventually enacted that outlawed the sale of wild birds for food and feathers. While such action came too late to save the passenger pigeon, it provided vital support to the Audubon sanctuary managers.

But no matter how effective protection from nets and guns may prove to be, each species has special requirements for nesting, brood rearing, and escape from natural enemies. Meeting these requirements and protecting birds from hunter disturbance is the principal aim of the National Audubon Society wildlife sanctuaries.

Prior to the mid-1920s, the National Audubon Society's main concern was rallying and organizing interest in birds. In 1903 President Teddy Roosevelt established the first national wildlife refuge, Pelican Island, in Indian River, Florida.

In 1923 T. Gilbert Pearson persuaded the General Land Office of Texas to give the Audubon Society a fifty-year lease (renewed in 1973) on 3,871 acres in Laguna Madre. The lease included Green Island, east of Brownsville, site of the largest colony of reddish egrets in North America, and farther north near Corpus Christi, the group known as Three Islands, North Bird Island, and South Bird Island, all containing thriving wading-bird colonies.

In 1924 National Audubon established its largest wildlife sanctuary, the Paul J. Rainey, in the brackish marshes of southwestern Louisiana. This was the beginning of the wildlife management program that now embraces some 150,000 acres in one-hundred sanctuaries.

Prior to 1966, when National Audubon established its Wildlife Sanctuary Department, Alexander Sprunt Jr. was responsible for five sanctuaries in Florida, one in Louisiana, and six islands along the Texas coast.

Sprunt was uniquely qualified to be director of southern sanctuaries when the National Audubon president, John H. Baker, appointed him in 1935. Alex grew up in South Carolina's low country and was thoroughly acquainted with native wildlife, author of *The Birds of South Carolina*, and curator of ornithology at the Charleston Museum of Natural History.

In California, William Goodall, former director of the Audubon Camp of the West, was the logical man to direct the programs at three sanctuaries in California.

Alex and Bill reported to NAS president John Baker in the Audubon office in New York City.

Carl W. Buchheister succeeded Baker in 1959. Buchheister and executive vice president Charles H. Callison decided in 1966 that the growing number and diversity of Audubon sanctuaries necessitated establishment of a single department with overall responsibility for managing them. I became the first director of the National Audubon Society Sanctuary Department in 1966.

Before joining the National Audubon staff, I spent twenty years as manager of the oldest private duck-hunting club in North America. The Winous Point Shooting Club on Sandusky Bay, off southwestern Lake Erie, was founded in 1856 and is still active.

I was hired by Windsor T. White, president of the club and president of White Motors Corporation. After surveying the marsh, I told White it was dominated by cattail, a good muskrat food, but of no value to those flat-faced ducks and geese. I could replace it with choice waterfowl food plants such as Walter's millet, rice-cutgrass, and several species of smart-weed (a close relative of domestic buckwheat). But it would cost upward of a million dollars and could take six to eight years to establish the necessary water control.

White said, "Aldo Leopold suggested I hire you and I did. What you recommend, I will support. But you'd better know what you're doing."

"Fair enough," said I.

Fortunately, two club members were interested in general ornithology or bird watching; another was interested in botany. With allies such as these, I eventually persuaded the club to establish a scholarship program at Winous Point whereby graduate students could do research on any phase of marsh ecology. This program is still active, and today alumni hold important positions in various state, federal, and private wildlife agencies. Robert L. Meeks and Robert Hoffman of Ducks Unlimited are cases in point, as are John Koerner and Ralph Andrews with the u.s. Fish and Wildlife Service and Robert Donohoe and Karl Bednarik, formerly with the Ohio Division of Wildlife.

Working with wealthy duck hunters and advanced students of wildlife biology is not so different from working with the board of directors of National Audubon, administrators such as Buchheister, Callison, Elvis J. Stahr, and a competent staff of professional wildlife managers on Audubon wildlife sanctuaries.

In 1974 I realized that the national office in New York was a long way from the marshes of Louisiana, the islands along the Texas coast, the prairie potholes of North Dakota, the spruce-fir forests of Maine, the arid lands of Arizona, or the chaparral of California.

To keep the board, administrators, and sanctuary managers in closer contact, I started our newsletter entitled *Places to Hide and Seek*. Six issues of these newsletters were written per year, based on reports from the wardens. Each issue covered three or four sanctuaries and was usually about five printed pages in length.

I hope excerpts from those newsletters will give you, the reader, an intimate look at some of the people, places, plants, and animals found on National Audubon Society sanctuaries.

Deciding which sanctuaries to include in this book was not easy. Each has one or more unique features. Corkscrew Swamp in southwest Florida is the only remnant of virgin bald cypress on the continent and contains the largest colony of the endangered wood stork. On Lake Okeechobee, by educating duck hunters and by providing and protecting a safe nesting area, Rod Chandler brought the endangered Everglade kite population up to a safe level. At Beideler Forest in South Carolina, we saved a remnant of the virgin cypress-tupelo swamp forest and gradually restored most of the original Four Hole Swamp. Every duck species that nests in North Dakota nests at the Alkali Lake Sanctuary near Jamestown, North Dakota, and we restored much of its native grassland and stopped the disastrous soil erosion on the hillsides. We hope to use it as a demonstration of sound land management, which is relatively rare in North Dakota.

In Maine, Steve Kress brought the puffins back from the verge of extirpation, and the camp program is a unique educational effort in marine biology. At the Lillian Annette Rowe near Gibbon, Nebraska, migrating sandhill cranes find food and shelter every spring, and nearby fields contain restored native prairie.

The Starr Ranch in southern California is a stronghold for the endangered California gnatcatcher and the plant community called coastal sage scrub.

It is safe to say other sanctuaries are equally valuable from the conservation standpoint but may lack unique features and so are not included in this book.

"Stick with Old Dad if you want to win." From that time on, I was known as Old Dad to Lonnie, his brother Berton, and the other sanctuary managers.

JULY 1974   In the early 1970s, overharvesting of alligators for their valuable hides had caused an alarming drop in the population over most of their range. Louisiana state wildlife biologists, however, maintained that the species was still relatively abundant in their local marshes and were opposed to classifying alligators as an endangered species.

Ted Joanen, manager of the Rockefeller Wildlife Refuge about forty miles west of the Rainey, is internationally known as the expert on alligators. Ted maintained that the state-owned refuges, such as the Rockefeller and Marsh Island, had a surplus of gators that could restock some of the neighboring states. When I asked, "Well, why don't you?" Ted replied, "If you'll help us catch 'em, and haul 'em, I'll be glad to."

So it comes to pass that Lonnie Legé, Carlyle Blakeney (NAS southeastern regional representative), and Old Dad are cruising down a canal on the Rockefeller Refuge about midnight on July 15, 1974. Lonnie is in the front of the boat armed with a headlamp and a ten-foot pole with a wire noose on the distal end. Born and raised in the marsh, Monsieur Legé speaks French, blue goose, and alligator fluently. This is comforting to Carlyle and Old Dad, since they don't know much about how to handle gators without losing fingers and other useful appendages.

All three have spent most of their lives trying to catch something and trying not to catch something else. Now they're trying to catch small alligators and trying not to catch water moccasins or malaria. Number one on the most unwanted list is a gator over six feet, since a mad alligator in a boat with three human-type critters gets crowded more than somewhat. Futhermore, a transported gator that size is an adventurous beast, apt to take off across country from his release site, causing consternation among livestock owners who are not accustomed to perambulating alligators. It is also hazardous for gators. Since our objective is to restore the primitive reptiles to parts of their former ranges from which they have been extirpated, we try to catch two and three footers who will stay put.

We spot an alligator and cruise up to him. While the gator is blinded by the light, the noose is slipped over his head and tightened around his neck. It is a delicate operation, which gets more so when he is lifted into the boat. The man in the middle must kneel astride the writhing reptile, reach forward and clamp his jaws shut, and hold them while a stout rubber band slips over his snout. There remains the tail that thrashes about with gay abandon, causing black and blue marks, profanity, and mild confusion.

With three men manning his head, back, and tail bones, however, the rubber band is in place, the noose is removed, and he is placed in a burlap sack that is securely tied. Repeat this performance enough times and along toward morning you have a boat load of gators. You head for the landing where Audubon's truck is waiting to go to Jackson, Mississippi. As Blakeney throws the truck in gear, Lonnie says, "I'm sure glad I don't work in the New York office! All that traffic and noise would make me so nervous!"

While we were busy catching and transporting alligators, the least terns were busy making little terns out of big ones on the island in Belle Isle Lake, adjacent to the Rainey headquarters. Legé Island, which we built in 1967, produced about 250 least terns this year. This is the seventh consecutive year this threatened species has made it big on this island.

Berton and Lonnie Legé banded fifty terns in July, using all the bands they had. Rich Paul came over from the Audubon Research Department in Tavernier, Florida, to survey the terns for a couple days and brought more bands. Our research department is contemplating a thorough study of these little minnow-burners in the near future. If it happens, the Legé brothers have enough information on nesting success, life history, and food habits to make a statistician drool. These data will make a good foundation for a more detailed study.

This island, as far as we know, is the only one in the world built and managed for least terns. It is covered with oyster shells, presenting the bare beach effect that terns require. If grass, weeds, or brush invade it, the terns will not nest on that portion of the island. If you've never tried to keep vegetation from invading fertile soil with a year-round growing season, Lonnie and Berton have news for you. It ain't easy.

In summer 1974, a great many gator nests on the levee surrounding our fresh-water impoundment escaped the raccoons and other egg eaters. By late August, the place was crawling with six-inch reptiles. Survival of the adults has also been so good in recent years that there is no laughter on the levee coming from nutria, deer, turtles, and other items on an alligator's bill of fare. According to Lonnie and Berton, if Norman Brunswig, manager of the Beidler Forest Sanctuary in Four Hole Swamp, South Carolina, wants more gators, Rainey is ready.

SEPTEMBER 1975 The second year of cooperation with the Louisiana Wildlife Commission saw us reach the two-thousand mark on our alligator transplant program that we agreed to three years ago. Lonnie and Berton had lots of help this year, most important of which were Lonnie's sons, Ricky, Terry, and Patrick Legé. The boys and their Uncle Berton have scars to prove that gators would not make good pets.

Our least tern colony on Legé Island in Belle Isle Lake fledged about 250 young again. Lonnie and Berton banded 224 nestlings. We assume some of the young terns return to nest on the island where they were hatched. As yet, no one knows, but the banding should tell us. The Legés were able to erect an observation blind in the colony, from which they conducted close-up photography and behavioral studies. Lonnie's wife, Valla, says the female least terns had women's lib figured out long before people thought of it. When least terns are courting, the male does not bring flowers nor whisper sweet nothings to his mate. Instead he brings a minnow now and then, presumably with his compliments. This goes on until the clutch is complete (usually two eggs, occasionally three or four), and incubation begins. Unlike most birds, the male takes his turn at incubation, whereupon he stops delivering minnows.

Two years ago, a developer on the south edge of the Rainey decided his customers could use our private canal. We allowed as how Paul J. did not intend that his beautiful marsh should ever become a public highway. By the deed of donation, we were legally and ethically bound to keep the marsh safe for blue geese and alligators, not weekend cottagers. The developer said, "I'll see you in court," and he did.

We beat the developer in the circuit court, again in the appeals court, and the Louisiana Supreme Court. But he had much money and possibly a politician or two in his bag of tricks. Next thing we knew, the police jurors (county commissioners) announced their intention to expropriate our canal for public use. Our attorney, Silas B. Cooper Jr. of Abbeville, effectively argued the legality of such a move. It seems that our very generous developer-friend had donated several lots to members of the police jury, as well as to certain prominent businessmen. These civic-minded citizens claim that a Cajun Coney Island on the Gulf of Mexico would be great for business. "The geese and gators can go elsewhere," they say, "and besides, who needs them?"

Lonnie and Berton Legé, John Franson (NAS southwest regional representative), and attorney Si Cooper, have been working overtime to tell our side of the story. The Lafayette television and local radio and press have carried features on what the Rainey Sanctuary and National Audubon are all about. Thanks to information we supplied, the *Abbeville Meridional* told why and how Audubon helped the Louisiana Wildlife Commission's efforts to restore the gator throughout its former range.

We also favored changing the official status of the alligator from "endangered" to "threatened" in three parishes of southwestern Louisiana, which would allow a rigidly controlled legal harvest of surplus animals. Instead of this simple change, the u.s. Fish and Wildlife Service undertook a "study" of the gator over its entire range, which accomplished nothing but a great waste of time, meanwhile promising Louisiana it could open its gator season on September 20, 1975.

But instead of a well-controlled harvest limited to surplus animals, harvest loopholes in the proposed federal regulations were enough to make a gator poacher rub his hands in anticipation. In trying to salvage the situation, the feds had to delay the opening of the gator season until September 26. This, of course, they blamed on us in a press release that made headlines from New Orleans to the Texas border. The following day, Carlyle Blakeney and Old Dad, in the interior of the Interior Building, persuaded a certain bureaucrat to print a retraction. Perhaps the bureaucrat mistook Blakeney for Leroy Brown, who is not known for gentle persuasion; anyway, he complied.

Meanwhile, Lonnie and Si Cooper have been busy telling local people the truth. The Louisiana Wildlife biologists with whom we have worked in recent years are also telling it like it is. Lonnie says it sure would be nice to spend a month in the marsh with no developers, politicians, or bureaucrats to worry about. Who knows? Some day he may get the chance.

JULY 1977 Lonnie and Berton say extreme weather conditions are so common on the Gulf Coast that when it's not blowing, freezing, or boiling, they figure the meteorologist is just wondering what to do next. For example, take January 9. The morning's at 70 degrees, the rose is not dew-pearled, and all is not right with the world. It's raining, in fact. Night falls, and so does the temperature—to 18 degrees above. Next morning, the sex of all the brass monkeys in Louisiana cannot be determined externally.

Pushing a pirogue through inch-thick ice will cut it to ribbons, and it is not healthy to get out and walk, even though the gators and cottonmouths are nowhere in sight. So for a few days our marsh men were marooned. They spent the time repairing damage to the plumbing and wiring caused by the deep freeze in the Deep South.

But the eagle-headed brant (which the bird books used to call blue geese until the name changers called them snow geese) kept company with the immobilized Cajuns. A flock of about 150,000, about one mile long and almost as wide, the biggest Lonnie had ever seen, kept on eating up the marsh east of headquarters over on the nearby state wildlife refuge.

As soon as Lonnie and Berton could get around, they made some fresh burns in the wire grass on the Rainey, which attracted the geese and spread the big concentration around a bit. By February the geese had completely denuded large areas of the marsh. We're glad we are not in the muskrat-nutria business, since the carrying capacity of bare ground for herbivores is zero. Where possible, we kept the water off the denuded areas, and by July the severe "eat-outs" supported a fine stand of coffeeweed (*Sesbania exalta*). This will make the flat-faced fowl happy when they come back next fall because coffeeweed is a member of the bean family. Seed pods are three to four inches long, very narrow, and contain thirty to forty small beans, which during the winter are eaten by ducks and other birds.

In the adjacent McIlhenny Marsh, managed by Pierre Legé, the muskrat population exploded last winter. Lonnie and Berton are not jealous of their dad's success, since they claim it is due to all the free advice they gave him. Pierre's marsh was the only one in all Louisiana, however, that had a good population. The rest, including the Rainey, were far below carrying capacity. Biologists came from near and far to witness this unique situation and try to find an explanation. The Legé brothers hope the muskrats responded to a combination of water and salinity levels that they had recommended and that they hope to duplicate again next year. Meanwhile, the mysterious muskrat is showing strong signs of invading sections of the Rainey adjacent to the McIlhenny. They will be watched with some anxiety because an exploding muskrat population sets off a chain reaction that affects all the beasts, birds, and fish that occupy the marsh.

On Valentine's Day, the martins came back to dine on the billions of mosquitoes around headquarters. The shorebirds came in on February 16. On the twenty-fourth, clouds of dust from out Kansas-Colorado way made heavy exercise and heavy breathing difficult. Shades of the 1930s; remember the dust storms and Okies in Steinbeck's *The Grapes of Wrath*?

A few years ago, an attorney for a local developer tried to have our private canal declared a public thoroughfare. He lost in the local court, the appeals, and the state supreme court. Last winter he brought a couple of school board members out to Section 16, a square mile of marsh that we lease from the school board. Although it had been trapped every winter before we leased it, Lonnie pointed out to the school board that trapping was illegal and would not be allowed so long as we leased it.

Unbeknownst to Lonnie and Berton, this legal eagle tried to show the board members and a reporter evidence of trapping on Section 16. The mere fact that they were on Section 9 was overlooked in the newspaper story that followed.

Instead of suing the paper for their mistake, we brought the young reporter back to the Rainey, showed him where Section 16 was and the complete lack of evidence that poachers or personnel from the adjacent state marsh had trapped the section. A front page retraction appeared in the *Abbeville Meridional,* followed by a full-page article on our least tern banding, gator research, snow goose management, and other Rainey programs. It is possible that the attorney, who is seeking reelection to the state senate in fall 1977, will have an image problem.

Our least terns had their problems this summer—not with politicians but with the weather. They were nearly wiped out three times by thunderstorms. A sixty-mile-per-hour wind with hail is not recommended for nestlings. On May 21, about 30 downy young died from no apparent cause. Specimens were saved for autopsy. Lonnie and Berton have banded 111, whereas they expected to band about 600.

SEPTEMBER 1978 In February 1978, the rains all went around the Rainey, and water in the marsh got so low the muskrats were wading instead of swimming. Two months later, Lonnie and Berton were cleaning ditches to drain water off the marsh so grass could grow. Comes May and they pray for rain; comes June and July and they have daily showers and violent thunderstorms.

Lightning in Louisiana is a spectacular show, but Cajuns consider it very unhealthy to be cruising the bayous in an outboard when Thor is throwing those fireballs around and about. Fortunately the rains dampened the marsh grass, and we had no summer fires. The Legés say marsh fires are fine tools so long as they set 'em when and where they want 'em, which is in winter on the wire grass flats.

On March 29, Lonnie gathers up his fancy clothes and his Cajun Queen and heads for Old Dad's office at the Emily Winthrop Miles Sanctuary in Sharon, Connecticut. Here "Miss Valla" is exposed to snow drifts on the north-facing slopes, ice on the lake that she can walk on, Canada geese fighting for nesting territories, and Yankee dialects. Lonnie and Old Dad talk budgets, boats, marshes, and men, then Art Gingert, manager of Miles, and Lonnie compare hardwood forests with salt marshes, snow plows with marsh plows, beavers with nutria.

After a few New England boiled dinners, Yankee pot roasts, and Indian puddings, a Cajun is apt to lose weight. Old Dad remembers a frozen flat-faced fowl stashed away in the freezer. Lonnie makes a roux, which he calls a "roo," and after many hours of simmering, many dashes of Tabasco sauce, and many nips of Old Stumpblower, a blue goose gumbo restores him to health and happiness.

Meanwhile, back at the Rainey, Berton records the first brood of mottled ducks on April 10. The least terns are arriving at Legé Island, and they start nesting in earnest about April 18. By late May, they are big enough to band, so somewhere down South America way there should be about 322 young least terns sporting aluminum bracelets. There were five nests of gull-billed terns on the island this year. A few pairs of skimmers made the attempt but were wiped out.

Egrets and other sharp-faced fowl did well on Dead Man's Island in Southwest Pass, but our roseate spoonbills must have moved over to Buddy Whitehead's country at Smith Point in Galveston Bay.

Our cooperative alligator study with the state of Louisiana is in its third year. We monitor the populations on marshes where gators are legally hunted compared to the sanctuary. So far, the quality of the marsh habitat seems to exert more influence on gator populations than the closely regulated hunting. The notorious vagaries of the fur and hide market are again brought to our attention by the closing of the gator season in Louisiana this year. The reason? Buyers have more hides on hand than manufacturers can use. Or so they tell us.

Just so the boys would not get bored, we have a minihurricane on August 28. The storm tide rolls some four feet of water over the marsh, and next day Berton can stand up to drink on the front lawn at headquarters. Fortunately, there was no serious loss to buildings or equipment, and at last count there were no Frenchmen missing around Vermilion Bay. By and large, just another normal year on the Louisiana coast.

SEPTEMBER 1979 When a Cajun can't catch catfish, some unusual circumstances must prevail. Hurricanes, prolonged drouth, day after day in the high 90s, clouds of mosquitoes, no mosquitoes, thunderstorms with five inches of rain daily for a week—well, now, these may or may not be considered unusual for the Rainey. But when the water in the marsh turns chocolate brown as though it belonged in the Four Hole Swamp, it is bad news for catfish and Cajuns.

Lonnie and Berton say that Hurricanes David and Frederick did not do much damage to the marsh. But Claudette and a couple other tropical storms that stayed about one hundred miles offshore, raising the tides and keeping torrential rains from draining away—Mon Dieu!

Lonnie says the flood waters stayed high for several days, which *is* unusual, even for the Rainey. He believes much of the wire grass was drowned, and the decaying vegetation drastically lowered the oxygen content, increased the acidity, and brown-stained water, and poor fishing for catfish, blue crabs, and shrimp was the result.

And besides, most of the gator nests, except those on top of the levees, were flooded, along with nests of mottled ducks and blue-winged teal. Those high spoil banks along the canals, many of them built for us by oil companies, also came in handy for deer looking for dry beds.

Lonnie did a fair amount of gadding about this past year. He was up to Ontario giving a presentation at the North American Wildlife Conference in March. At the invitation of Michael Zagata, in our Audubon Washington, D.C., office, he testified before the u.s. Congressional Committee on Fisheries and Wildlife along with Jim Rodgers of Tampa Bay and Dave Blankinship from over Texas way. The lads did themselves proud and helped get the birds that nobody shoots at some extra money and attention. Jackson, Mississippi, was the one-time home of Paul J. Rainey, so Carlyle Blakeney allowed as how Lonnie should give a program for an Audubon chapter over there. Lonnie was glad to oblige.

Lonnie and Berton say the value of impoundments was well demonstrated last November. After a prolonged dry spell, about twenty-five thousand flat-faced fowl and a mix of eight thousand herons, egrets, and roseate spoonbills were feeding and loafing in the Goose Pond and adjacent impoundments. The rest of the marsh was in better shape for rabbits than for waterbirds.

In addition to regular migrants, visitors to the Rainey included Cree Indians and members of the u.s. Congress. On February 10, from Manitoba came six Cree, guests of the Louisiana Wildlife and Fisheries Commission, to see how a good marsh is run. The blue geese have been coming to the Rainey for thousands of years. They have been fed upon by the Cree on Hudson Bay and by the Cajuns on the Gulf of Mexico for centuries. But this was the first time the blues and snows and their black-haired predators from both ends of the flyway ever gathered at the Rainey. Languages used included English, French, Cree, and snow goose. These Indians and these French have been talking to these geese for generations. We hope their conversation never dies.

Congressman John Breaux, whose voting record does not exactly reflect a deep concern for the fabulous productivity of Louisiana marshes, has started to pay closer attention to the ecosystem that has kept the rollicking Cajuns in business for these many years. The black gold that gushes from the ground and from beneath the Gulf is worth many millions of dollars. But if the Cajun country loses its ability to produce shrimp, oysters, catfish, menhaden, snow geese, rabbits, deer, and muskrats, as well as rice and soybeans, we will have lost something of value that cannot be measured in dollars. The Legé brothers explained all this to Congressman Breaux at the Rainey last December. We can't think of a better classroom.

The purple martins arrived on Valentine's Day; the fulvous tree ducks, on March 4; the least terns, on April 3. The terns were nesting heavily on the island by early May, and Lonnie and Berton had banded about four hundred by the time Carol Taylor and her New York office camera crew showed up on May 26. In six years, Lonnie and Berton have banded over fifteen hundred young terns, but until Cousin Sharp-eyes Taylor arrived, they hadn't seen a banded adult. Carol spotted one wearing an aluminum bracelet. Besides a new banding record, Carol brought good weather for photography, and we're looking forward to seeing least terns and great Frenchmen on film.

SEPTEMBER 1980 The winter of 1979–1980 caught us with our three-square bulrush down. The prolonged flooding of the marshes the previous summer was probably to blame. Whatever the cause, we were unable to burn the marsh, and without three-square and fresh burns to work on, the geese seemed to prefer the rice fields to the north and west.

Meanwhile, for about ten years, Sandy Sprunt and Gene Knoder, of the Audubon Research Department, have been quietly trying to persuade the Mexicans that they have some of the finest marshes—wading bird and waterfowl habitat in North America—and that they should not do to theirs what the Army Corps of Engineers, Soil Conservation Service, and Bureau of Reclamation have done to most of the valuable wetlands in the United States.

Mexican officials who deal with water management and wildlife conservation decided they would like to see whether the Yanquis really practice what they preach. Thus it comes to pass that on February 13, 1980, Pideau Broussard's crew boat docks at the Rainey. On board are Guillermo Lugo and eight compadres, plus a couple of u.s. wildlife biologists, two or three state biologists, an interpreter, a couple of Mexican and American Ducks Unlimited representatives, and George Laycock of *Audubon* magazine fame, all accompanied by congenial Cecil Eugene Knoder.

Eugene Knoder, formerly with the u.s. Fish and Wildlife Service doing research on cranes in the Southwest, often followed the long-legged, sharp-faced fowl into Mexico. So he became familiar with Mexican wetlands and wildlife, as well as with wildlife administrators south of the border. He persuaded the latter to come see how the Rainey Sanctuary is managed.

The Mexican contingent were greeted by Audubon president Russell Peterson and wife, Lillian, as well as Lonnie, Berton, Old Dad and wife, known as Miss Nancy in Cajun Country. The Mexicans ate Cajun venison, blue goose gumbo, and fried catfish, drank Cajun coffee and Old Milwaukee, and decided that if Lonnie and Berton could manage a marsh as well as they could cook, then they would learn a lot.

They did, indeed, learn a lot. The state furnished a float plane, plus their best alligator expert and their best mammalogist. Pideau furnished his crew boat and his practical knowledge of pollution control in petroleum production. Lonnie took 'em for a buggy ride and explained the use of weirs, fresh-water impoundments, controlled burning, goose management, nutria control, least tern banding, how to tranquilize poachers, and the proper use of Tabasco sauce.

According to Gene Knoder, it was shortly thereafter that Audubon was invited to Mexico City to assist in developing plans for preservation and management of the vast wetlands of Mexico. And that's really what it was all about.

SEPTEMBER 1981 When a Cajun marsh man says mosquitoes are *bad,* he means that whenever you step outside your khaki uniform it turns gray in about three minutes. Such was the case in October 1980. But the wind finally went to the north, and by October 28, when Lonnie and Berton Legé were washing down the camp prior to painting the buildings, blue geese were coming in all day. Good flocks of wigeon and gadwalls arrived ahead of the front, and mosquitoes, though still around and hungry, were ignored.

Evinrude came out with a new model fifty-five horsepower motor

erally goes back in the marsh, builds her nest beside a pond or gator hole, and patiently waits for the sun to hatch her eggs.

Comes September, when gator seasons opens, the males are pretty much concentrated along the canals where the gator hunter (or gator fisherman) plies his trade. The latter suspends a baited hook a few inches above the water, and his catch is normally about 95 percent males. Polygamy has its price.

But in 1981, with low water in the marshes, the finicky females refused to take their family duties seriously. They hung around the bank of the old canal like liberated females well into September. Ted Joanen, the Louisiana biologist who probably knows more about the lives and times of gators than anyone in the country, was well aware of this. Therefore, the Fur Division of the Wildlife Department, under Al Ensminger, drastically reduced the number of gators each marsh owner could harvest because they anticipated a higher catch of females.

On the McIlhenny, Vermilion Corporation, and other marshes where gator harvest is allowed, the ratio of females taken in 1981 was nearly 30 percent instead of 5 percent. (It is extremely gratifying when biologists are allowed to apply what they know and know what they are doing.)

This summer the water levels were generally more favorable, and gator production and behavior responded accordingly. Nest counts were about 50 percent above 1981's. On those marshes where water levels can be controlled, the carrying capacity, not only for gators but for a wide variety of species, can be considerably enhanced. That explains why Lonnie and Berton plan to install a weir across Tom Bayou and some additional flumes in strategic places and to repair levees where necessary. They brought in a dragline and two hundred cubic yards of shell and repaired the big weir at Big Island Bayou last year. They hope to do Tom Bayou next year. The whole idea is to be able to provide water of the right depth and salinity in the right place at the right time.

Last December the men were able to get good burns over most of the marsh. The blue (snow) geese had largely ignored the Rainey for a couple of winters, but Lonnie's report for December 1981 reads, "It sure felt good to hear sweet music again." Some eighty thousand of the eagle-headed brant were on hand for the holidays. In contrast, the wintering duck population was the lowest in Cajun memory.

January 1982 was extremely cold. Vermilion Bay froze over when the temperature dropped to nine degrees. The nutria and muskrat populations were very low. This spring, the three-cornered grass (*Scirpus olneyi*), with no grazing pressure from rodents or flat-faced fowl, spread profusely. Some ten thousand ducks loafed in the Goose Pond fresh-water impoundment in February, along with about twenty thousand blue geese, before they said au revoir to the Cajuns and headed for Eskimo country.

One of Jerry Cutlip's swallow-tailed kites wandered from Florida as far west as the Rainey on March 24, 1982, a new record. In early April, Lonnie and Berton devegetated the tern island. The little terns returned shortly thereafter. Berton and family banded about two hundred young terns in May.

The list of visitors for the year included ten students from Tunisia who are studying and teaching in southern Louisiana. According to Professor Legé, the Tunisians spoke beautiful French and English, and he is not sure who learned the most from whom.

On July 22, Lonnie and Berton launched their new thirty-foot aluminum boat, with its 235-horsepower Volvo turbo-charge diesel engine. It runs "like a dream," burns less than five gallons per hour, which is less than our 140-horsepower outboard, and is a far more seaworthy craft. In their spare time, they remodeled both camps, glassing in the screen porches and making room for Sandy Sprunt's outlaws from the Research Department to eat gumbo and confer on research plans.

NOVEMBER 1983 Between Scotsmen, Dutchmen, Texans, Bostonians, news reporters, oil company executives, scientists, politicians, and blue geese, solitude around the Rainey was at a premium in 1982 and 1983. Frank Hamilton, director of the Royal Society for the Protection of Birds in Scotland, spent three days in October 1982, inspecting the Rainey and natural gas production. Don Moore and Peggy Keney of National Marine Fisheries spent two days inspecting our water management program: weirs, flumes, impoundments, and the merits of trying to backfill canals. After reading the Rainey master plan, and discussing our twenty-year water management plan, Don and Peggy recommended that the Corps of Engineers and the u.s. Fish and Wildlife Service issue us a general operating permit without further delay. This may have disappointed some critics who had never seen the Rainey, had no wildlife management experience, but still insisted that our management was biologically unsound. (Sometimes personal aggrandizement masquerades as environmental concern.)

The white-fronted geese arrived on October 13; the blues, three days later. At the time, Lonnie was at the Starr Ranch in California, where a

Sanctuary Wardens Attack Team was rebuilding a house for Jeff Froke. Lonnie describes the Starr Ranch country as beautiful, but the hills are too high for a web-footed Cajun to want to live there.

Small streams that meander through the marsh are called rigolets by Cajuns. Apparently navigation canals and other man-made changes have speeded up the rise and fall of tides in the marshes. So the rigolets tend to get deeper and longer, forming a network that, during low tides, can drain vast areas of marsh. This is very ungood for production of shrimp, menhaden, and other species that don't like to be left high and dry. Consequently, the Rainey plan calls for management units enclosed by a system of levees, flumes, and weirs. All this costs money.

Fortunately, we can often persuade the oil companies that want to drill on the Rainey to build levees and weirs at their expense, and our income from natural gas helps keep the marsh producing beaucoup shrimp, fish, muskrats, and ducks for hungry people, birds, gators, and such. Lonnie took advantage of the slowdown in the oil business to speed up his levee repairs. In recent years, local dragline operators were begging for time off; now they are begging for work. So we got three miles of levee built for $25,000, about half the cost of two years ago. In addition, the sand and shale that Conoco had to get rid of filled in the low spots around headquarters, and grass was soon established on it. This saved us another $15,000 in barge and fill expenses for maintenance.

Unfortunately, the 17,330-foot hole drilled by Conoco was dry. But in exchange for about three acres of marsh that was converted to open canal, Conoco installed a $30,000 weir at their expense. While the crew and equipment were there, we built a couple of small weirs at our own expense, thus saving the "move-in" cost. (We have several more weirs and flumes and culverts to install, and we'll have the Rainey doing more-or-less what it used to do before the engineers messed up Acadiana. But most of these must be built with our own money.)

On January 27, 1983, in New Orleans, at a hearing before the Corps, USFWS, State CZM, DNR, LWF, NMF, SCS, EPA, and a few other combinations of alphabet and bureaucrats, our twenty-year plan was approved. In recognition of this historical event, Old Dad suggested that we drink no longer water but use a little wine for our stomach's sake and often infirmities.

Meanwhile, back at the Rainey, some Rotarians from Holland stopped by for a day. Lonnie and Berton were plum delighted by a visit from the heirs of Paul J. Rainey. The warden's report says, "Matt, Roy, Patty, and

Sam Plum turned out to be the nicest folks ever to visit the Rainey. None of them had ever visited the Louisiana marshes, so they had no idea what to expect. We didn't either, but we found out those Yankees could be Cajuns."

Another new record was a black-necked stilt nest that fledged 4 young on the shell island. Berton and crew banded 107 young least terns. It would have been closer to 300 but for very severe thunderstorms. The storms also destroyed thirty-six gull-billed tern nests.

JANUARY 1985 In the fall of 1983, Lonnie and Berton saw their first blue geese on October 17, a cause celebre for fais-do-do, gumbo, and geaux-geaux. On October 9, a big wave of indigo buntings, nondescript flycatchers, and confusing fall warblers cluttered up the live oak trees around headquarters.

In November the metal roof on the boathouse was removed in one piece and replaced by a new and better job that we hope will resist salt air for many years to come. On November 30, 1983, the Louisiana Wildlife Department, which has a big refuge next door to the Rainey, hooked up a state radio and tower at our headquarters, which puts us in touch with wardens and planes all over the state—a big comfort to us and discomfort to poachers.

Around 400,000 geese, mostly lesser snows, winter along the Louisiana coast, and the Rainey and state refuges held about 250,000 to 300,000 in February 1984, the largest flock on record.

In March, when the yellow-throated, warbling, white-eyed, and red-eyed vireos were attracting the eager eyes of Cajuns, and some of those confusing fall warblers were coming back in their Easter clothes, the least terns and eastern kingbirds arrived. On March 26, les garçons saw twelve yellow rails from the marsh buggy.

On April 15, the least terns started nesting, right on schedule. This colony, on the island we built in 1967, has reproduced successfully ever since, which must be some kind of record for an ephemeral nester. It suggests that, if the habitat remains stable, the colony will return. But at the Rainey, with its year-round growing season, it takes a heap o' sweatin' to make a home for terns. Dense grass makes ideal cover from which boat-tailed grackles can ambush baby terns, so Lonnie and Berton have the same problem Rich Paul has at Tampa Bay in Florida: how to keep bare sand and gravel bare.

In May 156 least terns were banded. On May 23, a brood of black-

done. Berton, Margaret, and family, and Lonnie, Valla, and family then built some 275 feet of new dock for a much needed improvement. Total cost to Audubon: ten pounds of filleted catfish, twenty-five pounds of crawfish, two gallons of shrimp—all caught and cooked Cajun style.

On May 3–4, 1985, bucking a headwind was too much for waves of tanagers, warblers, and grosbeaks. They hit the beach and canal banks worn out, which made birding without binoculars very easy. For some unknown reason, 1985 was a disastrous year for our big little tern colony. The fuzzy chicks kept disappearing from the island without a trace. Instead of banding some two hundred, the count was two. The family of barn owls in the buggy shed has no comment, but they've nested there for years, presumably content with a diet of clapper rails, nestling kop-kops, boat-tailed grackles, marsh rabbits, and such. An unsolved mystery, containing no definite clues.

The film crew for *The World of Audubon* came by on May 14, and Berton and Lonnie made like Paul Newman and Robert Redford. Other May activities included Old Dad, attorney Si Cooper, and NAS member Emmet Putnam Birdathoning on the Rainey. In July, Durward Allen of Purdue University brought his tape recorder, binoculars, and vast experience to see if Cajuns might add a new dimension to our wildlife legacy.

Other visitors included Hurricanes Danny and Juan, on August 15 and October 28. Danny brought four inches of rain, one-hundred-mile-per-hour winds, and a tidal wave of eleven feet over the beach. Next day, Valla and Lonnie, Margaret and Berton, and children found our old and new buildings had come through in relatively good shape. But except for buildings, it was tres difficile to find any structure or critter that Danny hadn't done in. The headquarters lawn was buried under two feet of drift. Mixed in with all that wood and dead grass was an assortment of saltwater fish such as sharks, redfish, and shrimp, plus many fresh and brackish water species including cottonmouth moccasins, alligators, muskrats, nutria, deer, rabbits, and catfish. Also worthy of mention: hundreds of bumblebees and wasps that were still alive but very unhappy about the whole situation and wanting to punish somebody for the disturbance.

Some canals were level full of debris, and damage to levees, weirs, and flumes amounted to $50,000. Then along comes Juan. Whereas Danny had rolled over the marsh with destructive force, Juan's tide gradually rose to about five feet and killed very few if any marsh critters. Migrating birds, however, did not fare so well. Lonnie estimated one dead bird per linear foot along our beach, mostly rose-breasted grosbeaks, indigo buntings, catbirds, and one chimney swift.

In December 1985, the blue (snow) geese returned in record numbers, more than the Legés could ever remember. The duck flight also set a new record.

MAY 1987 Lonnie and Berton Legé report that in 1986 they got forty-seven inches of rain, while normal is sixty-five inches. Temperatures were above normal. All of which means the larval shrimp and menhaden, which came into the marsh by the millions between May 15 and 20, grew rapidly and survived in record numbers because they like high salinity. But the lack of rain and resulting high salinity caused les hommes to keep their fingers crossed. When the salinity hovers around twelve to fifteen ppt, it is dangerously close to the lethal level for three-cornered grass (*Scirpus olneyi*). Prolonged high salinity and salt water intrusion could do to the Rainey what has already been done to the great marshes in southeastern Louisiana. Roots of three-square and wire grass provide the threads that hold the marsh together.

Below normal rainfall and above normal temperature persisted through 1986, and the winter of 1986–1987. But in March, temperatures fell well below normal. This was a blessing because our muskrat population had exploded. The rats were eating themselves out of house and home. Cold weather is a great help to the trapper who is vainly trying to keep the marsh from becoming a lake full of starving muskrats and nutria.

On April 23, 1986, in the Goose Pond impoundment, wherein we built a circular levee and planted willows about 1964, cormorants were found nesting; a new record for the Rainey. Carl Safina, from the Scully Sanctuary on Long Island, New York, visited the Rainey, and on April 28 they discovered six nests of roseate spoonbills added to the cormorants. The big pinks increased to about seventy-five birds later.

Being able to lower the water in Goose Pond stimulated a vigorous growth of bull whip (*Scirpus californicus*) covering about five to six acres in the southeast corner. Comes mid-April 1987, and the bull whip is the site of a mixed rookery of white-faced ibises, glossy ibises, white ibises, snowy egrets, and Louisiana herons plus a few least bitterns. Lonnie, Berton, Bubba Perry, and Timmy Vincent promptly built a very substantial observation tower on the nearby levee from which to observe and photograph life in a waterbird colony.

The white-faced, glossy, and white ibises are new nesting records for the Rainey. They will cause much skepticism among the experts because the white-faced rarely nests that far east, while the glossy doesn't nest that far west. But ranges of birds do have a way of shifting.

While the taxonomists argue whether the official common name for *Butorides striatus* should be little green heron, green heron, green-backed heron, or shitepoke, the Cajuns have no such doubts. The right name is kop-kop; always has been, always will be. The worrisome thing is a marked decline in kop-kop nests along the canals. Lonnie and Valla did a nest count and found about 10 percent of the former numbers.

When Lonnie was a petit garçon about forty years ago, turkey vultures were abundant around the Rainey. But on May 2, 1986, he saw his first one in over twenty years. Why did they disappear? Other vertebrate records of unusual interest include a Harris hawk on July 29; Roberto Gonzales from Monterrey, Mexico, from August 10 to 30; and Noel and Louise Chandler from Okeechobee, Florida, from November 8 to 20. A mixture of Mexican, Cajuns, and Crackers only goes to show that diversity promotes stability. The u.s. State Department calls Old Dad to see if Simon Upton, Speaker of the House in New Zealand, could get in the act. It was all set, but on the appointed day, Upton's plane was weathered in at New Orleans, so he had to take a rain check.

In May 1987, from Holland comes a couple of engineers of the marsh-creating type to accompany Lonnie and Berton, Bubba Perry, and a few biologists from Louisiana State University. They look at marshes west of Rainey that are dying from salt water intrusion. (If the great promoters have their way, a deep water channel through Vermilion Bay, just east of the Rainey, will make our marsh look like Lake Pontchartrain.)

Visitors of the domestic type included Audubon's president Peter Berle, president of Continental Natural Gas Gene Smith, attorney Silas Cooper, petroleum geologist O. R. Carter, and nas member/local businessman Emmet Putnam, who inspected the levees, flumes, weirs, rookery, and gas wells on May 19. It being hot and sultry, the boss asked Berton about swimming in the main canal. Berton allowed as how his younguns do it all the time. Next thing Berton knew, Peter is down the canal about one-fourth of a mile. Says Berton, "He swims like a damned otter!" "But," says Lonnie, "gators is mighty fond of otters." So, when Peter clambers out on the bank with no parts missing, expressions of great relief are in order.

On November 28, Lonnie and Old Dad met with about twenty Aleut Indians and Eskimos from Yukon Flats and a dozen or so Exxon representatives to discuss the dos and don'ts of drilling for gas and oil in wetlands. The effects of same on the Cajun culture and probable effects on Indian and Eskimo cultures were discussed very frankly by Monsieur Legé. (He said it destroyed it.)

In June 1986, we gave the Louisiana Fur and Refuge Division one thousand alligator eggs from thirty-eight nests. The state hatches these eggs and returns 170 gators between four and five feet. This is approximately the same number those eggs would have produced if left in the marsh. The state uses the other gators for research and alligator farming.

Steel weirs are commonly used to control water levels and reduce salt water intrusion. Lonnie installed six rock weirs in various bayous to test their efficiency as compared to steel. We installed staff gauges behind the rock weirs to test rate and volume of flow through and over the rocks. If they work, we'll use rock weirs, since they cost about one-third as much as steel.

Last winter the blue (snow) geese on Rainey and State Wildlife Refuge peaked at about 250,000. Berton led a few field trips for local NAS chapter members, federal magistrates and judges who handle wildlife violations, and board member–geologist Bart Rea and wife, Liz, from Casper, Wyoming. By May 1987, fish were jumpin' in Belle Isle Lake, and the little least terns were making littler ones.

APRIL 1996　After thirty-three years as manager of 26,100 acres of brackish marsh, Lonnie Legé decided the early retirement package was too attractive to turn down. So he turned over a new leaf. He and Valla will travel far and wide, doing a bit of bird-watching, saltwater fishing, and providing relief for beleagured ranchers whose land is overrun with deer.

It comes as no surprise that the other sanctuary managers wanted to acknowledge Lonnie's contribution to the Rainey and to Audubon. It comes in the form of two Bausch and Lomb binocs. Why two?

"Because," says Lonnie, "Valla worked just as hard as I did."

Timmy Vincent majored in wildlife biology at Louisiana State University. Having spent most of his life in and around Louisiana marshes, it is not surprising that he carries on very well where Lonnie Legé left off.

But there have been significant changes in the ecology of the marsh. In the late 1980s, severe hurricanes swept the shells off our island in Belle Isle Lake, making is impossible to keep it from reverting to grass and eventually trees. Least terns require nearly bare gravel for nesting, so we have lost our colony. We are hoping a colony of egrets and herons will occupy the trees.

Essentially all of the marshes between the Rainey and the Mississippi River have been lost because of salt water intrusion. When the Corps of Engineers built levees along the Mississippi and deepened the channel, precious topsoil, that for centuries drifted westward and built marshes such as the Rainey, now goes over the continental shelf to the bottom of the Gulf.

We are trying desperately to get the powers that be to repair the damage so the Paul J. Rainey Sanctuary and adjacent marshes will not become part of the Gulf of Mexico. Currently the National Marine Fisheries Service will not grant us a permit to build the weir across Tom Bayou to slow down the current and stop erosion.

❧ 2 ❧

GREEN ISLAND

SANCTUARY

Rio Hondo, Texas

Although the National Audubon Society had always been interested in protecting all species of birds, the colonial waterbirds undoubtedly played a leading role in establishing our wildlife sanctuaries. Coastal islands in Maine provided the base on which our education-conservation program was launched, but in the early 1920s, the Texas islands became the apple of NAS president John Baker's eye.

From the Texas General Land Office, he leased Green Island in 1923; farther north he acquired the Second Chain of Islands in San Antonio Bay, and the Vingt-et-une Islands in Galveston Bay. Second Chain harbored the largest roseate spoonbill colony in the United States, with Vingt-et-une a close second. Lydia Ann Island near Port Aransas, which had no colonial nesting birds when acquired in 1934, had eight hundred adult reddish egrets, five hundred Louisiana herons, three thousand laughing gulls, and two hundred spoonbills when surveyed by J. J. Carroll in 1939. Carroll was a wealthy lumberman from Houston with the interest and financial means to establish a lasting Texas coastal chain of sanctuaries.

Green Island, east of Brownsville, was of special interest because it contained a large colony of reddish egrets. For some reason, the reddish egrets did not seem to recover from the plume hunting days as well as did the other wading birds.

Our first warden for this area was R. D. Camp, a very competent coastal boatman, thoroughly familiar with the colonial waterbirds. He

On various islands up and down the coast that we have posted and patrolled, Friday figures 250 black skimmers reached flying stage. Production estimates for terns on these islands were as follows: Sandwich, 126; royal, 190; Caspian 126; common, 11.

A great horned owl's nest with three eggs was found on one island on February 25. Friday was not too pleased about this, but later on a raccoon took care of the owl's nest; then Friday took care of the coon. It's just Nature's way.

Hook-and-line anglers like to wade close to Green Island, some coming in for flounder at night. Their presence scares the nesting birds, so Friday scares the wading fishermen, and only the fishermen get their feathers ruffled for very long.

Friday wishes our neighbors in Mexico no bad luck, but he was relieved when Caroline went ashore way south of Green Island. He and his wading birds, terns, and skimmers have enough trouble without help from hurricanes. His December warden's report shows the great blues getting their gonads in gear for another go-round. It just goes to show that, in spite of raccoons, horned owls, boat-tailed grackles, freezes, helicopters, low tides, and hurricanes, life on Green Island goes on pretty much as it has for thousands of years. Since 1923, when Audubon established the sanctuary, we have fairly good records.

In January 1976, wading birds around Green Island were running out of groceries because water temperatures were too cold for small marine life from December until early March, and tides were extremely low.

On January 6, a flock of white pelicans was sighted on the mainland near Harlingen at 5:00 A.M. Normally no one but bird-watchers and drunks would be up at that hour, so when the 10:00 P.M. news reported that "the bird they saw was white, wingspread fifteen feet, six feet tall, and has a three-toed foot twelve inches across," Friday allowed as how the dawn patrol did not consist of birders. Anyway, his phone kept ringing with folks wanting to know who, what, and where. Friday soon got tired of that, jumped in his boat, and headed for Green Island, even though he knew he'd have to drag his boat the last one hundred yards to get there. At three-score years and ten, Friday observes, "I'm not the horse I used to be." But he can still maneuver a boat better than most of us.

He never did find out what the dawn patrol might have seen in the way of a "giant white bird." He suspects they might have seen a very compact flock of white pelicans and have mistaken it for a single bird. But he was grateful for the lack of telephones and electricity on his Green Island Sanctuary.

It was February 29 when the first big flock of reddish egrets, around three hundred, settled down to nesting among the great blues. More came in late until his nesting flock built up to several hundred pairs. For some reason, the reddish like Green Island. They started hatching on April 27.

As the weeks went by and summer came down, the usual complement of nesting herons, egrets, spoonbills, and white ibises were tolerating the vagaries of south Texas wind and weather. Something new had been added, however, when about 400 glossy ibises, mostly white-faced, nested there. (Sue Bailey, our warden up at Sydnes Island, some three hundred miles north, was also invaded by glossies for the first time!) In former years, glossies shied away from Green Island, and those that tried to nest failed. This year, in spite of hail and low water, the droop-snoots hatched and raised a good crop of young.

In mid-July Friday noticed snowy egrets were dying at Green Island, and he notified our biologist, Rich Paul, up at Rockport. Rich was doing research on the reddish egret and acting as warden for Second Chain of Islands up near Port Aransas. Friday explained that the Lower Rio Grande Valley had nine to eleven inches of rain July 5–11. A fish kill followed promptly, limited to the Arroyo Colorado, which empties into the Gulf by Green Island. Large numbers of snowy egrets fed on the dying fish, which were nearly all menhaden, although he and Rich did find a few redfish, black drum, gafftop catfish, speckled trout, sheepshead, and one Spanish mackerel. Friday first noticed dead birds on Green Island on July 11. Snowy egrets were most severely affected. By July 13, every snowy nest contained dead young. At the same time, he saw dead adults along the banks of the Arroyo Colorado. He did *not* find dead birds in a search of numerous farm ponds in the area. As Friday reconstructs it, the adults fed on fish carrying high levels of some toxic chemical and died. The young starved to death. He estimated the loss to be 2,500 adults and young snowies, plus 100 young Louisiana herons, 30 great egrets, 30 little blues, and 15 black-crowns. Fortunately, the reddish egrets were not affected.

The Texas Parks and Wildlife Department has had an office staffed by two fisheries biologists on the Arroyo Colorado since the 1950s. They say menhaden commonly go up the Arroyo Colorado to lower salinity levels and are often killed by sudden influxes of fresh water. This could have not nesting. But they managed to devour quantities of egret eggs. Friday learned that a great grackle roost some miles west had been bulldozed and burned. A familiar story in the Valley, which is also bad for nesting doves and other songbirds.

All things considered, 1978 was relatively unproductive. Even so, the sanctuary produced over 600 reddish egrets, 200 little blue herons, 170 great blues, 900 Louisiana herons, 400 white ibises, 150 white-faced ibises, 550 snowy egrets, 400 black-crowns, and 250 roseate spoonbills. Cattle egrets were hardest hit as they started late, and shade was nil from mid-July to mid-September.

Weatherwise, 1978 was a bad year, and production was down. In spite of adverse conditions, which are so frequent in the lower Laguna Madre, Green Island's contribution to wading birds, especially the relatively rare reddish egret, is very significant year after year. Much of this is due to the devoted attention paid by our warden.

It was June in January down on the Rio Grande in 1979. Friday attended an Audubon chapter meeting in McAllen. His report says, "Very good attendance, over a hundred. Had a good dinner, heard a good speech, and met a lot of almost strangers interested in Green Island."

On January 16, 1979, Friday goes down to our Sabal Palm Grove Sanctuary near Brownsville, along with Dave Blankinship and Old Dad to see how warden Ernest Ortiz is making out with the red-billed pigeon, buff-bellied hummingbird, and cat-eyed snake.

We became painfully aware of Friday's great contribution to reddish egrets and wading birds when he was forced to retire for health reasons in 1985. He will long be remembered for his colorful language, his colorful character, and his devotion to reddish egrets and other sharp-faced fowl.

In July 1986, Greg Silstoff, who replaced Friday on March 1, 1986, and Jesse Grantham, assistant Sanctuary Department director for western sanctuaries, concluded that Friday's absence explained the presence of a dozen or more raccoons on Green Island. Breeding pairs of reddish egrets numbered about fifty in 1985, only ten in 1986, and four in 1987.

In 1988 an excellent Sanctuary Wardens Attack Team tore down and rebuilt the observation tower on Green Island, and twenty Audubon Expedition students arrived to cut trails, paint the tower, create tern habitat on the shoreline, and start rebuilding the old cabin. A fitting tribute to Friday Fluman will thus be available for his replacement.

Unfortunately, replacing Friday Fluman has presented problems. Due to financial constraints, having a full-time manager at this important sanctuary has been impractical.

In July 1998, our volunteer warden, Jim Palmer, found several dead roseate spoonbills. They were young birds in the early flying stage. One great blue heron appeared crippled from unknown causes.

Our nearest full-time sanctuary manager, Jimmy Paz, is stationed at our Sabal Palm Sanctuary, a few miles east of Brownsville, Texas. Jimmy Paz and Jim Palmer do their best to protect these wading-bird colonies. But on occasion, their best is not good enough.

gional rep Ron Klataske, and Nebraska Audubon chapters and cooperators had saved the staging grounds of some 200,000 cranes and had done the taxpayers a great favor.

According to Bob, whenever sandhill cranes are concentrated on the Platte, they use three general types of habitat: (1) shallow submerged sandbars in broad stretches of the river as night roosting sites; (2) wet meadows, especially those near roosting sites, for feeding, loafing, courting, and as secondary roosting areas; and (3) corn and milo stubble and alfalfa and hay meadows for primary feeding sites. The first type is gradually becoming scarce due to upstream projects by the Corps, BuRec, and the Soil Conservation Service, which stay in business by putting wild rivers out of business. In addition, the gravel bars are being sold for construction material; then the gravel pits form a lake on which a new "waterfront" cottage is built. The second type, wet meadows, is also subject to drainage and conversion to croplands or gravel-mining operations.

As is always the case with any wildlife sanctuary, somebody somewhere figures he or she could make more money if the land were put to some other use. The National Audubon Society has to fight those changes that would destroy the natural resources that the sanctuary is intended to save. The Rowe is no different from the Rainey, the Corkscrew, or the Starr Ranch in this regard. It's an old familiar struggle that will never end. We win some and we lose some, but we gray-haired warden types can remember when we didn't win any.

The corn, milo, and hay stubble are normal by-products of farming operations, so they are plentiful. As in the case of flat-faced fowl, landowners do not object to sharing their waste corn, milo, weed seeds, and insects with the bugling cranes.

The sandhills prefer to roost at night in shallow water that flows over the sandbars. They leave the river about daybreak for the adjacent wet meadows where they spend a couple hours feeding, bugling, dancing, and carrying on like cranes. Bob thinks the high protein content of the animal life and plant tubers in the wet meadows may be very important to female cranes on their way to the nesting grounds up north. The flocks move out to grain fields by midmorning, back to the wet meadows around noon, to the grain fields again in the afternoon. Around sunset and into total darkness, they come streaming back to the wet meadows and finally hop over to the river shallows for the night.

The presence of a large food supply of high quality, wet meadows, and shallow but submerged sandbars in a broad open river is apparently why the Rowe and other stretches of the Platte are major staging areas. A substantial reduction in any or all of these components would probably spell disaster for a dominant feature of Nebraska land.

Our management plans, which Bob Wicht, Tom Logan, and Ron Klataske have developed and are implementing, call for maintaining and restoring all components of that dark and bloody ground we call prairie. Upstream dams enable trees and brush to take over the sandbars. Either the trees or the cranes have got to go. The native grasslands must be maintained by judicious use of substitutes for the prairie fires and buffalo that once enabled big bluestem grass to win the eternal struggle against oaks and willows. Persuading human critters that the enjoyment of cranes and all that goes with them is part of our standard of living is the greatest challenge of all.

While Bob was waiting for the cranes last fall, the stork came by on September 19 and dropped off son Jason. As soon as Jason can tell a whooping crane from a sandhill, we'll see about getting him an Audubon badge. That is, unless mother Janis decides that one crazy crane-chaser in the family is enough.

NOVEMBER 1976 Bob Wicht says he is glad to be out from under the shadow of the Midstate Reclamation Project, which was defeated at the polls in November 1975. On the other hand, he could have used many more rain clouds because the drought on the prairie hurt our hay and corn crops. Of the 782 acres in the Rowe we have about 32 in corn, of which we keep two-fifths and give the sharecropper three-fifths. He picks a strip twelve rows wide, then leaves a strip of eight rows. These alternative strips are used by sandhill cranes and other critters. The harvestable hay fields cover about 160 acres, and in a good year will produce about 150 tons. We leave some standing for food and cover; we sell some for cash; and we give the farmer half. Our long-range goal on the Rowe is to restore the native prairie grasses over most of the area. Any cash received is plowed back into the sanctuary.

In 1976 by late August, the Platte River, which runs through the Rowe from west to east, was as dry as Old Dad at the start of happy hour. It was about September 10 before any water came down the Platte. Although the drought was bad for domestic crops, it helped slow down the spread of brush and trees that ruin the riverbed habitat for roosting cranes.

Although Bob has seen whooping cranes on the sanctuary (the last time was October 30, 31, and November 1, 1974), verified records for Nebraska are scarce. The average for the Rowe region is about two per year. Last fall Bob decided to see what would happen if the Rowe Sanctuary offered a reward of ten dollars for every *verified* sighting. Executive vice president Charlie Callison gave us the green light, thinking Audubon probably would not lose too many green dollars.

We expected a flood of false alarms, all of which would have to be investigated. Bob wisely had the federal game wardens, state wardens, biologists, and reliable birders lined up to help check out each sighting. Members of this assemblage drove many a mile only to find every kind of white bird from avocets to white pelicans. But alas! no whooping cranes.

Meanwhile, down at Aransas and Second Chain of Islands, Texas, Dave Blankinship was scanning the skies and chalking up a record number of whoopers arriving on the wintering grounds. When returns from upstate were in, the count was fifty-six adults, twelve young, total sixty-eight; the highest count of whooping cranes since the 1930s. Although no one saw them going through Nebraska, they obviously got from Wood Buffalo Park in northwest Canada to Texas by some route or routes.

Sandy Sprunt, Research Department director, says the Whooping Crane Recovery Team is adopting Bob Wicht's idea for rewarding verified whooping crane sightings on a flyway-wide basis as of next year. It just goes to show you those high-powered scientists will eventually come to the rescue of endangered species if the Audubon research and warden staff will show 'em how it's done.

JANUARY 1979 Bob Wicht, Keeper of the Sandhill Crane, is bracing himself for the spring flood of visitors who come to put the long eye (sometimes called telescope and/or binoculars) on the long-legged birds. The best wildlife show in Nebraska is almost too popular for one warden to direct. Bob has made every possible effort to accompany as many people as possible on the sanctuary. But one man working seven days per week from daylight until dark can only accommodate so many, so we are in the market for additional personnel. As Bob's annual report states, "If the use of the Sanctuary is to be fully understood, and the area adequately protected against unauthorized visitors, the manager cannot be tied to visitor pressure all season." Bob suggests that a minimal entrance fee would offset the cost of additional help.

Unfortunately, the spring migration comes at the busiest time of the year, when the manager has patrolling, spring planting, control burning, and many other management duties. To try to be all things to all people when the air is full of bugling cranes and the motel is full of breathless birders is like convincing Sandy Sprunt and Carlyle Blakeney, of Florida and South Carolina, respectively, that Ulysses S. Grant was America's greatest general.

People on the Platte present a problem, but they are probably easier to handle than the pork-barrel projects to dam and divert the water. As the volume of water and the flushing and scouring action of the current are altered, brushy vegetation is able to invade the sandbars and shallows. Cranes want bare sand or shallow water for roosting, so vegetation control in the river channel remains a perennial problem. Time, money, and energy to develop new methods of controlling this vegetation are very high on Bob's want list.

The Rowe has about three hundred acres of grasslands of varying quality. Some areas, heavily overgrazed in the past, are recovering under Bob's management. Others could be used as a source of native seed in our efforts to restore the native grasses. If we're going into this program in a big way, however, Bob recommends that we purchase our own equipment, which should pay for itself in a few years and could be used for other purposes as well.

An observation tower that we built some time ago has been heavily used and much appreciated by visiting biologists and birders. It has been a great help in handling visitors, and Bob wants it kept in good repair and another tower or two added at strategic points along the river.

Bob is seriously considering going back to college for an advanced degree next fall. Although this is a worthy project on Bob's part, and we will help any way we can, replacing him at the Rowe will be extremely difficult. The U.S. Fish and Wildlife Service, through its Northern Prairie Wildlife Research Center in North Dakota, has been working on the cranes and the Platte, centering around the Rowe. The Nebraska Game and Parks Commission has also been very cooperative. We must make sure that, if we have to replace Bob Wicht, his successor will be able to talk the language of the feds, the state, the farmers, the birders, the television crews, newspaper reporters, and especially the cranes.

JULY 1983 Ken and Marie Strom successfully made the transition from the steaming Four Hole Swamp Beidler Forest Sanctuary in South Carolina to the drying-oven known as Gibbon, Nebraska. Ken's first report as manager of the Lillian Annette Rowe Sanctuary is most enthusiastic. They miss the cypress trees, tupelo gum, and prothonotary warblers; but when the sandhill cranes pile in next March, we suspect they will more than fill the void.

SEPTEMBER 1986 Russian olives, musk thistles, and the Bureau of Reclamation were not found on the unbroken native prairies of North America. From the standpoint of big bluestem, blazing star, piping plovers, least terns, sandhill cranes, and whooping cranes, they should not be there now. But they are.

Consequently, for days on end, an army consisting of Ken and Marie Strom attacks the Russian olive. On some days, reinforcements armed with front-end loader and chain saw, arrive from the Omaha Audubon Society, local Boy Scouts, Girl Scouts, state parks, and hired hands. More than one thousand trees about one foot in diameter make way for prairie grasses in a single day, and many musk thistles lose out to the natives.

As troublesome as exotic plants may be, they are not in the same league as the Bureau of Reclamation. As usual, while federal, state, and private agencies are fighting to save and restore wetlands, and the Endangered Species Act says the feds can't spend money to destroy the habitat of endangered whooping cranes and least terns, BuRec goes blithely on with colossal schemes to dewater the Platte River.

So Ken goes to countless hearings and meetings from Boulder, Colorado, to Grand Island, Kearney, Lincoln, and Omaha, Nebraska, and Washington, D.C. He lobbies appropriate members of Congress; briefs congressional staff members; and gives countless lectures at schools, Audubon chapter meetings, service clubs, and business groups. He is on radio and television and in the newspapers. He is on BuRec's hit list.

The promoters stare at one another and wonder, "Why would anybody want to keep *any* water in the Platte where it just goes to waste?" BuRec solemnly swears their "research" shows that reducing the flow in the Platte to only 890 cubic feet per second would provide optimum habitat for whooping cranes! Marie testified (very effectively we are told) at a hearing wherein developers tried to repeal Nebraska's Endangered Species Act.

Generally speaking, local business people, bankers, and politicians believe their fortunes fluctuate in direct proportion to the amount of federal dollars spent in their bailiwick. It is perhaps too much to hope that they will question the wisdom of irrigating more land to produce more surplus crops. On the other hand, the chamber of commerce types around Kearney and Grand Island are aware that sandhill cranes bring thousands of tourists in March, and they are thinking, "There's gold in them thar birds." Thus, a new interest in the Platte, the cranes, the Rowe, and Ken and Marie is awakening.

At present, Ron Klataske, regional rep and his staff, are helping Ken play David and Goliath. Only trouble is BuRec has more than one head, so Ken's slingshot must hold many, many stones. It has been said, however, "Truth, crushed to earth, shall rise again."

Even though Ken and Marie spend twenty-five hours per day fighting the diligent destroyers, they find time for many wildlife observations. On November 21, 1985, Marie found three whooping cranes on the Rowe, the third time whoopers have been seen in the same spot in eleven years. It is the cranes' favorite spot in Nebraska. But we only own one side of the river at this spot, and when blinds are hunted on the other side, it's of no use to cranes. Ken immediately measured width, depth, height of vegetation, and other features at this cross-section of the Platte, trying to guess what the whoopers like about it.

On July 4, 1985, with Professor Hal Nagel from the University of Nebraska at Kearney leading the annual Xerces Society butterfly count, 278 butterflies of fifteen species were found on the Rowe. Alfalfa butterflies, regal fritillaries, and large wood nymphs were most numerous. The regal fritillary is usually found only on virgin tall grass prairies, especially wet prairies, and the Rowe usually has the nation's highest count.

On June 5, 1985, Marie found the first piping plover chicks of the year and later found five least (little) tern nests, with a total of fourteen eggs. They found another least tern nest and three piping plover nests on July 4.

Because of low water in the Platte, dirt bikers use it for a highway, which spells disaster for these endangered species. If the birds escape the dirt bikers, the engineers at Kingsley Dam open the gates during the nesting season, which eliminates bikers and birds in the river channel. So far, the state and federal wardens only pursue gunners, not bikers or dam tenders.

The past year was good for several "first records" for the Rowe Sanctuary, including sanderlings, white-rumped sandpipers, least sandpipers, stilt sandpipers, Virginia rails, and a clutch of bluebirds. And during prescribed burning on May 7, 1986, the first smooth green snake was captured. This is only the fifth record for Nebraska. Needless to say, the specimen was returned to the area where found. November 9, 1985, was also the first time large flocks of snow geese were seen. They usually stay farther east.

Although prescribed burning is accepted by all prairie ecologists as a necessary management tool for preserving and restoring prairies, Nebraska farmers put it in the same category as Communism, spitting on the flag, and mixing ginger ale with good Scotch. Ken says it will take a long time, even for Marie, to change the neighbors' minds on this one.

As a substitute for burning, and to keep controller Jim Cunningham happy, Ken usually sells about $1,800 worth of hay. But with farmers going bankrupt and selling off their cattle, who's buying hay? Nobody.

Ed and Sil Pembleton, assistant regional rep and wife from Ron Klataske's office, spent a few days helping Ken and Marie with the tower blind project. Papa Joe Edmonson, versatile leader of Audubon's Sanctuary Wardens Attack Team, helped design the new blinds that are set on telephone poles twenty feet tall and will hold up to 15 people. Some 535 people climbed in to peer out at the long-legged bugling birds last March. Among them were NAS board member Bart Rea, Dick Plunkett of our New York office staff, and a couple of congressional staffers who work on water projects in the House of Representatives in Washington, D.C.

November 1986 was the coldest on record. The geese and ducks concentrated on our stretch of the Platte and kept it open. This further concentrated the flat-faced fowl, the mighty nimrods, and the game wardens. It also meant before-dawn-till-dark patrol by Ken and Marie. The game wardens often say they wish Audubon owned the entire six miles, both sides of the river, between the two bridges. We do, too.

On their return from the Audubon Convention, Ken and Marie stopped at Aullwood Farm in Dayton, Ohio, to consult those pioneers in prairie restoration, Paul Knoop, manager-naturalist of Aullwood, and the former owner and NAS board member, Marie Aull.

Like the hero of medieval romance King Tristram, Ken Strom is "one of the time-tested few who leave the world, when they are gone, not the same place it was." From the standpoint of cranes, plovers, prairies, and people, the Platte River country is better off because Ken and Marie have been there. Although they are badly outnumbered and their financial resources are but a tiny fraction of those available for dewatering the Platte, support for their efforts to save the cranes and their habitat continues to grow. This is not too surprising in view of the incredible schedule they maintain.

In addition to the dozens of illustrated lectures, countless meetings with federal bureaucrats, state wildlife biologists, and Audubon staff, Ken and Marie, as an extra added attraction, put on a show called "The Platte:

Treasures of a Prairie River" at the prestigious Smithsonian Institution in Washington, D.C. In the large audience were such notables as Elvis J. Stahr, president emeritus, NAS, and Glenn Paulson, vice president for science, NAS.

The spring staging of the sandhill cranes along the Platte in March has made the news far and wide. With help from Ken and Marie, the delighted chamber of commerce and travel bureaus put out an attractive folder called *Crane Watch,* a guide to spring viewing of cranes. Newspapers— and television and radio stations—across the state feature this wildlife spectacle and even give credit to Audubon and the Rowe! Chris Palmer, NAS film maker, has visions of an Audubon TV special on the Platte that should equal his other smash hits, such as *Ducks under Siege.*

Articles appeared in *Life,* the *New York Times,* and *Midwest Living.* Bruce Reitherman of BBC-TV came by, as did Swedish photographer Sture Karlsson and NAS board members Donald Stokes and Bill Riley and their wives.

But you ain't heard nothin' yet. On April 2, 1987, Ken teams up with Mr. Whooping Crane, a.k.a. Dave Blankinship, en route to China for an International Crane Workshop. Comes May 5, in Qiqihar, China, and Ken presents his lecture. The international gathering passes a resolution to save the Platte for posterity, news of which promptly makes the *Omaha World Herald.* Some two hundred scientists from twenty-nine nations attended. In addition to the paper sessions, several field trips through plains and marshes of northeastern China gave Ken and Dave insight into the management problems and techniques used by Chinese biologists.

We've never been very good at telling folks what Audubon is and does. That's not what prompted Lillian Annette Rowe to donate money for a sanctuary, but look what she set in motion! But please don't get the impression that Ken and Marie spent all their time on public relations. Perish forbid! Their first loyalty is to the wild plants and animals on the prairie. Whenever whooping cranes are sighted on or near the Rowe, the state and federal biologists rely on Ken and Marie to monitor when, where, and (maybe someday) why cranes do what they do. Some 50,000 Canada geese with a few snows and white-fronts attract attention. On January 10, 1987, 160 bald eagles are counted along fifty miles of the Platte.

In March it's handling visitors before dawn until after dark, seven days a week. On March 21, about 4,500 sandhill cranes made lots of noise, attracted hundreds of folks, some of whom were trapped by two blizzards in late March, which paralyzed the area and changed the behavior of the cranes. They fed in the fields until after dark, and many apparently roosted in the fields instead of the Rowe. Students from the Wyoming Cooperative Wildlife Research Unit came by to study the effect of power lines on cranes. On April 9, 1987, a sandhill wearing band number UP 11 appeared for the third consecutive year in the same part of the sanctuary. On April 16, Craig Faanes, well-known ornithologist, recorded an Eskimo curlew just east of the Rowe. Ken spent a week in May uprooting musk thistles, the worst infestation in four years. (Pete DeSimone, at Starr Ranch, California, says, "Welcome to the club!")

In July 1987, piping plover and least tern nests were again flooded when engineers opened the upstream dam for reasons known only to engineers. On July 4 the annual Xerces Society butterfly count found the regal fritillaries back in goodly numbers. On August 7–8, for the first time in ten years, several short-billed marsh wrens (erroneously called sedge wrens) were present.

In February 1987, Ken and the game warden trapped a pair of trappers who were trapping where no traps are supposed to be. One of the most promising ornithologist-photographer-writers in the business, Art Gingert (former manager of Miles Sanctuary in Connecticut) came by in late June to ply his trade.

Ed and Sil Pembleton have been a great help in building blinds, handling visitors, and in the fight to save the Platte. So their farewell party brought mixed emotions to Ken and Marie. But Ed promises to keep up the good work in the Audubon Washington office.

In the general election of November 1986, Ken was (believe it or not) elected as a director of the Central Platte Natural Resources District. This august body has been promoting the infamous Prairie Bend and Twin Valley water diversion projects! What hath got rot?

In their spare time, Ken and Marie are doing a feasibility study for a visitor center at the sanctuary. (If we don't build it, our competition is almost certain to try to steal the show.)

Speaking of competition-turned-ally, Dave Wesley is offering help from Ducks Unlimited in the struggle to save the Platte. Now that is something of which two great organizations can be proud.

There is much talk nowadays that the Bureau of Reclamation has run out of rivers to dam or divert and so are making noises about being good guys. Maybe the Ken and Marie Stroms of this world are giving BuRec pause. Or is BuRec playing wolf in sheep's clothing? We shall see.

JUNE 1990 When you take an old boy off the Platte and plunk him down in Pakistan, you might expect he would need a period of adjustment. Ken Strom says such was not the case. He and Mumtax Malik took to each other like sandhill cranes to wet meadows.

Ken left for Pakistan in late November 1989, via Switzerland, where he contacted some Pakistani biologists attending the International Union for Conservation of Nature (IUCN) Population and Environment Conference. They gave him some ideas on what to look for. After calling on Pakistan government officials, the U.S. Embassy, and the USAID Mission, he visited the major riverine wetlands used by migrating cranes in the Northwest Frontier Province. These are on the Indus River and two tributaries, the Kabal and Kurram.

Ken says the Indus River offered a glimpse of what the Platte must have looked like one hundred years ago. His observations and comments were gratefully accepted by Pakistani wildlife officials, and he says the visit was "extremely beneficial for me."

He spent a week in Nepal, primarily looking at a project dealing with human impacts on wildlife at Chitwan National Park, which could provide another site for our Population and Wildlife Project. Because humans are the greatest enemy of humans and other animals, be it in Nepal or Nebraska, Ken inspected some rather remote wetland areas that are threatened by humans hungry for money and food. The King Mahendra Trust and USAID staff had several ideas about Audubon participation in this work.

The end of the year found our guy from Gibbon in Rajkot, India, attending the Asian Crane Congress. Over 150 cranologists from Asia, Europe, and the United States discussed critical conservation and research needs for the cranes that pass through Pakistan and Afghanistan.

Mumtaz Malik had never seen the Platte, and Nebraskans had never seen him, but this was all changed in late March and early April 1990. According to Ken, Mumtaz made a hit at several chapter events. They flew the Platte and, all in all, had a grand tour of crane-cornhusker country.

Although cranes and some of the flat-faced fowl have been crossing the Bering Straits without passports for thousands of years, a two-day visit to the Rowe by five Russian ornithologists in April was something new. They had been up at Baraboo, Wisconsin, visiting the International Crane Foundation. Ken had met one of them in India. Only one spoke English, but crane talk is more or less universal, so the three Russian refuge managers from Siberia and the one from the Platte had much in common and made out well.

While all these international crane conferences were taking place, things back at the Rowe were in high gear. Another storm was brewing over the relicensing of Kingsley Dam. The Federal Energy Regulatory Commission (FERC) keeps an eye on various water development projects. To the consternation of the local public power districts and other water users, the FERC recently allowed as how the dam had damaged the Platte and accepted the U.S. Fish and Wildlife Service's recommended flowage for endangered cranes, terns, and plovers. Those who firmly believe growth can and should go on forever—in population, pollution, water consumption—are staring in disbelief! They are asking, "What is water for if it ain't to be used? What good is a least tern, or piping plover, or them damn cranes?"

Meanwhile, back at the Rowe, that master plumber, carpenter, and contractor Papa Joe Edmondson, with wife, Char, arrives on April 15, 1990, and proceeds to make an old farmhouse into an office building. This means a new well, new floor, new bathroom, new wiring and plumbing. Believe it or not, the whole project saved us a lot of money, and the job is done right. Such is not always the case in the modern world.

Once again, the number of cranes and visitors sets a new record. And, as every sanctuary manager knows, managing hundreds of visitors is wildlife management of a different sort, the kind they don't teach you in college. Plans for a long-awaited visitor center are taking shape.

In November 1989, Ross Medcalf, who was hired as a part-time warden, was soon clearing brush on the islands and riverbanks and patrolling along with Marie and volunteers during hunting season. Marie continued to monitor depth in our ground-water wells and stay on top of the myriad goings on at the Rowe. Because of the very bad drought, the Rainwater Basin was without rainwater, so over fifty-thousand flat-faced fowl spent most of the winter on the sanctuary stretch of the Platte.

Ken Strom says in July 1991 rainfall was way down, irrigation way up, and so the Platte at Rowe resembled the Rio Grande at Sabal Palm, our sanctuary below Brownsville, Texas. Because the spring breakup no longer scrapes the brush off the sandbars, the only bare sandy spots the least terns and piping plovers can find is in the bottom of the channel. Along comes a summer cloudburst, aggravated by massive releases of irrigation water, and away go the nests of these endangered species.

Ken and naturalist Bill Dunn are considering building sandy, brush-free islands, probably dredging up sand to create tern and plover habitat. Over twenty years ago, Lonnie and Berton Legé created an island in Belle Isle Lake at the Rainey Sanctuary in Louisiana, and a colony of least terns was established the following spring. It is very much worth a try at Rowe.

Restoring 140 acres of native prairie is another project that dickcissels, grasshopper sparrows, and birders will appreciate. At the Research Ranch Sanctuary in Arizona, we are restoring the semidesert grassland; at Rowe, it's native prairie. Because big bluestem, blazing star, and sandhill cranes don't vote, the u.s. Department of Agriculture looks askance at grasslands restoration. But Pheasants Forever, a private sportsmen's group, furnished milo seed to plant as a cover crop on 140 acres to be restored. The usfws, as part of its biodiversity program, also contributes to the project. The feds are also contributing about $5,000 toward the cost of clearing the brush from the sandbars. Seeing as how the Platte, cranes, fish, and grasslands are a public resource, it is fitting and proper that we should get a little help in conserving them.

The River Conference in March 1991 was a big success. So much so that the chamber of commerce types are beginning to see that corn and cows are not their only source of revenue.

Last September, Hal Nagel, professor at the University of Nebraska, Kearney, published a paper, "Regal Fritillary Butterfly Population Estimation and Natural History on Rowe Sanctuary." On 180 acres of our Harris-Day Prairie in 1990, Hal indicated a population of over fourteen hundred. Rowe has produced the highest count of regal fritillaries every year since 1970. Ken says Rowe may be more critical for butterflies than for cranes.

Andre Ivanov Smolenski visited last September. He and Ken planned an exchange program under the expanded Sharing the Earth Project, matching the Platte with the Amur River in Siberia. Andre gave a program on Russian natural areas to local Auduboners.

Chandra Gurung of Nepal came by last November. He toured the Platte and gave several programs locally. Pakistan, Russia, and Nepal are all working together on saving crane habitat and the burgeoning human population that threatens it.

Heather Whitaker, coordinator for Sharing the Earth, arrived February 1991. She set up poster displays in Russian and Chinese for use in those countries.

Ken was in northern California and Oregon November 18–21 to give five programs for Audubon chapters. His attendance at the Platte River

Instream Flow Water Rights meetings have paid off. For the first time in history, wildlife was granted some rights to the water in the Platte! Audubon sanctuaries do make a difference.

1 9 9 3   In 1973 National Audubon, using a modest donation from Lillian Annette Rowe, acquired 757 acres extending two and a half miles along the Platte, including the riverbed itself. We wanted to have the standing of landowner should it be necessary to take on the mighty U.S. Bureau of Reclamation (we called it "wreck-lamation") to protect the trickle of water that remained in the Platte.

For a few years we could afford only a part-time manager at the magnificent salary of fifty dollars per month. (Having lost both arms in Vietnam, Bob Wicht received a modest pension to supplement his income.) Nevertheless, with the help of local chapters, local voters, and Ron Klataske's regional office, we defeated the infamous Midstate Project that would have diverted the last of the water.

The Kingsley Dam, 150 miles west of the Rowe, often releases enough water to flood the nests of the endangered piping plover in one fell swoop. Ken Strom and staff are urging the Federal Energy Regulatory Commission to require dam operators to provide adequate seasonal flow for wildlife, rather than an occasional flood. But, as our ex-boss, Glenn Paulson, can tell you, the Department-of-Energy mind can be almost impervious to reason.

In spite of its humble beginning, Rowe has become known across the nation and around the world. As part of our Sharing the Earth Program, from October 15 to 30, 1992, Ken is off to Pakistan to meet not only his counterpart, Mumtaz Malik, but also Pakistan's minister for population and forests as well as the inspector general of forests. He toured the new Lakki Crane Refuge and explored the possibility of a "Sister Sanctuary" project with Lakki. He made presentations and took part in discussions on the Platte's cranes and the human pressures on them for a camp of twenty crane hunters near Lakki, for seventy students in a Peshawar High School Wildlife Club, and for thirty-five biologists and sportsmen at a special provincial conference on wildlife management challenges.

Meanwhile, back at Rowe, Bill Dunn and Kent Skaggs (naturalists and interns) do to an island in the Platte what the scouring currents used to do; that is, clear the island of brush so the cranes could roost on it. They also shingled the roof of the newest observation blind and built a new entrance gate and split-rail fencing at headquarters.

Kent and Heather Whitaker collected seeds of native forbes and grasses from the sanctuary's prairie areas and bought some additional seed to plant in the meadow south of headquarters. We hope eventually to restore all of the native prairie, both here and up in Bruce Barbour's bailiwick at the Edward Brigham Alkali Lake Sanctuary near Jamestown, North Dakota.

Ken and Heather are much in demand for lectures in Nebraska, Iowa, and elsewhere. The Christmas Bird Count found forty-eight species braving the Nebraska winter. Three grad students from the University of Nebraska worked with Ken on plans for using the Rowe as a study site for "Influences of Riparian Vegetation on Wildlife and Fisheries Populations in the Central Platte River."

Newspapers, magazines (including *Audubon*), and programs feature the Rowe. To give them something to write and talk about, the first sandhill cranes arrived February 7, 1993, but the first big push of cranes and geese came on the twenty-seventh, about two weeks later than usual. The remote sensing crew reported that thermal infrared imagery data collected in 1989 show that Rowe has by far the largest concentration of cranes on the Platte, over 110,000, or almost 25 percent of the Platte's cranes, which is probably the single largest concentration in the Western Hemisphere.

And, if that ain't enough, we normally have the nation's highest count of regal fritillary butterflies on the annual July 4 Xerces Society butterfly count.

That crew at Rowe must be doing something right. At least the cranes, butterflies, and a million-plus ducks and geese must think so, as does the chamber of commerce. Planning for 100,000 visitors during March and April keeps our staff busy and the merchants happy.

After an unusually snowy winter, a chinook wind in March gave the ducks and cranes the wettest wet meadows they've had in five years.

The Nebraska Audubon Council met with our staff to plan for the Spring Crane Watch activities, as well as strategy for the upcoming policy issues affecting the Platte and its wildlife.

Heather worked with the Institute of Soviet-American Relations, planning for the two Russian wildlife managers who started their six-week fellowships in March.

Also in March, well over a million ducks and geese came to the Platte-Rainwater Basin Region—over a half million snow geese—a new record this far west in the Central Flyway. Over twelve hundred people used our well-built crane-watch blinds. For lagniappe, five whooping cranes visited

Rowe, using the same spot they were seen in last year. We had visitors from thirty-four states and seven foreign countries, including Russia, Japan, Bangladesh, Germany, Canada, and Egypt.

Lillian Annette, look what you started!

1995 After Ken Strom retired from the Rowe, Paul Tebbel very adequately filled Ken's big shoes. He has an MSc in zoology and spent many years working on sandhill cranes and other wildlife in Michigan, Wisconsin, and Ontario. Bill Dunn is still the assistant manager. He has a BSc in business management but is no beginner in electrical contracting and packing house management.

Kent Skaggs is our naturalist; born and raised in Nebraska, he received his BSc in biology from Kearney State College.

We are sure Lillian Annette Rowe would be pleased to see what is taking place on the land that bears her name. The sanctuary has up to twenty-two hundred acres with more visitors every year.

MAINE COASTAL ISLANDS

SANCTUARY

Medomak, Maine

Since its beginning in 1935, the Audubon Camp in Maine has been an outstanding center for education in the various fields of natural history. The teaching staff for that first summer session reads like a Who's Who in biological science. It included men who later became famous in their fields: Roger Tory Peterson in ornithology; Allan Cruickshank, who became a famous author and wildlife photographer; and entomologist Donald J. Borror, who, among other accomplishments, made great strides in recording the songs of birds.

Thus, the Maine Coastal Island Sanctuaries provided Steve Kress an outdoor classroom and research center par excellence. As we can see, Steve was able to take full advantage of these wildlife resources.

Had you visited these islands about four hundred years ago, you would have seen puffins on Eastern Egg Rock, Western Egg Rock, Matinicus Rock, Large Green Island, Machias Seal Island, and Seal Island. Had you been a typical pioneer, meat from those puffins would have gone down your gullet; their feathers, into your pillows and mattresses. In the 1880s, the demand for puffin wings and feathers to adorn women's hats exceeded the supply. By 1901 the last pair of puffins south of the Canadian border had Matinicus Rock all to themselves. Europeans of the genus *Homo* had extirpated the rest.

In 1901, just before the National Audubon Society was organized, a group of scientists and concerned people hired one of America's first

The puffin restoration project is a success!
(Photo: Steven Walker)

wildlife wardens, the Matinicus Rock lighthouse keeper, to protect the puffins. From this humble beginning, as with brown pelicans, Everglade kites, several plume birds, and wood storks, Audubon sanctuary managers have brought the u.s. population of puffins from the brink of extirpation to relative abundance.

Once adequate protection was established, puffins begin to come back to Matinicus Rock. In 1999, you'll find not one, but about 150 pairs doing what puffins do when we take time to care and act in their behalf.

In 1972, Steve Kress (Ph.D. scientist and seabird expert on staff of NAS Research Department) and Old Dad discussed the possibility of using Todd Sanctuary, specifically Eastern Egg Rock, as an outdoor lab to test whether or not puffin chicks could survive the one-thousand-mile journey from Newfoundland, be placed in man-made burrows, fed by hand, and fledged. Old Dad allowed as how it would be a long shot, to say the least. No one had ever attempted such a far-out scheme. On the other hand, puffins had once nested on Eastern Egg Rock. What prevented their return?

As Kress observed, "While they thrived on Matinicus Rock, puffins never came back to Eastern Egg Rock and those other islands. Why?"

Since it is well known that gulls will eat puffin eggs, chicks, and adults, he suspected the population explosion of gulls of several species, due to an increased food supply in the form of garbage, factory wastes, dead fish, and fish parts from commercial boats, prevented puffins from even landing there—to say nothing of raising chicks.

Biologists from the u.s. Fish and Wildlife Service agreed that gulls would prevent puffins from reestablishing a colony on any of the islands they had once occupied. Suffice it to say, a gull control program was highly essential to our plan for the puffins.

As any veteran wildlife manager can tell you, managing wildlife is relatively easy; managing people can be very difficult. While restoration of an endangered species has wide public support, reducing the population of another species that may be limiting your restoration efforts can arouse an emotional storm of protest.

Without too much publicity, federal biologists sprayed the eggs of the black-backed and herring gulls. With the predatory gull population somewhat reduced, the restoration of puffins to Eastern Egg Rock was made possible.

The Canadian Wildlife Service agreed to help Steve, so in 1973 he flew to Newfoundland with a couple of graduate students. They were taken by boat out to Great Island, site of the largest puffin colony in North America. They stuck their arms into puffin burrows and collected a total of six chicks that were ten to fourteen days old. They placed the chicks in soup cans nailed inside a wooden box, flew them safely back to Eastern Egg Rock, and placed them in man-made burrows.

A female puffin lays one egg in a rocky crevice or in a long earthen tunnel; some of the latter are eight feet long, dug by those strong, comical beaks and sharp toenails. By using chicks that were ten to fourteen days old, the puffineers did not have to keep the nestlings warm. Since the adult usually drops fish into the burrow and leaves to go fishing again, the foster puffin parents adopted the same technique—they placed a fish at the burrow openings twice a day—which was adequate in all respects.

When old enough, the chicks were color-banded, so each could be identified in later years. A month later, in mid-August, the chicks were ready to fledge. At night the crew hid behind rocks and watched as a chick stumbled down to the water's edge and out to sea.

According to Steve's reports, "In 1973, we began with 6 baby puffins. The next year we took 54 chicks, and increased to about 100 chicks per summer until 1981 . . . . by then we had brought 954 tiny fuzzballs south to Maine, probably the only time suitcases have been filled with downy puffins."

Steve hoped that, like wild ducks, the offspring would return to where they learned to fly, not to where they hatched. Unlike wood ducks and mallards, however, puffins do not come back to nest as yearlings. They spend two or three years on the ocean before returning. Steve says only about 30 percent to 40 percent of them survive and return to land.

As puffins are colonial birds, he assumed a few decoys would help. In 1979, four years after beginning his project, he was looking at a large rock with three decoys on it, plus one live puffin! From its leg band, he knew it was one of his 1975 transplants from Newfoundland.

On July 4, 1981, a puffin was seen carrying fish, which meant a newborn chick was waiting for food. Eight years of hard work had paid off. For the first time in one hundred years, puffins were nesting again on Eastern Egg Rock.

To make a long incredible story short, Steve and his team have also restored puffins on Seal Island in nearby Penobscot Bay. There are now about nineteen pairs nesting on Eastern Egg Rock and about forty-five pairs on Seal Island.

The millinery trade had also eliminated terns from Eastern Egg Rock

Adult puffin brings food to the burrow containing young puffins.
(Photo: Stephen W. Kress)

Visitors at Eastern Egg Rock Sanctuary.
(Photo: Steven Walker)

and Seal Island. Since decoys worked so well with puffins, Steve and crew set out tern decoys and played tape recordings made in another tern colony. Common terns and occasionally an endangered roseate tern almost immediately were attracted to the islands, but three or four years elapsed before they started nesting.

The methods developed by Steve and his staff in Maine have since been used by an Audubon team in the Galapagos Islands on the dark-rumped petrel. Their ideas are employed in seabird colonies in Canada, Hawaii, Japan, and other places around the world.

❧ 5 ❧

VINGT-ET-UNE

SANCTUARY

Smith Point, Texas

In 1923 the National Audubon Society leased several islands from the General Land Office of Texas. These included Green Island, our southernmost island sanctuary down in Laguna Madre, Second Chain of Islands in San Antonio Bay, North Bird and South Bird Islands near Corpus Christi, and Vingt-et-une near Smith Point in the mouth of Galveston Bay.

Vingt-et-une supports a very significant colony of roseate spoonbills, and since 1967, when A. E. "Buddy" Whitehead was hired as our first warden, we have kept adventurous fishermen, picnickers, and frolicking dogs from disturbing the big "pinks" during the nesting season.

Excerpts from Old Dad's Sanctuary Department newsletters may provide some idea of the wildlife around Vingt-et-une.

SEPTEMBER 1974   As protector of the biggest colony of roseate spoonbills on the Texas coast, Buddy Whitehead is much in demand by photographers, birders, and scientific types. This spring and summer were not exceptions.

After a very mild winter with only one light frost, some herons and cormorants started nesting in early February and had young about ready to fly by April. Roseate spoonbills arrived about March 1 and were building nests by April. But in the latter part of April, Old Mariah started moaning and whining with high tides and waves that flooded all the ground nests and those on the lower branches of the salt cedars.

In spite of that, by mid-May Buddy reported about fifty young rose-ates ready to fly. Later that month, about two hundred pairs of the pink, flat-faced fowl were incubating, and by May 30 another two hundred adults arrived.

In June, according to Buddy, he had a spell of real Texas weather: hot and still. Tides were back to normal or below, all of which make for ideal nesting conditions. At least nine hundred spoonbills were using the island by then, including two hundred immatures. Several hundred apparently came in from elsewhere in the first half of June.

Cormorants kept nesting and reached peak numbers by mid-June. About fifty white ibis were on hand by then but were apparently not in the mood for love, June or no June.

We can remember when the Texas Parks and Wildlife Department was interested only in game birds. This summer the department was carrying on a wading-bird banding project. They banded twenty-four young common egrets on the Vingt-et-une Islands. Buddy kept track of these and thinks all but two of them reached flying stage.

A flock of fifteen wood storks arrived about June 10. Whether or not they had a Spanish accent, Buddy does not say, but you can ask Sandy Sprunt, of the NAS Research Department, whether he thinks they wandered over from Corkscrew Swamp in Florida or came up from Mexico.

A welcome newcomer to the islands was the black skimmer. About one hundred young were raised on a spoil-bank island. The spoil island nearest Vingt-et-une played host to green herons all summer long, producing about two hundred young.

All in all, it was a rather unusual season: very windy and wet the first half; dry and hot the last half. Nevertheless, we came through with a very good crop of birds. The estimated number of young fledged is 700 spoonbills, 200 great blue herons, 200 green herons, 100 little blues, 500 common egrets, 225 snowy egrets, 100 Louisiana herons, and 70 black-crown herons. The cattle egrets were still nesting in August, but they seemed fewer in number than in former years.

We had to get a new Mon Ark boat and a twenty-five-horsepower Evenrude, since our old equipment was ready to make a dry land sailor out of Buddy.

Buddy's son, Joe, a veterinarian, helps keep an eye on the islands, for which we're profoundly thankful. He is also interested in the red wolf and hopes a few may persist in the vicinity of Smith Point and Anahuac.

John Franson, southwest regional representative, has been dickering with the Texas Parks and Wildlife Department and the Corps of Engineers over placement of spoil from maintenance dredging. Vingt-et-une has been eroding, and the oyster shell has been shifting in recent years. Rebuilding with spoil from nearby channel maintenance, as we have done in Tampa Bay, Florida, is a possibility. The water is too shallow to get a barge in without digging a new channel, however, in which case the disturbance would outweigh the benefits. The Corps of Engineers is considering the possibility of running a discharge pipeline to the islands, which might work.

SEPTEMBER 1975 Buddy Whitehead's roseate spoonbills, for which "Van Toon" is famous, had a very good year. About one thousand adults built four hundred nests and fledged five hundred young. Buddy says he can't recall a year in which the weather behaved better: no real bad storms or tides. In the early part of the season, the waters were unusually fresh, so the fishermen went elsewhere, leaving the wading birds in peace and quiet. Yet, the supply of shrimp and fish were adequate for our star boarders.

By April 10, Buddy had about four hundred adult spoonbills, but only four nests. In late May, a flock moved in that may have been broken up at another site. They had some grown young with them and showed no interest in setting up housekeeping. By mid-June, however, the early nesters were fledging, and some of those May arrivals got in the mood. Buddy and his wife, Bernice, kept their fingers crossed as a "toad drowner" dumped seventeen inches of rain in two days nearby but missed Vingt-et-une.

By the end of June, the early nesters were out and gone, while about four hundred of the big pinks had some fifty nests just starting to hatch. The latter did very well, and by the end of July, most had left the islands except for about thirty young that hung around in the daytime.

The cormorants also had a good year with six hundred adults building 250 nests and averaging two fledglings per nest. They were about gone by the end of June. They get the jump on the spoonbills by arriving in February and March and usually have half-grown young by the time the spoonies start nesting in April.

The great blue herons are also early birds, having young in the nest by early April. First arrivals came in February, but kept on coming until May. By June 15, some four hundred adults had built two hundred nests and fledged about four hundred young. By the end of July, a few great blues were still fledging. They'd been at it since February. Black-crowns, about one hundred in number, arrived with the great blues, built fifty nests, produced seventy-five young. Little blues and Louisianas arrived in April; about ninety blues built forty nests, fledged one hundred young, while fifty Louisianas made twenty nests and cranked out fifty young.

In May one hundred little green herons arrived, built 50 nests, and fledged two young per nest. About nine hundred American egrets arrived in February and March, being second in total adults to the spoonbills. They out-produced the spoonbills, however, with some 450 nests and 650 young. Maybe that's why the name changers call 'em "common"? Two hundred snowies, with 100 nests, added 200 young to the Smith Point countryside.

Cattle egrets had a hard time making up their minds. They left the area completely by May 1, perhaps to nest elsewhere. About two hundred came back in June and began to nest—considerably fewer than in former years. By the end of July, when Buddy went off duty, they still had several half-grown young in the nest.

All in all, Buddy says it was a very good year. The various species seemed to be healthier than usual. No rookery is complete without a lot of dead birds of all ages, but there were very few at any time around Vingt-et-une this year.

Last year a flock of black skimmers nested for the first time on a nearby spoil bank. This year three flocks produced about two hundred young, nearly twice as many as last year. The lack of storm tides this year was a blessing for these and other ground nesters.

SEPTEMBER 1976 Although the poet T. S. Eliot says April is the cruelest month, Buddy Whitehead says it was not that way around Vingt-et-une. After a mild season, with only one freeze down to twenty-eight above last winter, the great blues and cormorants started nesting in February. Young cormorants were leaving the nest, and great blues were about half-grown by late April. At least one hundred pairs of roseate spoonbills moved into some salt cedar trees Buddy had planted about four years ago; the big pinks were the first waders to show appreciation for Buddy's hard work.

An oil spill in the Houston ship channel did not drift toward Smith Point, and Buddy uncrossed his fingers when it was cleaned up with little damage.

A larger flock of great blues than he had seen in many years came through with three young per nest and good survival. About ten years ago, Buddy planted salt cedar (tamarisk, if you prefer) on a spoil bank of about two acres some three miles east of Vingt-et-une. A whole new colony of birds, the same species as on Vingt-et-une, had built about three hundred nests thereon by early May of this year.

To the long list of pestiferous exotics that have invaded our sanctuaries, such as melaleuca at Corkscrew Swamp in Florida, nutria at the Paul J. Rainey in Louisiana, and the ubiquitous starlings and sparrows, the fire ant may be the most troublesome. On Roll-over Island, Buddy found production of wading birds reduced to near zero. Buddy and Joe got the entomology department at Texas A&M University interested in our problem. The good news is that the insecticide with the trade name Logic has proven very effective.

On the untreated half of Roll-over, production of wading birds was zero; on the treated half it was about 98 percent successful. Logic is a hormone that affects the fire ant queen. The Houston Audubon Society is using it on its sanctuaries. Bart Brees of Texas A&M has published a paper on it.

Over in Tampa Bay, Florida, Dusty Dunstan figures it takes about twenty years for trees to reach the size where the fussy fowl will use them. By planting trees as Buddy did instead of waiting for wind and tide to transport the seeds, the time required may be cut in half. Dusty plans to try Buddy's system on some new islands those old bird lovers, the Corp of Engineers, are going to build.

Buddy noticed that some of the spoonbills moved on without nesting on the sanctuary. The temperamental critters established four nesting colonies, and by late June, two of these had young about ready to fly. The other birds laid a few eggs, then for reasons known only to roseate spoonbills, headed for parts unknown. Buddy speculates that with the islands getting somewhat smaller because of erosion, and with great blues, cormorants, and great egrets on the increase, the place is getting like Manhattan and the spoonbills won't stand for that. Over thirty years ago, Robert Porter Allen noticed that spoonies are spooky and will abandon their attempts at reproduction at the slightest disturbance from raccoons, photographers, and other varmints.

According to Buddy, black-crowned night herons also appreciate elbow room and seem to keep other birds at some distance from their nests.

A nice colony of four hundred black skimmers nested on a shell island that was pumped up for a drilling pad for an oil well some time ago. As every coastal warden knows, high water very often wipes out entire colonies of this species. You'd think a bird that's stuck with a pair of scissors with which to do a skimming job at meal time should have troubles enough without having to worry about storm tides. But nobody asked our opinion on this.

At least fifty pairs of least terns nested on the largest of the Vingt-et-une Islands and brought off a good crop. This is the first year we've had more than a few pairs of least terns here. All in all, except for the two contingents of spoonbills that went AWOL, it was a very productive season at the Twenty-one Club.

SEPTEMBER–NOVEMBER 1977 Buddy Whitehead reports that we oughter do something about otters. Either that, or he's going to have to teach the ground-nesting least terns and skimmers to nest in bushes. Buddy thinks even the great blues, egrets, spoonbills, and cormorants that nested on the lower branches of his salt cedars had their eggs scrambled by the sleek cousins of the mink. If otters would read the books, they'd know they're supposed to eat fish and leave birds alone.

All of the nests of the least terns and skimmers were broken up by otters the last week in July. But the least terns had a good many young already flying by that time, as did a few skimmers.

In February the cormorants and great blues were moving in. About four hundred cormorants built two hundred nests and fledged about three young per nest. Great blues also numbered about two hundred pairs and averaged a shade under two young fledged per nest. Snowies and great egrets came in March. About one hundred pairs of greats brought two hundred young to the flying stage, while forty pairs of snowies also averaged two young fledged per nest.

The glamour-puss around Vingt-et-une, of course, is the roseate spoonbill. Buddy had 250 adults, but the temperamental critters only built fifty nests. By the end of June, the early nesters that arrived in April had flying young, and another batch were about all hatched. By the end of July, 125 young spoonbills were flying, but a few had yet to leave the nest.

Little green herons had a good year. Some fifty nests fledged 150 young. Over on the Rainey, in Louisiana, where every bush along the canals seems to have a green heron nest (Cajuns call 'em kop-kops), fifty pairs would be a poor year indeed; but on the islands of Vingt-et-une, that's not bad.

The first part of the summer was dry and hot, and with salt water coming back into the bays, so were great schools of menhaden. The waders had a good supply of groceries until those thunderstorms started in July and kept it up for the rest of the season. As all the Texas wardens know, too much fresh water means skimpy rations for birds that depend on salt-water fish. But, all in all, Buddy says it was a good year at "Van Toon."

SEPTEMBER 1978 After a rough winter, Buddy Whitehead reported the cold weather letting up about mid-March, so spring was about one month late. By the middle of April, great blues, great egrets, and cormorants were nesting, and about thirty pairs of spoonbills were setting up housekeeping. March and April were very dry around the islands; the rains and floods of nearby areas missed Vingt-et-une.

In late April, a writer and photographer from Exxon who are doing an article on the wildlife on the spoil islands along the coast paid Buddy and his birds a visit.

The lack of rain around "Van Toon" continued throughout May, with very high winds and high tides but no real damage to the nesting birds. About seventy-five white ibises hung around but did not nest. Some fifty least terns occupied a nearby spoil island, but in June, Buddy noticed that their eggs were disappearing. In the case of the terns, he could not identify the egg robbers.

From June 1 to 15 about seven inches of rain fell, but no really bad weather or winds. Some great blues and cormorants were still around, but their numbers dwindled daily. Fishing was very poor, so Buddy had no problems with boats around the islands. Lots of shrimp showed up in June, but they were very small and so was the number of people after them.

In July a new colony of roseate spoonbills developed on a spoil island that they had never used before. They were so late in arriving that Buddy thinks they were a colony that had been broken up elsewhere. At least twenty-five sailboats anchor on this island on nice weekends. But the island is large, and the birds are in the interior and so disturbance is minimal.

Buddy says the main islands of Vingt-et-une are still overrun by otters. The only birds to nest successfully were in the very tops of the trees. Hodge's Reef, about two miles east, fledged about 150 great blues, 200 great egrets, 225 cormorants, 80 roseate spoonbills, 400 cattle egrets, and 30 black-crowns.

Redfish Reef, which was dredged up from Anahuac Channel in 1949, is about two miles west of Vingt-et-une. It produced about 20 young great blues, 20 spoonbills, 40 snowies, 60 Louisianas, 300 cattle egrets, and 150 black skimmers. On both these islands a few years ago, Buddy planted salt cedars that provide good nesting habitat.

It is interesting to speculate on the factors that may govern the production of wading birds at the various Texas sanctuaries. Food supplies fluctuate with salinity levels. Fledging success is affected by such predators as otters, raccoons, boat-tailed grackles, and gulls, as well as fire ants. We hope Sandy Sprunt's lads and lassies (NAS Research Department—who are already spread too thin) can continue to study these environmental factors.

SEPTEMBER 1979 In contrast to the wind and flood damage at the Rainey in Louisiana and Sydnes Island, Texas, Buddy Whitehead reports a very successful season in spite of the weather. In early April, Buddy said, "The season seems to be starting off better than it has in years." He had two beautiful flocks of waders on a couple of new spoil banks, including a new colony of Louisiana herons, also a few pairs of reddish egrets that Buddy had never seen nesting on Vingt-et-une before. He had about twice as many roseate spoonbills as in 1978. They were just starting to nest in early April.

Throughout May, Buddy dodged severe thunderstorms and fifty-mile-per-hour winds, but out on the island it was business as usual for the herons, egrets, spoonbills, skimmers, and terns. The young great blues and great egrets, in greater numbers than in 1978, were practicing solo flights by late May.

For those who believe in reincarnation, we don't recommend coming back as black skimmers. Not on the Texas coast, at least. Not only do they make hard work out of gathering groceries, they insist on nesting on low, bare sand spits. Otters come by for a taste of omelette or tender young skimmer, and floods such as Tropical Storm Claudette caused are very bad for reproduction. Between the otters and the waters, some six hundred adult skimmers managed to fledge about fifty young.

The least terns had similar problems, plus something new in bird mortality. A flock of white pelicans decided to roost on "Van Toon," and when a twenty-pound pelican steps on a tern nest, things get very squishy.

On the other hand, the glamour-puss roseate spoonbills did very well. Buddy's report for early July says, "The flock of spoonbills on one spoil bank are doing better than any I have ever seen. Have at least two hundred young that are flying, some nests just hatching, and a nice bunch of young in all stages."

Fortunately, the season for wading birds (except cattle egrets) was about over before Claudette blew in. Shrimp were plentiful in the bays, and they figured prominently in the diet of the sharp-faced fowl. All of which helps explain Buddy's comment, "We have more birds of all kinds on Vingt-et-une Island than we have had in several years."

Cattle egrets led the production parade by fledging 950 young. Spoon-bills fledged 400; great blue herons, 475; Louisianas, 105; black-crowns, 90. Great egrets did great with 525; snowies, 200; and cormorants had a good year with 375. Black skimmers made 50, and the least terns got a lot of experience.

SEPTEMBER 1980   Buddy Whitehead says things got off to an early start last spring. Great blues were courting up a storm in February, but a lot of them decided to go elsewhere. He later found two colonies west of Anahuac Refuge in a reservoir and big lake. Maybe they didn't like the salty bay water. A cold spell about April 10 set a forty-year record. Buddy lost about forty young cormorants that probably got too wet and cold. Others survived the chill and were flying well by mid-April.

Late April was beautiful weather, and Buddy reported more spoonbills and Louisiana herons than he had seen in years. Dave Blankinship, super-visor of the Texas Coastal Audubon Sanctuaries, came by with Kirke King, a U.S. Fish and Wildlife Service biologist. They were checking on the amount and kinds of food available to the sharp-faced fowl; also look-ing into possibilities for getting the Corps of Engineers to pump spoil on the islands. Buddy says, "The silt they pump from existing channels is too soft to stand up. We have no sand or clay. I am sure it won't do any harm. May help the trees to grow. Lost about twenty of the big trees last Octo-ber in the high winds and tide we had on the Texas coast."

Things were looking good by May 15. In spite of a six-inch rain and forty-five-mile-per-hour winds, the tide was not too high. One colony of skimmers had to abandon their new nests and move to higher ground, but that was no hardship. Young spoonbills, great blues, and cormorants were just starting to fly. By the end of May, most of the young spoonbills were flying, which was about a month earlier than average, and most nests averaged three young. Skimmers and least terns were still doing well. The supply of food fish and shrimp was above normal, and Buddy suspects this explained why the birds did so well.

June was very hot and dry around Vingt-et-une. Buddy had no varmints chomping up eggs and young on the islands this year but had the usual number of eggs eaten by other birds such as grackles and gulls. The hot, dry weather seemingly posed no problems for the colonial birds, and the number of dead and weaklings usually seen around the colonies at the end of the season was lower than usual. Populations of all species, except great blues, increased around the Vingt-et-une Islands in comparison to recent years.

As usual, cattle egrets led the parade with about 950 young; great egrets raised 470; snowies, 230; great blues, 115; black-crowns, 155; Louisianas, 215; white ibises, only 12; spoonbills, 415; and skimmers, 100.

In the past two years, Buddy planted about four hundred salt cedar trees on Smith Point Island, which has helped stabilize the sand and shell and provide nesting habitat.

SEPTEMBER 1981   Buddy Whitehead's reports for 1981 are full of new records. When he started patrol on April 1, the area around Smith Point was about twelve inches below normal rainfall. Hurricane Allen, in the fall of 1980, had filled nearby swamps with salt water, and with the lack of rain, salinities rose to the point where the alligators were wishing they were crocodiles.

In spite of the mild winter, the wading birds came in about one month later than usual. But with the exception of great blues, Buddy had more egrets, herons, and spoonbills than he had had in the last five years. About 350 pairs of roseate spoonbills started building in mid-April. By that time, a pair of oystercatchers—the first ever to fledge from Vingt-et-une—were about ready to fly.

By late April, Buddy had replaced all the big signs that were done in by Hurricane Allen, and he made like Dan Connelly, manager of Silver Bluff Sanctuary in South Carolina, as a planter of trees. While Dan, at Silver Bluff, with tractor and planter, sets out many thousands of longleaf and loblolly pines, Buddy starts with cuttings of many dozens of salt cedars, which he transplants on the shifting sands of Vingt-et-une. This stabilizes the island and provides nesting habitat for spoonbills, cormorants, and sharp-faced fowl.

By late May, the drought broke; the salt cedars grew rapidly; and most of the young wading birds except cattle egrets were leaving the nest. On the highest ridge, some three hundred pairs of black skimmers were nesting.

In June at least three cyclones missed Buddy's bird factory, but managed to dump some twelve inches of rain round and about. This caused a few young spoonbills to become orphans, with no chance to learn the spoonbill trade. By and large, however, the wind and rain did little damage. Young skimmers were hatching at the same time more adults were arriving from points unknown. Unlike the Cubans and Haitians that flock into Florida, the skimmers found plenty of food, adequate housing, and were immediately employed making more skimmers. One colony did very well, fledging about three hundred young. Another colony on a large spoil island did not fare so well because sailboats were often anchored on it. According to Cap'n Wimby's Bird Atlas, a mixture of sailors, skimmers, and Texas sun is very bad for the baby bird business.

In July about 500 least terns were flitting about the islands. Some of them nested among the black skimmers. Buddy's son, Dr. Joe, and granddaughter, Dawn, did a least tern survey on August 10 and came up with 493 adults in five colonies. This was more than Buddy had seen for several years. They built only thirty nests and fledged fifty young.

Buddy's summary of the 1981 season shows the following:

Species	Adults	Nests	Fledged
Great egrets	200	100	175
Snowy egrets	150	75	150
Cattle egrets	1,000	500	1,500
Great blue herons	150	70	150
Louisiana herons	80	40	90
Green herons	90	40	150
White ibises	20	10	10
Spoonbills	300	150	300
Black skimmers	1,200	500	300
Least terns	493	30	50
Oystercatchers	4	1	2

And so, to a new record for nesting oystercatchers, more least terns than in several years, a record-breaking number of black skimmers, a complete lack of otters looking for eggs, and no high tides to flood the skimmer nests, we can add the best record of all. We had three generations of Whiteheads protecting birds, counting birds, planting trees, and typing reports on the same day at Vingt-et-une when Buddy retired in 1981!

SEPTEMBER 1998 Following Buddy's retirement, his versatile veterinarian son, Joe, looked after the islands of Vingt-et-une. Today their number is closer to *trois* or *quatre,* but other spoil-bank islands around Smith Point provide suitable living space for long-legged fowl with sharp beaks and spoonbills, as well as those fish eaters that tend to live dangerously, such as skimmers and least terns.

The Houston Audubon Society, one of the most active and effective chapters in the nation, is no stranger to the avian goings-on around Smith Point. From the two-story observation platform, a couple of volunteers monitor the "hawk watch" during migration. Their data are of much interest to National Audubon's Science Department, Cornell University, the Texas Parks and Wildlife Department, and the u.s. Fish and Wildlife Service.

Joe's mother, Bernice, at the tender age of eighty-eight, plays the computer like Van Cliburn at the piano. She writes the history of Smith Point, from the standpoint of its wildlife and people, from a firsthand view. Needless to say, her contribution equals that of her late husband, Buddy, her son Joe, and the grandchildren.

All of which makes Vingt-et-une rank very high in wildlife management and the ecotourism business.

❧ 6 ❧

EMILY WINTHROP MILES

WILDLIFE SANCTUARY

Sharon, Connecticut

Although Governor John Winthrop's name may live on in the history of Massachusetts, Emily Winthrop Miles left a permanent mark on the wildlife and natural history of Sharon, Connecticut. When Emily's father and mother landed at Le Havre, France, about 1915, word that their two daughters had eloped awaited them. Emily had married the chauffeur, Corey Miles; her sister was wedded to the gardener. The exasperated parents returned immediately to the United States and tried in vain to annul the marriages.

Emily acquired about 740 acres about four miles east of Sharon on which she protected flora and fauna, both wild and domestic. Her goats, pigs, and cattle were housed better than some humans in the region. She enlarged the millpond by installing a new dam on Carse Brook. Not to be outdone by mere humans, beavers made the two-and-an-half-mile-long valley a series of beaver ponds that they and the otters, wading birds, wild geese, and ducks enjoy to this day.

In her will, to the pleasant surprise of Carl Buchheister, then president of the National Audubon Society, she left her beautiful estate to the society. Her house and grounds became the Emily Winthrop Miles Wildlife Sanctuary, and Old Dad, director of the Sanctuary Department, made his office there in January 1966.

Today the sanctuary consists of fifteen hundred acres of hardwood forest, steep mountain slopes, fields, and wetlands. It is a key wildlife management area in a five-thousand-acre block of federal, state, and private land.

MARCH 1976 'Twas an unseasonably warm day in mid-February when Art Gingert, Miles Sanctuary manager, heard a faint honking way down the valley. Miles Lake was still locked in ice, which made a fine landing strip when sixteen mated pairs of Canada geese came slanting down from the blue. There followed a great session of tail-wagging, wing-flapping, and neck-stretching as everybody, including Art and Miss Nancy (a.k.a. Mrs. John M. Anderson), carried on about how good it was to be back where they belonged.

The advance guard was later joined by about sixty yearlings, most of which were probably hatched on the sanctuary. They have nothing much to do except loaf around the sanctuary this summer. Many of them, without benefit of clergy, wll pair off this year, and if they make it back next spring, they will get on with the business of making little geese out of big ones.

Meanwhile, the beavers up and down the valley have several lodges on which the old pairs nest. At present our goose population is increasing faster than the beavers, so Art has a small man-made island in Miles Lake that has been used by a pair of geese for several years, and he is working on some additional nesting platforms for the honkers.

Since Miss Nancy insists on detente with the coons, skunks, possums, and foxes, Art has a hard time trying to save the nests of the flat-faced fowl from all sorts of egg eaters. Hence, the honkers, mallards, and blacks are encouraged to nest on islands. The boxes for the wood ducks and hooded mergansers are equipped with predator guards.

In addition to his housing projects, Art is doing a breeding bird survey in cooperation with the United States Fish and Wildlife Service. He also acquired a banding permit and has caught and banded the odd kestrel in recent months. He has discovered that college students looking for practical experience in wildlife management or research are a good source of brains and brawn. This year his labor is supplied through an agreement with Penn State University.

In this bicentennial year, Art's plans for the Miles Sanctuary will allow some six hundred acres of second-growth hardwoods to continue to recover from a couple centuries of clear-cutting, grazing, and charcoal making, while maintaining the diversity resulting from abandoned fields, lawn, shrubs, and domestic crops. He will also maintain about four miles of nature trails, lead a few field trips, and lend a hand if director Bob Moeller gets in a real bind over at the Sharon Audubon Center.

JANUARY 1977 Art Gingert says this is the first time a few black ducks have not spent the winter on the open water below the waterfalls behind his house. That's because the open water is closed, and ducks are too smart to stay here if they don't have to. Now that it's twenty degrees below most mornings, Art likes to recall events of last summer. For example, on May 9, it was warm enough to bring Jim Rod, manager of Constitution Island Sanctuary on the Hudson River, and two golden-phase timber rattlers out of hibernation, and they exchanged greetings on Mine Mountain across the road from the Miles Sanctuary home-office of Old Dad and Miss Nancy. As a spring ritual, Miss Nancy announces at the local beauty salon that the rattlers are out at Miles, and that automatically eliminates visitors who don't know why a wildlife sanctuary cannot be a picnic grounds. It's just another way of teaching Nature Appreciation.

Art's warden reports include other visitors such as a bobcat on May 2, a pair of minks, otters frolicking in the stream on several occasions, the deer that completely finished off his garden so all he and Susan got was exercise, and beavers persistently damming up the spillway on Miles Lake. The nesting Canada geese, black ducks, mallards, wood ducks, and hooded mergansers had a good year.

He operated five mist nets off and on from which he banded dozens of warblers, swallows, and other dickey birds. He and a couple of other raptor enthusiasts also banded several young red-tails and a brood of goshawks.

Art found a starving downy goshawk, evidently pushed out of the nest by its older siblings. Had he put the chick back in the nest, it probably would have been eaten. So he took it home, and he and Susan hand-fed it for several weeks. It progressed from a downy chick to fully feathered young adult, ready to return to the wild.

On June 27, at 1:30 A.M., Art heard the goshawk making a fuss from its platform in a nearby tree. Art tore out of his house as a hawk-napper jumped into his car and tore away. The state police and falconers in three states are still hoping to catch the thief. Goshawks bring a fancy price on the falconry black market. The moral of the story is that as long as human animals can make money selling other animals or plants (they're now rustling cactus in Arizona), they are going to do so. That's why the first Audubon employee, in 1902, was a wildlife warden, and Audubon wardens will probably be around so long as there's an Audubon Society.

Last year about thirty acres of additional property were donated to the sanctuary, on which Art posted the boundaries.

In addition to supervising college students who worked here on various projects, Art took a week off to go back to Michigan State University, turn in his thesis, take his oral exams, and receive his master of science degree. He also found time to show many visitors (including an Audubon life member from Ohio) around the sanctuary, led several field trips for the Housatonic Audubon Society, lectured at the Sharon Audubon Festival, and gave Dick Rhindress, NAS regional representative, a generous hand with his regional conference up at Williamstown, Massachusetts.

Meanwhile, back at the Miles Sanctuary, while the Canada geese and bluebirds were incubating, so was Susan Gingert. Daniel Ethan Gingert was hatched on January 7, and so far he does not claim the Miles Sanctuary is a cold, cruel world even if the black ducks are gone. Daniel is a most welcome addition to the fauna of the sanctuary.

MARCH 1977 We are aware of the mention made of the Miles in the January issue. 'Twas this March, however, that Miss Nancy decided Old Dad should go down to Florida and help Sandy Sprunt, Joe Linduska, and other research types plan their perilous course. Naturally Old Dad objected strenuously, pointing out dangers from sunburn, sharks, athlete's foot, and other hazards of travel in the Southeast, but Miss Nancy would hear none of it.

One day after Old Dad departed, the first of ten inches of heavy, wet snow began to fall on the Miles. Then the lights went out. The electric stove in the kitchen wouldn't cook; the electric pump in the well wouldn't pump; the electric switch on the oil furnace wouldn't switch; the TV wouldn't televise. This went on for forty-one hours. Meanwhile, Art Gingert fetched firewood, and Miss Nancy cooked in the fireplace as in days of yore. Before the first limb fell across the power lines, she had drawn many buckets of water. She also had access to Old Dad's life-saving brandy (sans Saint Bernard), so this pioneer from the plains of Kansas suffered no stress. And all the time Old Dad faced hardship duty in the Florida Keys. There is no justice.

MAY 1978 Art Gingert's geese were late returning to this frigid corner of Connecticut, where Miles Lake was firmly locked under a foot of ice until mid-April. Love laughs at the locksmith, however, and on May 6 the first brood of Canadas sawed their way out of eight eggs on the top of a beaver lodge. At least a dozen pairs are nesting on the Miles, plus a flock of yearlings and two-year-olds that are too young to take on the trials and tribulations of parenthood.

Once again the Miles is headquarters for Mike Root, Pete DeSimone, and Mike Redmond, students who specialize in raptor ecology. Last year they located nests of twenty goshawks, seven red-shoulders, seven barred owls, and three great horned owls. They made no special effort to locate the more common red-tail nests. In 1976 they found one Cooper's hawk nest, which was the only known record for the state, but could not locate a Cooper's nest last year. They feel this accipiter is very uncommon in this region and deserves special attention.

Likewise, the red-shoulder has declined drastically since the days when A. C. Bent did his work in New England. Last year, of the seven nests only four were successful. Pesticides, shooting, and loss of habitat in recent decades are possible causes of the decline. In some areas, the red-shoulder is still declining according to an article "Keeping Track of Hawks" in the July 1977 issue of some magazine called *Audubon*. So far this spring, the red-shoulders are doing better, and our researchers are hoping the trend may reverse.

As Connecticut farmers are gradually forced out of business, their lands revert to second-growth forests that apparently benefit the barred owl. Last year these charter members of the Fowl and Owl Society found seven nests, but as in the case of red-shoulders, only four were successful. The research trio has observed goshawks nesting very close to red-shoulders, barred owls, and horned owls. From their observation blinds, they saw no evidence that the chicken hawks ate the hootie owls or vice versa. In any case, when the summer is over, we should know more than we do now about the lives and times of these uncommon raptors.

Art had a couple of students, Susan Fitch and Gordon Whitbeck, working on an inventory of mammals, reptiles, and amphibians. Supervising all these goings-on, plus his regional nest box program for wood ducks, hooded mergansers, bluebirds, sparrow hawks (sometimes called kestrels), and all sorts of hole nesters, plus maintenance of 760 acres of sanctuary, buildings, and equipment, plus lecturing, leading field trips, and giving Bob Moeller and Joe Edmondson a hand now and then at the Sharon Center—all this keeps Art very busy in his spare time.

MAY 1979 May at the Miles finds manager Art Gingert followed about by birders of various brands and sizes. And they all tell him what a paradise he lives in with all these birds to be watched up, wildflowers to be keyed out, wild geese to be tamed down. The bank clerks, bus drivers, schoolteachers, and other envious souls all agree, "Son, you really got it made!"

But it's like those blind men who felt around the elephant and decided it was like a rope, a tree, a snake, or a wall—depending on what you felt. For days on end last summer, Art Gingert, Pete DeSimone, and Mike Root worked from daylight till dark and convinced everyone they were professional builders. They put a new roof on a building that was once a dairy barn, painted it, and replaced windows, plus much of the plumbing and wiring. The barn has been the manager's residence for about fifty years, and time was beginning to tell us that something had to be done to keep out wind and water. If Emily could see her cow barn now, we think she would be proud and pleased.

But living quarters for those who study and protect the birds and bees cannot occupy too much of an Audubon warden's time. Come around at another time, and you find these guys perched in a tree. No hammers, saws, or paint brushes—only binoculars, bands, pliers, ropes, and climbing gear. Mike Root does not climb trees, he walks up them. That's what comes from gathering data on the nest of nineteen goshawks, sixteen red-shoulders, thirteen barred owls, and a Cooper's hawk or two. Art, Pete, and Mike have a three-hundred-square-mile study area under its third year of observation. They have data on how many eggs are laid and when, how many hooked-beaks take to the air per year, what they eat, and what they wear.

Compared to 1978, this spring is only fair for Falconiformes. The boys have only five goshawk nests, fifteen red-shoulder, only one barred owl. They are somewhat cheered, however, by finding two Cooper's nests, compared to one in 1977, and none in 1978.

Possibly a shortage of prey, especially chipmunks, a favorite item on their menu, has caused the meat-eating birds to curtail production and not even try to nest.

Bearded men and hook-beaked hawks do not entirely steal the show at Miles. In 1978 Susan Fitch conducted an intensive inventory of the vertebrates on our 760 acres. Her report is filed here and at the Sharon Audubon Center, the Hotchkiss School and Scoville School libraries in Lakeville, and the State Library in Hartford. This year she is also assisting the Root-DeSimone team in the raptor work. But, alas! In August she leaves us to begin her studies at Yale for a master's degree in forest science. If her teachers are smart, they will learn a lot.

Although we have no computers nor electron microscopes, our hawk banders do require some money for sleeping bags, peanut butter, gasoline, and lumber. Fortunately, the Housatonic Audubon Society is aware of this, and their support enables Art and his interns to monitor thirty nesting boxes for the sparrow hawk on a forty-square-mile study area. This is a year-round effort to observe adults and fledged young, band, and color-mark the birds, and learn which kind of nest box is best for them.

This year they also began work on another cavity nester; consequently, northwest Connecticut's first "bluebird trail" is established. Four experimental designs are approved by the North American Bluebird Society. Which ones the bluebirds approve of is being determined by Lisa Solometo, who is checking the fifty boxes located on the property of more than twenty-five landowners round and about. Lisa is a graduate of Penn State University, where her grades were nearly all *A*'s. She speaks Spanish fluently, swims like an otter, and gets around the woods like Aldo Leopold, wildlife management's patron saint. The bluebirds never had it so good.

In their spare time, the lads and lassies help the Ralph T. Waterman Bird Club in Millbrook, New York, banding nestling bluebirds from their one hundred boxes. They also give the many lectures throughout the Northeast, lead bird counts, do breeding bird surveys, and carry on with all sorts of woodsy lore. In the spring of 1980, they will undertake an intensive botanical inventory of Miles Sanctuary. It barely leaves time for the guitar strummin' and banjo pickin' that Messrs. Gingert and De-Simone do mighty well.

Quite often in nature, Cupid and the stork are inclined to give up easily on people who are so intent on birds of prey, wee beasties, and sleeping bags because people who can get by for days on biological surveys, peanut butter sandwiches, and an occasional beer are often too busy for romance.

But it comes to pass that on September 29, Pete DeSimone and Sandra Mervis, naturalist at the Sharon Audubon Center, are united in matrimony. The ceremony takes place in a beautiful outdoor setting at the Sharon Center. Following that, there is a bit of a do at the Miles Wildlife Sanctuary—what Lonnie and Berton Legé, in Abbeville, Louisiana, would call a faise-do-do. There is many a toast to the bride and groom, which eventually leads to guitar and banjo music and finally to dancing on the lawn. Next morning Old Dad is seriously wondering about the wild life on the wildlife sanctuary, but his outlook brightens considerably by afternoon.

Comes January 12 and our Mr. Gingert participates in the bald eagle census for the region. He reports, "Lots of geese, coots, gulls, no eagles." On January 19, he leads the Housatonic Audubon Society on a winter bird trip. He reports, "Very few birds, five-thousand geese, a few red-tails, and a lone female bufflehead." Meanwhile, back at the Miles, Susan Gingert is observing an eagle feeding on a deer carcass on the ice on Miles Lake. Old Dad tries to make this a golden eagle, which would be a splendid record for the sanctuary. But when Art and Pete return they put the long eye on the bird and declare it to be a young bald eagle—mostly because that's what it is! Which shows you that birders who don't yet have white hair and bleary eyes are totally unreasonable.

On March 10, Jim Higginson, a student intern from Penn State, arrives to learn from Art the science of sanctuary management. A week later, Jim is joined by Barbara Shockey from Hartwick College in upstate New York, and another spring is under way. On March 21, Mike Klemens, of the American Museum of Natural History, keeps them up all night working on salamanders: hundreds of spotted salamanders in migration, one Jefferson's, and larvae of the marbled.

In the morning, the bluebirds are courtin'; in the twilight the woodcock are singing. In the midst of all this, the stork puts in an appearance, delivering Jacob Koenig Gingert on May 7. It is predictable that some future naturalist will be climbing Jacob's ladder, although the wildlife hunters have not yet found one on the Miles Sanctuary.

MAY 1981 Art Gingert says critters such as hootie owls, bobcats, bluebirds, golden eagles, and wild turkeys kept life interesting around the Miles last year. On May 14, the first wild turkey since 1813 was gobbling up a storm around Miles Lake. On January 31, 1981, the first golden eagle we've ever seen at the sanctuary was dining on a dead doe that our game warden donated to the cause. One deer carcass brings one golden eagle, one eagle brings forty birders, forty birders bring a concoction called Wild Turkey. As John Muir said, "In Nature everything is hooked to everything else."

With help from graduate students Joyce Simeroth from Missouri and John Bergquist from Maryland, Art expanded his bluebird trail around

Sharon from 60 to 140 boxes. Time spent talking with landowners and erecting nest boxes on their property pays off in birds, public relations, and financial support for the Miles. In Dutchess County, New York, just west of Sharon, Florence Germond becomes Art's right hand in bluebird banding. Art says she can band up to 150 nestlings on her twenty-year-old, highly successful nest box trail. Formerly, he drove over there three or four times in spring to band her birds, but Florence accepted Art's do-it-yourself kit which saves time and gas.

Trapping and banding adult sparrow hawks were given high priority in Art's program. He has twenty-one pairs of the little falcons using boxes in twenty-eight territories, a very high ratio of box use. This project offers an unexcelled opportunity to study a "managed" population long enough to learn whether adults return to the same boxes annually, to compare production in boxes versus natural cavities, and to measure recruitment rates and mortality rates. The feds from Patuxent Research Center, in Maryland, are fascinated by this project, in addition to the five-year study by Mike Root and Pete DeSimone of other winged critters, such as goshawks, Cooper's hawks, red-shoulders, and such. The feds even sent Janet Partelow and Barbara Dowell to do a botanical inventory within a 11.3-meter radius of each nest.

In her second summer of study of the sanctuary's plant communities, Sandra DeSimone discovered a healthy colony of the spreading globe-flower, a member of the buttercup family, so rare that only three specimens are known from the entire state. Because birders and botanists are people, the existence of this flower and its exact location will remain known only to a tight little group, what the Moral Majority calls the "elitist few."

In addition to playing director of wildlife research, grad student adviser, educator, field trip leader, lecturer, and photographer, Art completely remodeled the kitchen in Emily Winthrop Miles' former residence, kept the road passable in a typical Connecticut winter, and kept tractor, truck, and cars running. He also dabbled in the forestry trade, deer habitat management, and landscape architecture, plus hawk and owl rehabilitation. Sometimes, on Sunday afternoons, he goofed off and played soccer for the Cornwall Uniteds. Obviously, his ever-loving wife, Susan, rules him with an iron hand.

MARCH 1982 The crows and turkey buzzards are complaining because Art Gingert gets to all the road kills before they do—gathering up squashed squirels, chipmunks, and such to feed some injured and or-phaned hawks and hootie owls. The great horned and barn owls kept him in the raptor recovery business for most of the year.

His kestrel housing and banding project is yielding some interesting results. Intern John Bergquist finds a female, banded as a nestling in an elm snag in 1978, captured again in a nest box in 1980, happily raising a brood in another box on June 9, 1981. This time, she chose an experimen-tal box in a two-acre white pine clear-cut.

This spring, Diane DeLuca of Cornell University, who spent last sum-mer keeping an eye on puffins at the Cruickshank Sanctuary in Maine, and Jeanne Anderson of Bucknell University will carry on with the kestrel nest box research and the bluebird trail studies along with a thousand other assignments that provide Miles students with a rich experience.

On September 29, law enforcement officer Peter Robinson, of the Royal Society for Protection of Birds (Great Britain), spends a day with Old Dad to learn how protecting birds in the United States compares with a warden's life in jolly old England. They conclude that the British poacher carries on in much the same manner as his Yankee counterpart, but our Audubon wardens get better support from state and federal enforcement agents. They also compare the relative merits of Scotch and bourbon and conclude, after due deliberation, that both are a boon to mankind.

Pete and Sandra DeSimone gave Robinson a tour of our newest sanc-tuary, Rheinstrom Hill, near Craryville, New York. Art took him up to Mount Riga, in Salisbury, Connecticut, for a go at hawk watching before Robinson went off to visit Heinz Meng and other famous Yankee bird-brains.

In October, Art took in the North American Bluebird Society confer-ence at the Holden Arboretum near Cleveland, Ohio. Also in October, Art, Pete DeSimone, and Carl Safina, manager of the Scully Sanctuary, Long Island, journeyed up to Montreal to attend the Raptor Research Conference.

A wave of evening grosbeaks, red-breasted nuthatches, pine siskins, and pine grosbeaks in October had Art and Susan wondering if they should lay in an extra supply of firewood and tune up the snowplow. Ac-cording to Cap'n Wimby's Bird Atlas, these birds were a sign of high drifts and low temperatures to come. Our average snowfall for the entire winter is forty-one inches, but by late January, fifty-two inches of the white stuff had fallen. And it kept on falling until after the spring peepers were peeping, Canada geese, wood ducks, and hooded mergansers were nesting, and skunk cabbages were blooming.

But Art had five cords stacked in his basement for his wood-burning Jotul, and another five on Miss Nancy's back porch, which kept her warm while carrying in all that wood. It pays to read Cap'n Wimby's Bird Atlas.

In November, while Art was laying in his winter wood supply, the beavers were laying in theirs. Emily Winthrop Miles was very fond of trees and planted many a sycamore, tulip poplar, honey locust, northern white cedar, and shagbark hickory round and about the place. Beavers are also very fond of all these, plus apple, white ash, white birch, hawthorn, and several conifers. If any of these are to survive around Miles Lake, their trunks must be encased in half-inch wire mesh at least three inches high. Tree protection and beaver control sometimes go hand in hand.

The temperature for the Christmas Bird Count was below zero, and the number of species seen was only thirty-four above zero. Art interrupted a poacher dragging out a deer. He explained that although we have too many deer in the area, this is an expensive no-no on a wildlife sanctuary. The state game warden took over, and the poacher, not knowing about birders, is still wondering why an Audubon warden would be in the swamp before daylight when it's below zero.

Art's report for February has several notable entries. "We enjoyed the grand sight of nine wild turkeys feeding in a sensitive fern patch behind the warden's residence on the third, despite the rain and sleet on that day. Mike Dudek (a new intern) and I caught and banded three gray-phase screech owls that were using our wood duck boxes as winter apartments. One of the highlighted wildlife observations for the year occurred at 10:30 A.M. on the twenty-second, as the season's first pair of Canada geese returned to the main swamp. On the evening of February 27, under the glow of the red light from our nocturnal wildlife shelf feeder, we were privileged to observe a pair of mating striped skunks. A series of careful approaches and hasty retreats by the camera and flash-armed resident manager may have resulted in a few interesting photos for our sanctuary slide file. We shall see."

Horries! Under pressure to raise funds to support sanctuaries, various wardens have come up with various schemes. But, so far, there is only one red-light district in operation.

MAY 1983 The weather from May 1982 through May 1983 was as changeable as the Miles manager's duties. Art Gingert's reports for the year show him plowing snow, banding bluebirds, counting eagles, remodeling houses, teaching classes, repairing plumbing, thawing pipes, cutting firewood, raising orphaned great horned owls—and sometimes he just looked at birds.

His "bluebird trail" stretches from the Miles into nearby New York and into Massachusetts. It just happens that prime bluebird habitat (which Art can now define more precisely than previously) is often found on large estates in the tri-state area, owned by people who like lots of elbow room, generally resent intrusions on their property and privacy by their fellow humans, but might welcome a family of bluebirds. When this diplomatic, clean-cut, handsome young man offers them a new lease on life in exchange for a lease on their property on which to erect a house in which bluebirds may be the lessees, paying off in song and insectivorous work, many a blue-nose takes a flier on the bluebird. All of which often results in donations to Miles Sanctuary for various wildlife projects where needed. There's nothing like a winsome bluebird to help you win some friends for the work you are doing.

In making their rounds on the trail, Art and his trusty volunteers, Sue Fitch, Mike Root, Pete and Sandy DeSimone, and a couple of interns, also check some thirty kestrel boxes, about twenty wood duck boxes, six barn owl shelves, and a few saw-whet owl boxes in addition to over two hundred bluebird houses.

In the spring of 1982, the weatherman showed no sign that he gave a damn about birds or birders. On April 6, Storm Olaf dropped sixteen inches of snow, accompanied by gusts up to fifty miles per hour, a temperature of sixteen degrees above, which meant snowdrifts higher than the Jeep, and two days behind the plow. Just ten days later, it was in the seventies and muddy underfoot.

Apparently, June got tired of hearing that "April is the cruelest month," so on June 5 and 6, just when Art, Miss Nancy, Susan Gingert, Sue Fitch, Sandy and Pete DeSimone, and Mike Root are having their great tag sale of valuable and not-so-valuable antiques, farm equipment, useful tools, and some not-so-useful, comes a deluge of eleven inches in two days. In spite of such adversities, they made a handsome profit of about $1,500. "'Twas not all beer and skittles" though, as his warden's report says, "Pete and I were kept busy, what with loading purchased items on cars, aiding mud-stranded motorists, and fending off some of the less well-mannered human types that came trooping in." It took five full days preparing and cleaning up after the great event. Old Dad was in Milwaukee and missed all the fun. Alas!

The big rain did not set well with the bluebirds, either. Many nestlings were killed in their boxes. The total fledged was thirty-two for the season, which is below par and probably due to the cold, wet spring and summer.

Comes August 4, 1982, and Connie Anderson and Craig Bielert fly in from Johannesburg, South Africa, where they are doing research on a troop of chacma baboons. In comparing the troop with the Sanctuary Department, many similarities are noted. An individual chacma can get the job done with little or no help. On the other hand, the entire troop pulls together on the slightest notice. Sanctuary personnel are generally better looking than chacmas.

By coincidence, some fifty select local folks also come by on the evening of August 4 for a bit of a do. There is shrimp, catfish, ruffed grouse, Famous Grouse, venison, tame turkey, Wild Turkey, turnip greens, Old Milwaukee, and New York Taylor. Entertainment is more or less spontaneous, aided and abetted by a musical group known as The Non-Game and Endangered Species. The latter consists of Joe Edmondson on bass, Pete DeSimone on mandolin, banjo, and guitar (a real virtuoso, that lad!), Art on banjo and guitar, Gene Krupa (alias Miss Nancy) on snare drum (Carl Safina, eat your heart out), and Scott Heth on piano. Old Dad alternates between vocalist, guitarist, band leader, and bartender. Along toward morning, things quieted down.

By November, Art was recovered enough to go down to Silver Bluff, in South Carolina, and learn about southern hospitality and softwood timber management from Sally and "Cooter" Connelly. He returned to Miles with "Cooter's" John Deer tractor, which we decided was a bit too small for our wildlife, agriculture, and forestry programs at Silver Bluff, but just right for the hills and hollows of Miles.

On November 14, Art presented a slide program on sanctuary management and research to a group of biologists at the Audubon Center in Greenwich, Connecticut. The meeting was arranged by Dusty Dunstan (assistant director, Sanctuary Department) and included members of the Wilidlife Society's Non-Game Wildlife Group for the Northeast. The Connecticut Department of Environmental Protection borrowed many of Art's slides for use in a how-to-do-it program on land management. The Sanctuary and Research Departments have been exporting this kind of know-how for about eighty years.

So far, the 1983 season has been just as interesting. On February 19, a very large bobcat was feeding on the road-killed deer out on the frozen lake, while two otters were playing tag and eating fish on the ice in the swamp. Lonnie and Berton Legé would be happy if all coyotes, coy-dogs, and feral dogs would leave Louisiana and go to Hartford; but at the Miles, the novelty of a real live coyote, with a reasonably good pedigree, has not worn off. At least three have been seen this year on the sanctuary. By the end of May, about thirty nestling bluebirds had been banded.

MAY 1984 According to Art Gingert's records, the past twelve months were notable for setting records of various kinds: in the wildlife department, he was well satisfied; but not so with some weather events. In the that's-more-like-it department, his sixty-five boxes on the bluebird trail fledged over one hundred young. With the capable help of Sue Fitch, he banded ninety-six nestlings and several adults for a new record. Says Art, "Looks like we're beginning to see the return of bluebirds as summer residents in the town of Sharon."

In late August, hooded mergansers and wood ducks were holding beauty contests on Miles Lake, while unusual numbers of red-breasted nuthatches were creeping around and about the trees. On August 29, some two hundred tree swallows up and left for Brazil. On September 21, a young red-headed woodpecker made the third record for the Miles; the first since 1974. Another youngster, possibly the same bird, was seen again on November 17. Next day a lone immature snow goose showed up and hung around about two weeks—another record.

On December 30, after Dusty Dunstan had filleted most of the venison from the bones, an immature bald eagle dined on a deer carcass put out for that purpose. The pity of it all!

December and January were very hard on the firewood supply and gave Art and his trusty snowplow lots of business. Then February comes off the warmest on record. On Groundhog Day, Roger Cohn, from over at Buttercup Farms Sanctuary near Millbrook, New York, comes to Miles to see his shadow and to pick up a pickup in the form of a 1975 Scout. Art bids his faithful Scout a fond farewell and wishes Roger much happy motoring over the hills and hollows of Buttercup in Dutchess County. Art, meanwhile, is sporting a new Chevy equipped with snowplow and dump bed. There is no justice!

On March 4, ten deer begin their late afternoon visits to the backyard for their daily handout of corn. This may not be extra sound wildlife management, but it keeps the pregnant does and the local chapter and other visitors happy. On March 12, the first woodcock is all atwitter in the grassy areas Art and Pete DeSimone keep mowed for such performances. A bobcat is seen in the valley on March 31.

On April 3, the second official record of a red-shouldered hawk on the sanctuary occurs. Which means Ed Carlson at Corkscrew in Florida sees more red-shoulders in twenty minutes than the Miles manager sees in twenty years.

In the last decade, the intern programs at Miles, Corkscrew, Buckley, and Beidler Forest have taught dozens of college students what it's like out there in the wide, wild world. They've learned about climbing trees and banding hawks, wading in swamps full of moccasins and mosquitoes, mowing lawns, painting outhouses, running vegetation transects, censusing breeding birds, and leading canoe trips, bird trips, wildflower trips, night walks, and boardwalks, teaching six-year-olds and senile citizens all sorts of woodsy lore.

Housing interns has been a problem at every sanctuary, including Miles. Now Joe Edmondson, leader of the Sanctuary Wardens Attack Team, aided and abetted by Gingert, DeSimone, and Dunstan, remodeled Emily Miles' old carriage barn. When finished, Old Dad will guarantee a comfortable, efficient dormitory-laboratory complete with the best in electrical systems, insulators, plumbing, and hot and cold running blacksnakes. What the SWAT did for Starr Ranch in California, it can do for Miles in Connecticut, and, in time to come, at other sanctuaries across the country.

Recently, the Jackson Peck Land Company writes to Art, "We are trying to formulate a management plan for the 710 acres . . . based on the best possible information and guidance with respect to soil and water conservation, wildlife habitat, and timber stand improvement where needed." They point out that "Audubon's long-standing and close relationship to the town of Sharon . . . and its interest in protecting the Carse Brook watershed all serve to strengthen the argument for donating a conservation easement to Audubon—if Audubon would be interested."

We see no problem with helping them draw up their management plan and possibly managing the land for them. The Audubon Sanctuary managers have been demonstrating this kind of land and wildlife management for eighty years. Our motto has always been, "Don't just do as we say; do as we do."

JULY 1985 After ten years and seven months as manager of the sanctuary, Art and Susan Gingert had put the Miles on the map. Due to his "bluebird trail" of nest boxes throughout Sharon and environs, Art was able to write on May 9, 1984, "There seems to be bluebirds everywhere in town this spring, though it has taken six years to reestablish them."

Art and Susan's dedication not only benefitted the bluebirds, kestrels, golden-winged warblers, deer, grouse, and woodcocks, it did a superb job of public relations for Audubon. As of July 1, 1984, Art began a two-year leave of absence to concentrate on his photography, lecturing, writing, and research. In his spare time, he does a bit of carpentry to keep his hand in the trade and the wolf from the door. It pays to be versatile when it comes to conservation.

Pete DeSimone and Dusty Dunstan kept the place under control until Mike Dudek, a former Miles intern, took over on January 1, 1985. It didn't take Mike and Jan long to adjust to a deer cluttering the yard, coyotes howling in the hills, and great horned owls hooting defiance to the Connecticut winter.

Some thirty-five mourning doves also decided there was enough food and cover to get by. This wintering flock has been growing steadily for over ten years. In view of its great adaptability and tough, feisty character, it hardly seems appropriate for the symbol of peace to make such mournful noises.

February 1985 was a fairly birdy month. Robins came back on the thirteenth and blustered about the yard, complaining about the weather. Four pairs of Canada geese arrived on the twenty-third and started honking and fighting over the nesting platforms and beaver houses. Red-winged blackbirds and red-faced blackbirds (what the bird books call turkey vultures) showed up on the twenty-fourth; grackles, on the twenth-fifty; hooded mergansers on the twenty-sixth. And all this time, a family of otters was belly-slamming across the snow and ice.

In spite of such distractions, Mike managed to get all the wood duck boxes ready to rent and refurbished the goose nests. Meanwhile, Pete DeSimone, Papa Joe Edmondson, and Mike just about finished conversion of the old carriage barn. From now on, instead of housing surreys, buggies, cutters, bobsleds, and other vehicles of by-gone days, it will house interns whose eyes are on the future.

Intelligent beavers are supposed to eat aspen, blue beech, alder, willows, and other species of no commercial value. But those who have not read the book chomp up sugar maples, red maples, red oak, white oak, apples, and other species that keep a sanctuary manager warm in winter and feed the squirrels and deer. It's no good trying to livetrap the excess beavers and move them elsewhere in the state because Connecticut is plumb full. Tacking heavy duty hardware cloth around the trees is expensive and time-consuming but Mike says it works. To offset the busy beavers, Mike and Pete planted 365 trees of various species this spring.

On March 4, one of the most important members of the Class Aves arrived. For thousands of years, black ducks have probably nested in the valley that transects the Miles Sanctuary. The noble bird is in trouble throughout New England, and it's gratifying to see them still using the swamp and beaver ponds of the Miles.

On March 10, 1985, Pete DeSimone got the first record of a raven for the sanctuary, and a flock of eighty Atlantic snow geese flew over on the twenty-ninth. Other species, such as woodcocks, fox sparrows, phoebes, tree swallows, great blue herons, and wild turkeys were on hand to greet the black flies and no-see-ums.

Aldo Leopold once said, "What a dull world if we knew all about geese!" One goose nesting at Miles managed to keep things interesting by mysteriously disappearing. An island built by Warren Rumsey (Mrs. Miles' former caretaker who remained on the sanctuary after her death) and Old Dad back in 1968 has been occupied every spring, and the goose brought off a brood. On April 13, 1985, the incubating female vanished overnight, leaving seven eggs, a perplexed gander, a perplexed sanctuary manager, and no trace of a struggle or evidence of a predator. Mike reports, "The male continued to circle the nest and defend the area for a full week before retiring to the front lawn seemingly as perplexed as we."

On the seventeenth, another nest was abandoned, this one containing six eggs. Again, no evidence of disturbance was found, but the goose and gander both stayed near the nest site a full week after leaving the eggs.

Down at Pine Island Sanctuary, North Carolina, Ernest Brickhouse reported a similar situation, except that the eggs disappeared with no evidence of predation such as broken shells. Do we call in Sherlock Holmes or a goose psychologist? Has the Canada goose population in New England reached carrying capacity, and is some subtle population curb operating? We know a lot more about geese today than Aldo did in 1948, but the world of the geese at Miles is far from dull.

Fortunately, no such mysteries surround our hooded mergansers and wood ducks. The hoodies brought off ten young, and the wood ducks produced several broods.

In June, Peter Tinkham (intern) began a study of beaver food preference and habitat selection. Mike reports, "Pete started his project by slosh-ing through the sanctuary swamps in an effort to 'guestimate' population numbers and locate all active and inactive lodges; no easy task, that. By the end of his stay at Miles, Pete will attempt to ascertain who is managing whom as far as the beaver populations is concerned."

As usual, Mike found time to lead a few field trips (the golden-winged warblers attracted folks from far and wide), attend a few professional con-ferences, and put on bird-banding demonstrations for school classes.

NOVEMBER 1986 Human population pressures being what they are, it's not surprising that golden-winged warblers, the endangered globe-flower, river otters, white-tailed deer, and dragonflies must share the Miles Sanctuary with primates. Manager Mike Dudek makes like a major professor advising graduate students doing research on birds, beasts, and botany; or like a forester thinning out the big-toothed aspens; a lumber-man cutting, splitting, and chipping logs; a carpenter remodeling his resi-dence or putting a new roof on the barn, while operating a tractor, slide projector, snowplow, and other machinery common to New England.

Interns for 1985–1986 include Pete Tinkham, who livetrapped, tagged, and released beavers to study their movements, food, and habitat prefer-ence. Mike Barrows undertook a forest inventory which supplements the earlier vegetation survey by Sandra DeSimone and so provides a better background for management. Jennifer Cofer monitored the use by blue-birds of the nest boxes erected by former manager Art Gingert. She also followed the fortunes of the wood ducks, hooded mergansers, and Can-ada geese nesting on the Miles. Joe Buzzo continued to build on our data-base pertaining to beaver food habits and dispersal of young adults.

Terri Donovan added to our knowledge of breeding birds. Using *American Birds* standards, she established a breeding bird census. Art Gin-gert, who had originally laid out a study area for this purpose, came back to give Terri a hand. Using mist nets, she managed to band many resi-dents and offspring. Steve Majetich studied the feasibility of water control structures that might enable us to draw down and reflood sections of the swamp to manage the vegetation. Rebecca Wertheim began a study of limnology of Miles Lake.

These interns usually spend twelve weeks at the sanctuary learning all sorts of woodsy lore, observing practical wildlife management firsthand, and measuring the response of flora and fauna to management. They are comfortably ensconced in the old carriage barn, which was completely remodeled by Joe Edmondson and Pete DeSimone. The program got off the ground about twelve years ago under the direction of Art Gingert. As interns, Mike Dudek and Pete and Sandy DeSimone got hooked on the Audubon Sanctuaries and vice versa. Hence, they are now well trained for running the Miles and Starr Ranch. When Pete and Sandy left for California and the Starr Ranch on August 17, 1985, Mike's report stated, "Miles will miss the flash of Sandy's smile and Pete's head, as well as Jake, the wonder dog."

As usual, the lives and times of the wild critters were most interesting. A bluebird occupying a box on the front lawn had been banded the year before as a fledgling in Lakeville, ten miles away, by Art Gingert. More wild turkeys and coyotes are seen and heard every year. On the 1985 Christmas Bird Count, December 22, at minus five degrees to eighteen above zero, Mike and five rugged birders sallied forth at 5:00 A.M. in search of hootie owls. The latter, being smarter than humans, snuggled down in their cozy cavities. Mike's crew did see a sharp-shinned hawk and a winter wren, which helped boost the Sharon area count to seventy-three species. Two female red-bellied woodpeckers spent the winter at Miles, usually ignoring suet in feeders and feeding on corn on the ground with the blue jays. On January 28, 1986, a redpoll was the first record since 1984. Mike's report says, "The daily blue jay picnic was interrupted one snowy afternoon as a Cooper's hawk dropped by uninvited and made short work of a somewhat startled jay."

Why can't they be nice?

Mike's notes for February 1986 include bluebirds, goshawks, saw-whet owls, flocks of snow buntings, horned larks, sixty turkeys, busy beavers, and otters. In March a gray-phase screech owl occupied a wood duck box. Mike finds occasional blue jay feathers and the beaks of evening grosbeaks in screech owl pellets.

The Miles crew is very much into the nest box business. They built fifty more bluebird boxes and twenty for wood ducks. In addition to screech owls, hooded mergansers, and wood ducks, they find boxes used by starlings, white-footed mice, and gray squirrels. Jennifer Cofer monitors eighteen of Art's bluebird boxes, plus thirteen wood duck boxes on Miles and fourteen on the adjacent state marsh. She follows up on three hooded merganser nests, three wood ducks, plus those of other ducks and geese.

May 1986 was a great birding month. Some species of note include solitary sandpipers, Canada and Wilson's warblers, and olive-sided fly-catchers. Photos were made of the golden-winged warblers. Of the seven pairs of geese, with a total of thirty-eight goslings, only three broods with a total of four goslings made it to flying stage. Predation such as bobcats, great horned owls, snapping turtles, and perhaps coyotes kept our population down. This 90 percent loss of goslings probably makes regional golfers happy.

In August 1986, three great egrets fed in the marsh for most of the month, a new record for the Miles, since the great has never been common or even seen there. Terri Donovan prepared a report and a slide show on her summer's work. She mist-netted a pine siskin, a blister-raising female cardinal, a hermit thrush, some chestnut-sided warblers, endless house finches, a Canada warbler, five bluebirds, a veery, a very irate kingfisher, plus a song sparrow with an adopted cowbird fledgling. After banding, the sparrow continued to feed the cowbird for a solid week. Says Mike, "This makes a strong case for planned parenthood."

Mike, Joe Edmondson, and Art Gingert made three trips down to the Scully on Long Island with chain saw, log splitter, chipper, and dump truck to help Carl Safina dig out from under the trees blown down by Hurricane Gloria.

MARCH 1988 Mike Dudek says the Miles has more beavers than any other Audubon sanctuary, but that is not an unmixed blessing. A tree that may in summer wear a nest of robins in its hair may damn well be in a dam that floods the road in fall. Its branches may be stuck into the bottom of the lake and, come freeze-up, serve as groceries for the flat-tailed varmints who swim about under the ice in the safety of their dining room. Dragging aspens for one hundred yards across West Cornwall Road into Miles Lake has a marked effect on the landscape, and on the temperament of the manager, motorists, and road crew.

In times past, at the request and behest of the township highway department, we have had professional trappers supply the fur industry with raw material; we've livetrapped and moved "excess" beavers; we've been thankful they haven't caused serious automobile accidents. What long-term effect, if any, this has on the Miles beaver population, no one knows. Therefore, Kevin Maurice arrived on March 23, 1987, for a ten-week internship and his third field season of our beaver-monitoring project. By livetrapping and tagging, studying food habits, and keeping tabs on population numbers and ages, Mike and Kevin hope to get a fair notion of how to keep the beaver a permanent member of the Miles fauna without eliminating the woody flora within one hundred yards of the lake. After all, the deer, yellow warblers, red squirrels, and woodpeckers can't get by without trees and brush!

But never let it be said that rodents can derail audible boy bird-watching. Perish forbid! The Christmas Bird Count for 1986 was not especially noteworthy, although accipiters and saw-whet owls were more numerous than usual. Art Gingert recorded an immature northern shrike; a pair of ravens stayed just outside Mike's count area. Wild turkeys continue to increase on and around the Miles. In January 1987, there was heavy activity at the feeders by nineteen species. Flocks of redpolls, pine siskins, and a pair of red-bellied woodpeckers added interest to the list. Mike vowed to find nesting red-bellies come spring, and they thoughtfully nested in a willow in his yard for the first bona fide record. Other January sightings included bluebirds, kingfishers, pileated woodpeckers, black ducks, and screech owls. A gyrfalcon, just west of the Miles, was a new record for Dutchess County, New York.

In March additional mallards, blacks, goldeneyes, and wood ducks arrived. Redpolls and siskins were gradually replaced by swamp sparrows, phoebes, and bluebirds. An immature bald eagle benefited from a road-killed deer that was donated by a game warden.

In April, Jan Dudek, Kevin Maurice, and Judi Murray began monitoring the boxes on the extensive bluebird trail. In mid-April four mist nets kept the bird banders busy with siskins, rose-breasted grosbeaks, goldfinches, yellowthroats, song sparrows, cowbirds, and a male red-bellied woodpecker. Mike operates under Art Gingert's master banding permit. Art, former Miles manager, provides priceless help in the bird-banding business.

On May 17, Janet Steele, grad student from Eastern Illinois University, began work on two breeding bird censuses. She continued last year's census of the mixed habitat (swamp, old fields, openings, etc.) and established a new plot in the second-growth forest habitat. The latter was not easy because of hilly, rocky terrain and biting blackflies. In the forest, she found twenty-one breeding species—the most numerous being oven-birds, wood thrushes, wood pewees, sapsuckers, red-eyed vireos, and scarlet tanagers.

The first goslings appeared May 8, 1987; by the twelfth, there were four broods with nineteen young holding court on the front lawn. The anserine debate was a welcome relief from the politicians running for

U.S. President. A Brewster's warbler was on hand again. On May 16, Mike and Jan Dudek participated in the Housatonic Audubon Society Birdathon, with sixty-seven species found on a two-mile stretch of West Cornwall Road.

On April 5, 1987, Judi Murray, from Virginia Polytechnic Institute, began a five-month study on the nesting ecology of nothern goshawks, red-shouldered hawks, and barred owls. This study was begun about eight years ago by Pete DeSimone and Mike Root. It is very gratifying to have Judi continue to build on the database established by Pete and Mike. Her work is sponsored by the U.S. Fish and Wildlife Service. On April 6, Pete arrived from the Starr Ranch in California. He spent a week showing Judi the nests of former years and getting acquainted with the overall area. While checking hawk nests, Judi found a saw-whet owl's nest. Later, she and Art Gingert banded the owlets. Judi measured vegetation parameters at sixty-seven nests and fifty random plots. Using her data, future woodland managers should be able to evaluate habitat for raptor management.

Other summer notes include young red-bellied woodpeckers pestering the adult male for food at the feeder, young pileateds peering from a cavity (Janet's breeding bird plot) and a new record: immature double-crested cormorants feeding in Miles Lake.

JUNE 1990 Mike Dudek says January 1989 was the warmest in the memory of northwestern Connecticut folks. The meaning of "typical New England winter" and "old howler" was lost in the melting snow.

He continued Cornell University's Feederwatch program—a sixteen-week feeder count of wintering birds— and completed his annual banding data report forms for the U.S. Fish and Wildlife Service. His February report shows a mink, otters playing tag, a mockingbird off and on, a noisy raven, an osprey fishing in the open water in the swamp, and the return of geese, red-wings, and hoodies on the twenty-third.

On March 27, the ice on Miles Lake broke up and went over the spillway, whereupon the beavers promptly dammed it up, and Mike had to unplug it every other day to keep the water from flooding West Cornwall Road. When not undamming the dam and damning the beavers, Mike cleaned and repaired our twenty wood duck boxes, three goose platforms, and bluebird boxes. Three pairs of geese immediately claimed the baskets. To keep the nesters in business, Mike bush-hogged some meadows, cleared a new one, and kept water in the swamp. In response, song sparrows, veeries, wood thrushes, bluebirds, red-tails, wood ducks, hooded mergansers, and such cluttered up the place. Three fox sparrows (a record number) spent a week around the feeder en route to parts north.

May 1989 was the wettest on record, with 10.1 inches of rain, proving that the weatherman is another environmental extremist. Not content with excess spring rains, on July 10 he arranged a tornado in nearby Cornwall, while Miles got 2.3 inches of rain in two hours.

Jessica Eskow arrived May 7 to continue our small mammal trapping project in field edge habitat, which will correlate mammals' use of specific vegetative types. Jennifer DeCecco arrived May 15 to continue the two breeding-bird censuses in a mixed habitat and a woodland plot. The ladies also monitored a stretch of bluebird trail established by the intrepid Art Gingert. Five mist nets were set up and banding began in earnest in late May.

By the end of August, 275 birds were banded, including 56 young and 6 adult bluebirds, 12 sparrow hawks known as kestrels, 58 house finches, and 41 tree swallows. Added interest was provided by the recapture of 50 birds from previous bandings, including a chestnut-sided warbler banded in 1986.

Eric Kelchin continued our beaver research, trapping and tagging twenty-four. He estimates a total population of thirty for the lake and adjacent swamp.

Robin Cohen caught 331 small mammals along field edges, mostly white-footed and deer mice. These data will be used in managing the sanctuary for optimum species diversity.

To add diversity to his own schedule, Mike assists Papa Joe Edmondson in SWAT projects at Constitution Island Marsh (on the Hudson River in New York) and the Todd Sanctuary in Maine.

After Hurricane Hugo devastated Beidler Forest, in South Carolina, it swung inland and passed west of Miles. But 13.22 inches of rain (norm is 3.9) shattered September records.

Woodies and mallards were "bunching up" in September, along with about fifty Canada geese. Because the spillway and dam at Miles Lake need repairs, a meeting on September 25 included three state agencies such as Connecticut Dam Safety, Wildlife Bureau, DEF Inland Wetlands, plus four federal agencies including FWS, SCS, EPA, and good ol' Corps of Engineers. Says Mike, "Unbelievably, all these agencies will have their hands in the various permits required to accomplish this project."

Says Lonnie Legé, "Welcome to the club, son. Just wait till the seven of them start fighting among themselves." (It took Lonnie and Berton about three years to get a permit to patch a hole in the levee to keep salt water out of the Rainey Marsh in Louisiana.)

It kept on raining in October with 8.43 inches. But the Miles was brightened by a red-breasted nuthatch in the hemlocks, sixteen wild turkeys, and some fifty geese having a bit of galliform and anserine conversation on the lawn. After being mysteriously absent in 1988, evening grosbeaks showed up in November 1989 and made like grocery-beaks all winter.

Summarizing the goings-on for 1989–1990: 308 birds were banded in 1989; 225 conifers and 10 shrubs were planted; woodies shucked out seven broods and hoodies, five broods for a mixed bag of 120 ducklings.

WINTER 1991 Mike Dudek's reports give the distinct impression that wildlife research and management go hand in hand. On May 20, 1990, Beth Anstet, University of Maine student, and Amanda Merwin, of Swarthmore College, began their twelve-week studies of the relationships between birds, mammals, vegetation, and various environmental factors.

Amanda conducted our two annual breeding-bird censuses, which include vegetation plot analysis. By the end of June, she had finished twenty-four census runs on the mixed habitat plot and the forest plot. This marks the fourth year for the woodland; the fifth for mixed habitat. If, as seems likely, our native breeding birds face habitats diminishing in quality and quantity, wildlife managers hope to know what tools to use and how to use them to reverse this trend.

In the forest plot, dominated by red oak, Amanda found thirty-six species of birds, six of which accounted for 50 percent of all territorial males. This group of tropical migrants, in order of greatest abundance, included ovenbirds, eastern wood pewees, wood thrushes, black-and-white warblers, veeries, and scarlet tanagers. These species are undergoing stress on their wintering grounds as well as on their breeding grounds. If these numbers hold true for a substantially larger forest of this type, we will have a pattern to go by in restoration efforts.

The mixed habitat produced sixty-five species (fifty-three breeders) of which nine accounted for 55 percent of the territorial males. In order of greatest abundance: catbirds, yellow warblers, chestnut-sided warblers, red-winged blackbirds, common yellowthroats, American redstarts, robins, song sparrows, and veeries. Most of these species are indicative of the "edge" habitat dominating this plot.

Beth Anstet completed her forestry project and designed an operation that would selectively cut certain kinds of trees. Her target species are red maple, white ash, and black birch. If a timber tract needs thinning to produce maximum dollar returns, and if this operation can also benefit breeding birds, it's a win-win situation. By removing some competition for the more valuable red oak and white ash, both birds and landowner can benefit. A stand of uneven age is also more productive of birds and dollars. So, if done right, cutting trees, like burning marshes, is not automatically bad.

Permits to repair the dam that makes the lake that pleases beavers, ducks, geese, bass, and chain pickerel are wending their way through a maze of state and federal bureaus. The SCS promises plans by next August. What would Emily Miles think of that?

For ten years, Bill Borck has been studying the timber rattlers in and around the Miles. He monitors about eight den sites, has found four or five color variations, is attempting to measure their reproductive rate, has many pictures of pregnant females, and, in cooperation with the American Museum of Natural History, is preparing a long-term research-management plan.

Moving up the evolutionary scale to critters with scales on their feet and feathers on their back, five pairs of Canada geese produced about thirty-five goslings. In cooperation with state biologists, Mike caught and neck-collared nine adult honkers. No one knows where our locals go, but we'll find out. They also leg-banded five young and five adult wood ducks. Eight pairs of woodies and three pairs of hoodies held the franchise on our nest boxes.

In the dickey bird category, 470 were banded by early November, including 55 baby bluebirds. Of much interest are 84 recaptures from former years, including a five-year-old downy woodpecker and four-year-old chickadee.

Included among the unsung wildlife management success stories is the big upsurge in the bluebird population in the northwest corner of Connecticut. In the 1990 Christmas Bird Count, bluebirds were high on everybody's list, whereas they were "very good birds" back when Old Dad and Miss Nancy lived at Miles. This is unquestionably the result of Art Gingert's establishment of a trail of bluebird nest boxes in the Sharon-Lakeville area some ten to twelve years ago.

MAY 1995 Providing suitable habitat for native plants and animals in northwestern Connecticut is something worth doing. If done well enough, neighboring landowners who, at first, may want to distance themselves from the "bird-watchers and tree huggers" will get interested in the way Miles Sanctuary is managed.

In the 1970s, Manager Art Gingert persuaded a few landowners to let him install a bluebird box on their property. No one has ever accused Art of being a crusader, but Mike Dudek, current manager, says Art was certainly the icebreaker.

If there's a brood of bluebirds in the backyard, the once stand-offish neighbor is willing to talk about the value of nearby wetlands, hardwood forests, open spaces, and the need for caution in the use of pesticides, chain saws, and macadam. We have accepted responsibility for a regional bluebird box program.

Fortunately for the tri-state area (Northwest Connecticut, Southeast Massachusetts, Dutchess and Columbia Counties, New York), Mike is well versed in such topics.

Mike's report says, ". . . the focus at Miles is basically developing a regional habitat management strategy that will have at its core the four Audubon properties in the area . . . the two key ingredients to the program are organizing area conservation groups to promote long-term land use planning goals and a management plan program that would be available to private landowners. In both cases, Miles would have an impact on land use decision making and thus become more of a community asset . . . the expanded role of the Miles Sanctuary will have many spin-offs such as tighter connections to universities, tie-ins to NAS's migratory bird conservation program and expanded funding resources."

Positive effects are already in evidence. A state police request to build a telecommunications tower on Bradford Mountain, one of the most environmentally sensitive areas in the region, was denied by the Connecticut Siting Council, and a wetland in Sharon known as Bradford Fen was saved.

Mike cooperates with at least six private groups and one federal agency involved in various aspects of land protection in the region. In response to inquiries from three private landowners, he visited their properties and made recommendations for sound land use management.

Sterling College in Vermont expressed much interest in student work experience with Miles. A graduate student at Yale School of Forestry may design a forestry plan for Rheinstrom Hill Sanctuary (Hillsdale, New York) with 924 acres of hardwood forest and planted conifers. In 1994 six students from the University of Michigan, Connecticut College, College of Holy Cross, and Sterling College participated in our program.

Landmark Volunteers, gifted high school students from the eastern United States, also took part. The Emily Winthrop Miles has always extended its influence beyond its borders by serving as a model of sound wildlife and land management ideas. Today its influence covers roughly 100,000 acres in the tri-state area.

SYDNES ISLAND

SANCTUARY

Bridge City, Texas

For many years, Sydnes Island in Sabine Lake, near the mouth of the Sabine River, which separates southwestern Louisiana from Texas, was the site of a large colony of wading birds.

Susan Bailey had kept an eye on the great rookery of roseate spoonbills, egrets, herons, and cormorants. She had long felt that the 127-acre island should be an Audubon Sanctuary. Finally, on November 5, 1974, with assistance from John Franson, our Texas regional representative, and members of the Sabine Audubon Society, her wish came true. She became the official warden on January 1, 1975. The island was leased for ten years from the state of Texas.

So the great state of Texas, where men are men and women are governors and senators, could boast the first female wildlife warden in the Audubon Sanctuary Department. We are glad to note that the Texas Parks and Wildlife Department has taken an interest in birds other than those officially classified as game birds.

Establishing the sanctuary, however, did not meet with universal approval. Hook-and-line anglers, who are very numerous, vociferous, and excitable, were generally opposed on the false belief that we would prohibit fishing in adjacent waters. To their way of thinking, protecting fish-eating birds is the work of misguided bird-watchers. Fortunately, some fishermen are better informed and support our sanctuary management.

As is true of our other sanctuaries, we don't intend to lock up Sydnes Island and throw away the key. For the time being, however, visitors will be admitted only with permission of Sue Bailey and the Sanctuary Department.

JUNE 1975 In former years, photographers, gun-toting kids, and overzealous birders gave the wading birds here in Sabine Lake a bad time. This year, our warden kept the shutter-bugs some distance from the birds, diplomatically handled the birders, and gave the kids a bad time. On June 19, she enlisted the help of state and federal game wardens in persuading three adventurous boys that roseate spoonbills and egrets can be very expensive targets.

When we went to press, the case against the boys had not been settled, but the birds had settled back on their nests within twenty-four hours. With Sue on the job, we think incidents of this kind will change from fairly common to extremely rare.

Trees and bushes for nesting purposes are at a premium on Sydnes Island. Water gets about one foot deep during very high tides, so a nesting bird in the bush is worth two on the ground. To alleviate this situation, a schoolteacher and four Girl Scouts from Bridge City helped Sue plant some fast-growing Chinese tallow trees. About that time, 100 great egrets and 50 cormorants got in gear for the start of a good nesting season. Nesting cormorants increased to about 200 pairs, and, by late May, about 700 left the nests. Great egrets built about 200 nests and fledged about 500 young. About 125 pairs of snowies nested in late March and produced about 375.

Susan noted that in 1974 the great egrets averaged about four eggs per nest; this year, only three. Spoonbills dragged their nesting activities out this year. By April 12, many large young cormorants were dead in their nests. Sue thinks the very low salinity of the estuary may decrease the marine animal life on which her birds depend for groceries, causing late nesting and fewer eggs. The Toledo Bend Reservoir apparently lowers the salt content of Lake Sabine, which is bad news for fish-eating birds. This is a subject that John Ogden and Rich Paul, of our Research Department, may look into.

Some production estimates for other species are cattle egrets, 800 young; no great blues nested; little blues produced 4 young; Louisianas, 225; black-crowns, 580; white-faced ibises, 40. Susan says erosion on the channel side of the island caused by tugboat backwash could be lessened if she could persuade the Army Corps of Engineers to rip-rap the vulner-able stretch with rocks.

On March 21, 1975, her big signs proclaiming the island as a wildlife sanctuary were erected. Objections of a big fat cottonmouth in the grass nearby were overruled.

On June 6, Douglas Slack of Texas A&M, his assistant, Mary Cox, and Susan took an inventory of the island in preparation for the Fish-Eating Bird Conference. Her warden's report says, "Sampling is not possible on Sydnes, as Dr. Slack learned. Temperature 93, but about twice that in among the roseau canes. One-third of the island was counted before game was called because of heat, which is detrimental to baby birds, also to ornithologists. Dr. Slack finds the terrain on Sydnes far more rugged than that of other coastal sanctuaries."

1976 When Old Dad hired Susan Bailey, our first woman warden, he should have known that her sanctuary was going to get attention like it never got before. Comes April of our bicentennial year, and Sue Bailey and the Sydnes are visited by Phil Kahl, photographer on a project for *National Geographic,* and Frank Graham Jr., writer for *Audubon* magazine. Then came a Dr. Ramsey, ornithologist from Lamar University in Beaumont, a couple of research types from Louisiana State University and the Louisiana Cooperative Wildlife Research Unit, Hal Osburn of Texas Parks and Wildlife, an alligator, several folks from the Sabine Audubon Society, and the Houston Audubon Society. Everyone wanted to see, count, or photograph birds, with the exception of the alligator, for which Susan refused to be the gracious host.

On April 6, John Portnoy, of Louisiana Cooperative Wildlife Research Unit, and a colleague did a nesting survey of the island. Their method was to count all nests, by species, in strips two meters wide. The strips across Sydnes Island were twenty meters apart. Since Portnoy's strips covered about 10 percent of the island, he multiplied his actual count by ten to get the following estimates of nests: 394 olivaceous cormorants; 5,189 great egrets; 5,614 snowies; 2,548 Louisiana herons; 1,802 black-crowned night herons; 52 white ibises; 673 roseate spoonbills; 1,533 empty nests of various species, for a grand total of 17,805 nests.

Portnoy's complaint was that Sue ran him off the island a little too soon because his sampling technique was keeping too many birds off their nests too long. But he was happy to have had a place to work, and it doesn't hurt these recently hatched Ph.Ds to learn that science is spelled with a little *s*, and Susan is spelled with a capital *S*. Besides looking after her birds, Susan found time to show her slides to several groups in the Orange–Port Arthur area, disseminating a little Audubon publicity and education.

The Easter Bunny brought severe weather and extremely high tides to Sydnes Island, which did considerable damage to ground nesters. Her white ibis nests were all wiped out by tides four feet high. Spoonbill nests weren't hurt much, although a number of small young were killed, as were several great and snowy egrets. Little blues have always been very scarce on Sydnes; this year they built thirty nests in deep, heavy canes where they escaped damage from high water.

The white ibises renested this time on higher ground, eventually totaling about 125 nests that fledged over 200 young by early July. All in all, the weather was fairly stable, and production on Sydnes Island was better than average. Black skimmers nested on a construction site within the Texas Refinery at Port Arthur and, as of August 1, the job was being held up pending the fledging of the young. Susan talked the manager of the refinery into looking after the black skimmers. The Texas Colonial Waterbird Society concludes that skimmer populations are stable or declining slowly. In our experience with skimmers on our coastal island sanctuaries, they tend to nest on shell beaches close to the waterline, which often results in flooded nests. Sue believes they need all the help they can get.

Not to be outdone by Louisiana State University, the Texas Aggies Department of Wildlife and Fisheries Sciences sent Mike Morrison, graduate student, to study the olivaceous cormorant. Not much is known about the nesting chronology, success, or status of this cormorant, so with Susan's cooperation and advice, this should make a valid addition to bird lore.

1977 The cruel winter of 1977 was no respecter of birds or beauty. Reports from January through March 15 from Sue tell of blue northers, a deserted island, birdless beaches, and a desire to go down and visit with Ernest Ortiz and Friday Fluman to get warm. But as April draws nigh, a brighter iris changes on the burnish'd dove; the great egrets are staking out territories; and the olivaceous cormorants are getting in gear for another go-round.

Comes April 21 and Sue's report states, "Spoonbills seem to have been given a hormone shot. Or did the rains do it? Nesting is off to a great start. Where they were just starting to build last week, one nest now has six eggs."

At the same time, some of the female spoonbills were dropping eggs on the ground. Susan had noticed a bit of this in 1976, and she wonders if the cool spring and lack of early green vegetation got the spoonies unsynchronized. Instead of rings and rice, the male presents his bride-to-be with a broken stick, and the pair proceeds through a standard ritual without benefit of clergy. Nest building and egg laying follow. We daresent (that's a good old Texas word) speculate too much about this subject lest those who study bird behavior and call themselves "ethologists" have heart failure. But Sue thinks a female ready to lay may drop an egg here and there, and when a male finally comes along who is ready to bring her a broken twig, the sound track gets synchronized with the picture, and the show goes on.

The Chinese tallow trees Sue planted two years ago are growing nicely and are big enough to be used for nesting. She says her elderberry bushes were planted by the birds themselves. They grow very fast and are used by several species.

Requests to visit the island were not as numerous as in other years, and Sue was beginning to wonder if wading around in mud, twelve-foot canes, mosquitoes, cottonmouth moccasins, and bird droppings had lost its appeal. Then came the last week of April, and a group including some amateur called Roger Tory Peterson dropped in. It was too rough to view the birds from small boats, so Rob Bailey, who is a self-respecting commercial fisherman, took his big boat, loaded with birders instead of fish, and unloaded them on the beach.

That was probably fortunate because about five hundred roseates plus thousands of great egrets, snowies, cattle egrets, great blues, Louisianas, black-crowns, little blues, white and white-faced ibises, and olivaceous cormorants greeted them. When birders are on foot, they can't tip the boat over no matter how much they jump up and down.

Mike Morrison, the grad student from Texas A&M, is still studying the cormorants. Sue says he and his assistant are a big help in recording the lives and times of the various populations on Sydnes Island. When a Coast Guard helicopter spotted Sue and the Aggies poking around in the bushes, they called the game wardens, who responded with surprising speed. Sue was pleased to see the wardens' devotion to duty, and they said the same about her. A mutual admiration society involving an Audubon sanctuary warden and a Texas game warden must be another first for Texas. All in all, it was a very productive season at Sydnes, in spite of the Yankee winter.

1978   Sue Bailey has been busy this season, and her birds have followed her example. On January 22, 1978, myrtle warblers were the only feathered objects on the island, although a few olivaceous cormorants were cruising this stretch of the Sabine River. A month later, great blues and a few other herons were in the area but ignoring Sydnes. Spoonbills arrived March 12 and were staking out territories a week later. Meanwhile, black-crowns, snowies, greats, Louisianas, white ibises, and white-faced ibises started nesting.

All these species had a very good year at Sydnes Island, but the roseate spoonbills were the undisputed champs. They fledged 2,100, which is better than ordinary. Only one spring storm threatened the wading birds, although at one point an excess of fresh water moved their groceries out into saltier water. This put the nestlings on skimpy rations, and Sue suspects this held production down slightly.

Great egrets did very well, averaging about three young per nest. Snowies and little blues came out about the same as last year, while white ibises are on the increase.

Cattle egrets, as usual, nested later than other species, and a few were still around by the end of September. Sue says some cattle ranchers have finally observed that cattle egrets do not kill trees, and they do eat grasshoppers that compete with cattle for grass. So they have put away their shootin' irons and allow as how them cow cranes ain't all that bad.

Mike Morrison has finished his research on olivaceous cormorants, and Sue is awaiting a copy of his thesis.

Whenever you have a lot of birds in the glamour-puss class, such as roseates and snowies, they are bound to attract a lot of photographers, writers, biologists, and birders. Sue handles these with ease, but long-distance swimmers are something else. For April 29, her warden's report reads: "Weather dry, awfully windy and rough. As dark was about to fall, I had a feeling I should look out and see what was happening, and sure enough my birds were upset about something. Because of the late hour and rough water, Rob [her husband] insisted on taking me out. Small craft warnings were up, but when you gotta go, you gotta go. Why do they always do this in a gale? We had to approach from the south, where the water was roughest. Sure enough, there was a man on the beach struggling to put a large piece of styrofoam on the island.

"You must remember I am a sweet old grandma and would not lie. This young man claimed he had swum from the Port Arthur side and did not know he was not supposed to be there. The rough water and late hour prevented my making any decipherable notes, and also made it seem reasonable that we take him to shore. We did and he claimed to be a chiropractor. After that I probably needed an adjustment. . . ."

But such goings on did not prevent Sue from leading wildflower field trips to the Big Thicket, doing slide shows for the locals, and attending Park and Water Pollution Board meetings while keeping an eye on the sanctuary.

On one patrol, she was "treated to the sight of a very large moccasin eating baby ibises." Even though she knows that Lonnie and Berton, over at the Rainey, just love water moccasins, she tranquilized this one. Over on Vingt-et-une, off Smith Point, Buddy Whitehead has otter problems; down on Green Island, Friday Fluman has coon and coyote problems; and here on Sydnes Island, we are in need of a St. Patrick to drive out the snakes. Since saints are very scarce in this part of Texas, Sue relies on her snake stick.

This winter Sue plans something new in chapter activities. The beach at Sydnes Island gets cluttered up with garbage and trash from passing freighters and pleasure boats. So while the heronry is uninhabited, the Sabine Audubon Society will tidy up the place in anticipation of the 1979 season.

January 1978 had come and gone, and Sue was glad to see it go. Her reports say the weather, even by Texas standards, was poor. "The ones who live in Oklahoma and Connecticut might find it mild, but to east Texans it is dreary." But on February 15, great flocks of myrtle warblers brought promise of merry sunshine. The white-faced ibises, great egrets, cormorants, and spoonbills didn't believe it, so they waited until March to set up housekeeping.

There are no pear trees on Sydnes Island, but Sue had a Partridge, by the name of Karen, checking trees that contained olivaceous cormorant nests. Karen's research on these Mexican mullet-burners will help evaluate the role of Sydnes in Texas birdlife.

By early April, great egrets and cormorants were incubating, but the big flocks of spoonbills played it cool until the end of the month. The extremely high tides and strong winds eroded away some fifteen feet of the south end of Sydnes during April. More trouble was in store, however, from Tropical Storm Claudette, which rolled over the island on

July 24, when most young spoonbills were too young to fly. Sue estimated 125 young drowned in their nests. Damage was not restricted to nests, however, since fifty feet on the south and one hundred feet on the eastern end of the island disappeared.

Sydnes Island was created as a spoil bank about 1915 by the Corps of Engineers when it dug the Sabine-Neches Waterway to Beaumont. The island has eroded badly, and Sue is trying to persuade the Corps to re-build it. Since it is so susceptible to erosion, a retaining wall to hold it in place would be most practical. Then the island would not continually wash away, and the resulting vegetation would provide excellent habitat for the colonial birds. But the Corps is not too eager to reduce the necessity for constant channel dredging, and they are encouraged by people who fish and certain developers who would rather see the spoil placed elsewhere. We predict that members of Congress will be getting letters from schoolchildren in the area favoring restoration of Sydnes.

That restoration of Sydnes Island is well worth the time and effort is shown by the production from Sue's fish-eating friends. In spite of the weather, the number of flying young produced by the various species was as follows:

Louisiana herons	1,200	Cattle egrets	800
Little blues	150	Spoonbills	1,800
Black-crowns	300	Olivaceous cormorants	1,000
Great egrets	3,000	White-faced ibises	400
Snowies	1,200	White ibises	2,000

Although the water around the island was usually fresh, the birds apparently found ample food, since cormorants and spoonbills laid four or five eggs per nest. To help keep people off the island, an eight-foot alligator patrolled the rim, and Sue was careful to point him out to potential visitors.

1980 On Sabine Lake between Louisiana and the little ol' state of Texas, Sue Bailey had an interesting time of it. On February 8, 1980, she checked her island and found only myrtle warblers and no sharp-faced fowl. Five days later, several great egrets' nests had two eggs, and cormorants were in the building trade.

The morning of March 13 was too foggy to get out to the island, but from the amount of bird talk she could hear. Sue figures there were some territorial disputes going on. When the fog lifted, she found spoonbills, white ibises, Louisianas, snowies, black-crowns, and great egrets all trying to nest in the center of Sydnes.

Her report for April 1 reads, "The continued lovely weather has caused me to make so many trips out to throw off sightseers that there hardly seem time to make a regular trip. Today while chasing fishermen off the east end, I was able to head off a boatload of picture takers. The loss of the large signs (hurricane mischief) makes it very hard to keep people off or to make a trespass case." Sue guessed that the birds had concentrated in the center of the island because of the erosion on the east end and perhaps because of drilling activity in the lake.

Her May 4 report says, "I checked the island early so Rob could go fishing, and I would 'tend the store,' but in the middle of the afternoon, the birds got to flying so wildly that I had to get a fisherman to take me out to see the cause. Someone had decided to take a few pictures right in the nesting area. Rob saw him, and chased him off about the same time I got there."

Bob Arbib, editor of *American Birds*, has the black-crowned night heron on the blue list, which means they are not doing too well around and about. Sue Bailey has them on her black list because they have a gross habit of dining on roseate spoonbill chicks. The pure scientists can talk all they want to about ecological relationships and inherited behavior patterns and balance of nature, but in the Sanctuary Department we reserve the right to personal preference, bias, and bigotry when it comes to who eats what.

Gary James, of the *Eyes of Texas* television show, accompanied Sue one day and filmed the goings-on at Sydnes Island. The show was well received along the Texas coast. Old Dad's file on Sydnes contains letters from Rotary, Kiwanis, and similar clubs thanking us for Sue's fine programs. The slides she gave the Sabine Audubon Society in 1979 are still paying off, since the chapter uses them in schools, which saves Sue a lot of time and travel. She still did a lot of programs on butterflies and wildflowers while Sabine Audubon made good use of her bird slides.

On May 30, 1980, Theodore Cross, a long-time Audubon member from Princeton, New Jersey, revisited Sydnes Island. He was appalled by the changes caused by floods, but highly approved of the way Sue and the birds adjusted to the situation. So, he whips out his checkbook and writes a check for $1,000 for "Contribution for any Sydnes Island project."

On June 17, Sue said she would send in a comprehensive report as soon as the season ended and added, "I need to check on some late nesters and chat with a small alligator who is feasting on birds." Susan's chat, plus the fact that its pond dried up, and other environmental factors, persuaded the gator to take a leave of absence.

In spite of drought, heat, photographers, anglers, night herons, gators, and cottonmouths, the spoonbills fledged about 1,500 young; great egrets, 3,100; snowies, 2,000; cattle egrets, 1,500; black-crowns, 1,000; Louisianas, 2,000; little blues, 70; white ibises, 2,400; and white-faced ibises, 600.

A typical Audubon warden, Sue Bailey lectures to schoolkids in a classroom one day; next day she threatens to sink a trespasser's boat; then she helps some wide-eyed, open-mouthed college student working on his advanced degree; appears on CBS *Sunday Morning* show; does a radio program; and sees to it that about ten thousand colonial waterbirds make it through another season.

A story making the rounds in Beaumont is a case in point. It seems a party of vandals is harassing the colony on Sydnes Island. Whereupon our Susan takes possession of their boat. A passer-by considers rescuing the stranded mischief-makers, but is persuaded that it could be bad for his health. He looks up the sheriff and complains that Mrs. Bailey threatened to shoot a hole through his hull. The sheriff replies, "You're just damned lucky she didn't do it."

And next we see Sue Bailey in a beautifully illustrated article in *Friends*, the Chevy owners' magazine, September 1981. The photography would pass for *Audubon* magazine, and the text is reasonably accurate. "Shad" Northshield, producer of CBS *Morning* with Charles Kuralt, has seen fit to show Susan and the Sydnes several times.

Susan had new four-foot by four-foot signs built that she says are working very well. Buddy Whitehead, from Vingt-et-une Sanctuary in Galveston Bay, brought over one hundred salt cedar seedlings that are curently growing well.

1 9 8 2 Sue says 1982 was a good year at Sydnes Island. By March 1, great egrets were starting to build, while about three hundred roseate spoonbills hung around the shore. By March 12, great egrets were laying;

about thirty cormorants were building; and the spoonies were still thinking about it. By March 18, the pinks were starting to build, while snowies, Louisianas, and black-crowns were just arriving.

Dusty Dunstan and Dave Blankinship showed up on April 23, but they showed no signs of nesting. Since Dusty's past job with Audubon was warden for Tampa Bay, in Florida, he could identify all the big white and pink birds without his bird book and could even guess what the white ibises were thinking about from the way they carried on. He surmised that their nervous actions indicated the arrival of a new flock. Sure enough, Sue found about one hundred new nests a few days later.

Sue says dry, hot weather is good for hatching birds, and as long as the food supply holds up well, "It keeps them healthy and pretty." On May 10, she reported, "The birds all have chicks. The black-crowned night herons seem to be eating the baby spoonbills. The white ibises seem to be thriving, as do the great egrets. Cattle egrets are moving in and nesting. Cormorants are thriving. Overall, the sanctuary is doing the best ever."

On May 18, an exploration crew for Tenneco took Sue out to their recording barge to observe the effect of seismic shots near the island. Sue reports, "Several spoonbills were bathing in the edge of the water when the shot was fired but did not seem to notice. The blasts were undetectable to me, and the crew was most cooperative. The only thing the birds seemed to notice was the loud noise from their radios."

As usual, on her checklist of visitors were lawyers, doctors, state and federal biologists, wildlife photographers. Television reporters, garden variety birders, and outdoor writers, including Erwin A. Bauer of *Outdoor Life*. Old Dad has known Erwin—better known as Joe—Bauer for some forty years and suspects Joe smelled an article about a colorful character and a colorful bird sanctuary.

Speaking of smelling things, Sue's report for May 27 says, "Beautiful hot weather. Normal tides. Counting birds is interesting, if somewhat messy. The roseau canes (*Phragmites communis*) are about twelve feet high, and the small herons and ibises nest among them and roost atop them. I hope guano is as good for a person's skin as it is for the garden." (Estee Lauder, please note.)

In addition to guano, our gal Sue collects data on the producers of same. Counting all birds, including young in the nest, she comes up with the following:

Species	Nests	Total Birds
Spoonbills	300	1,200
Great egrets	2,000	6,000
Snowy egrets	1,500	4,500
White ibises	200	700
White-faced ibises	200	800
Black-crowned night herons	500	2,000
Louisiana herons	1,600	4,000
Cattle egrets	1,500	3,000
Common gallinules	1	7

The above count was made on May 27, 1982. Cattle egrets were just getting started at the time. Sue had not located a colony of little blues, although there was a couple of birds on the island. In late June, she noticed several nests that had produced young being used a second time. She wants to ask Alexander Sprunt IV, director of NAS Research Department, whether these birds are raising a second brood or whether they are newcomers, too lazy to build their own nests. And she doesn't want any smart-aleck remarks, such as, "Why don't you color band them so you can identify the individual birds?"

On July 4, she writes, "I noticed a large amount of very ugly oily substance on the water and on the shore. I called the Coast Guard as we are supposed to do. They sent out a very dressed up lieutenant whose only action was to call on his radio and say there was no oil. He told us there was no use to investigate because they didn't know where it came from and couldn't find out."

Later it was said to have come from two separate accidents at the mouth of the Neches River. Fortunately, no oil got on the sanctuary, and the Bailey Birds finished the summer without mishap.

1983   Ordinarily, we wonder if we'll have to bail Sue Bailey out of jail for shooting up trespassers on Sydnes Island. But 1983 was different. Nobody bothered the birds because there were no birds on Sydnes. By February 14, the weather was nice, but there was only one great blue on the island, and it got no valentines. In early March, many great egrets hung around with no apparent interest in the future of their race. Some white pelicans were developing horns on their beaks, but most individuals of all species were not horny in any sense of the word.

Was the water too fresh for the production of favorite food? Too many raccoons on the island? On the mainland in May, Sue recorded a black-necked stilt with chicks, a mottled duck with ducklings, and a clapper rail with railings. But on Sydnes Island, one lone great blue was singing the blues.

On June 10 Sue noted, "There does not seem to be any birds left in Orange County. Not only are there no birds nesting or roosting on the island, but very few of any kind feeding in the area."

In November Sue's husband, Rob, reports blue crabs dying in his holding pens. Are blue crabs and blue crab eaters affected by the same environmental factor?

Meanwhile, Sue continued her lectures and slide shows throughout the schools in her area, continued her radio programs, and kept the local chapters happy. The wildlife photographers, such as Roger Tory Peterson, who had planned to visit her and photograph the wading birds, were not happy.

To this day, we are not exactly sure what caused the birds to abandon Sydnes Island. Within twenty miles or so, there are some rookeries that Sue visits and records. And she continues to spread the gospel according to John James Audubon in schools from kindergarten through college, National Audubon chapters, business groups, bankers, and sportsmen's clubs, on television, in magazines, and newspapers.

1997 Sue still keeps track of the colonies in the region. But the environmental factor that caused the birds to abandon Sydnes Island is apparently unchanged.

❧ 8 ❧

CONSTITUTION ISLAND

MARSH SANCTUARY

Garrison, New York

Constitution Island Marsh Sanctuary lies next to historic Constitution Island, slightly upriver and across the main channel of the Hudson River from West Point. It not only provides a beautiful vista from the restored Boscobel Mansion at Garrison toward the towers of the U.S. Military Academy but also is the largest and healthiest expanse of tidal marsh remaining in the Hudson estuary. Its 267 acres became an Audubon sanctuary through a three-way arrangement that took years to negotiate. In 1969 the state of New York bought the property from the Greek Ladies Philoptochos Society with funds contributed by Laurance Rockefeller and the Reader's Digest Foundation. In 1970 the Taconic State Park Commission granted permission to the National Audubon Society to preserve and maintain the area "as a wildlife sanctuary and to perform such remedial work as may be necessary to improve and sustain the ecological quality of the marsh." The Reader's Digest Foundation has continued to supply financial support for operation and maintenance.

Constitution Island Marsh is an important nursery area for striped bass, shad, herring, and other fish of the Hudson River estuary. It is habitat for numbers of resident and migratory species of birds.

MARCH 1976 The influence of that sly Scotsman, David Seymour, continues to spread up and down the Hudson River Valley and into the Catskills and Peekskills. David says he can't confine himself to the sanctuary and hope to save the wildlife. In recent years, General Electric has been dumping polychlorinated biphenyls (PCB's) into the river. The Hudson River Fishermen's Association, of which David is currently president, took a dim view of this, since they depend on catching and selling fish for a living. When the PCB's built up to a certain level in the striped bass, they could still catch 'em, but sell 'em they could not, since they were declared unfit for human consumption.

At the request of Conservation Commissioner Ogden Reid, David arranged a meeting at Garrison and another at Bard College, which is upstream near Red Hook. Commissioner Reid explained the reason for his drastic action. Even though they had been put out of business and into the great army of unemployed, the fishermen did not blame Reid, who was doing what he had to do by condemning the fish. Instead they blame a company that claims it cannot economically produce a product for our convenience without eliminating a source of food for our bellies.

Constitution Island Marsh is considered a sanctuary for wildlife. Like all great marshes, such as the Rainey in Louisiana and the Guilford in Connecticut, it also acts as a filter for the sediment that would otherwise choke the aquatic life of the river. Waste assimilation for tertiary treatment is another service performed by the marsh.

One might think that people would be willing to pay someone to save the marshes. But since they can't see what goes on in the marsh, they assume that it offers nothing of value to them. They don't know what the plant growing in the marsh is doing, but they think they know what the plant that produces plastic-coated electrical equipment is doing. To them, the latter means employment that keeps our economy running. Dave and the Hudson River fishermen believe our economy should be able to run without running out of edible fish. They are gradually convincing more and more people that this is a reasonable expectation, and they intend to keep the pressure on until this source of pollution is eliminated.

In addition to this continued monitoring of potential pollution sources, David kept his house in order as far as wood ducks were concerned, and the woodies cranked out four broods from nine boxes. Ospreys still use the sanctuary in migration but have not accepted the three nesting platforms. Perhaps this is just as well, since they would have to feed their hook-nosed offspring on fish loaded with PCB's.

The College of Manhattan contacted Dave about using the sanctuary for inventories of the numbers and kinds of vertebrates and invertebrates.

Bard College students made several field trips to compare the vegetation types and animal species with another marsh several miles upstream. The local elementary school called on the Keeper of the Cattails for field trips on the sanctuary, as did those virtuous virgins from Vassar. That's what he gets for lecturing up and down the valley about the wonders of nature.

Sweet young things were not alone when it came to calling on Sagacious Seymour for advice. The Nature and Historical Preserve Trust of New York asked him to look over Cruger Island and Tivoli North Bay, a marsh and island complex similar to Constitution Island. Located up the Hudson near Red Hook, Dave and Old Dad consider this to be one of the finest examples of fresh-water estuarine marshes left in the Northeast. Well-known among Yankee ornithologists, it would make an excellent wildlife sanctuary. We are hoping that David's recommendations will help the Nature and Historical Preserve Trust find the money and political clout to preserve the integrity of the marsh, islands, and adjacent forested hills and valleys. Also, it contains more golden club (an endangered plant) than any area in the state.

JANUARY 1977 When we last reported on this sanctuary, the Hudson River Fishermen's Association, of which warden David Seymour is currently president, had been put out of business by PCB's in the river. Conservation Commissioner Ogden Reid then threatened to put the General Electric Company out of business if they didn't stop dumping PCB's into the Hudson. GE complied and paid a modest fine. Governor Carey may have gotten a little nervous at this point, possibly figuring an electric appliance industry might have more votes than a commercial fishing industry. Anyway, Commissioner Reid was put out of business, and his replacement doesn't seem overly eager to take up the cudgel in behalf of fish that are fit to eat, water fit to drink, or air fit to breathe.

Sagacious Seymour says trying to push backbone into some public officials is like pushing on a chain. Better you should go around front and show them what the public wants and needs. To do this, our Number One River Rat betook himself to the headwater, Lake Tear-in-the-Clouds, and walked the entire length of the Hudson, 285 miles, to its mouth at Battery Park. He had been asked to do this to raise money for the Hudson River Sloop Restoration.

Conservationists along the route joined Dave for short stretches. Motels offered in advance to provide overnight room and board. Some industries, as well as private citizens, donated money for the cause, which was to focus attention on the scenic Hudson and to unify demands to clean it up. State officials took note. Almost single-handedly, or two-footedly, Dave raised several thousand dollars and no blisters. As we went to press, David had just been asked by a state legislator to testify in Albany on toxic substances in the Hudson.

Last summer the wily Scotsman got an extra good buy on a couple of new Grumman canoes that come in very handy whenever he takes groups of students and other visitors through the marsh. The motor in his Datsun station wagon, after about five years and ninety thousand miles, was complaining so loudly that it kept Dave awake, both while he was driving and when he wasn't. He is now motoring about in a Volkswagen Rabbit. He says the front-wheel drive is a winner on snowy and icy roads. His good wife, Anne, has the never-ending task of trying to convince people that her husband is not crazy; he is just an ordinary Audubon wildlife warden.

MARCH 1977 Over on the Hudson River, Warden David Seymour is up to his elbows in number 6 oil. Downstream from the Constitution Island Marsh Sanctuary, an oil barge is hard aground and leaking worse than Washington. Oil-soaked ducks, geese, swans, and gulls are in deep trouble because their insulated underwear will no longer keep out the cold air and water. Local volunteers turn the Rockland County highway garage into a rescue station. Dave Seymour is the take-charge guy. From the Roosevelt Sanctuary on Long Island comes director Alan Ruppert. Sad to say, Alan has had much experience handling oil-soaked birds around Oyster Bay on Long Island.

Because of the emergency, Jim Rod, assistant to the Audubon president, and his brother, Doug, from NAS Nature Center Planning Division, go upstream to lend a hand. Since Pink Lux liquid has been used with some success in removing oil from feathers, the Audubon crew wangles a donation of 240 gallons from Lever Brothers in Edgewater, New Jersey. A neighbor offers his truck, and he and Dave drive down to fetch the pink detergent. Alas! It will not cut number 6 oil.

Alan Ruppert then fetches 110 gallons of Shell Sol 70 from Oyster Bay, which, it turns out, will take oil out of feathers, skin off human arms, and is very unhealthy when inhaled. David Seymour meets this challenge by calling NAS president Stahr, who contacts West Point, and a dozen gas masks are forthcoming.

Although the Audubon guys look very good in their gas masks, and although the local volunteers work very hard and manage to save several aquatic birds, Jim Rod says he and Doug got up the river with good intentions but the birds and people that depend on fish and aquatic vegetation for a living are mostly up the creek without a paddle. The heavily soaked birds are the only ones they can catch, and most of these are beyond salvation. Those that can recuperate will fly back into the oily waters. The only way to maintain the Hudson's capacity to support birds and people is to prevent oil spills.

We hope Stahr's letter to the *New York Times* urging tighter controls on oil tankers and barges will stir the public to pressure the politicians into putting an end to this incredible insult to our environment. The other President, Jimmy Carter, has said he is willing to put the oil transporters in hot water if they insist on trying to make a fast buck by hauling oil in antique buckets. Hang in there, Jimmy!

MAY 1978 From Constitution Island in the lower Hudson to the headwaters of the Connecticut River on the Quebec–New Hampshire border is about three hundred miles as the crow flies. Dave Seymour did not go by crow, however, he went by Rabbit, his Volkswagen that gets about thirty-five miles per gallon. 'Twas early in the morning of May 6 that Old Dad and Miss Nancy bid Dave a fond adieu beside Third Connecticut Lake whence the water flows south some 364 miles between New Hampshire, Vermont, across Massachusetts and Connecticut and empties into Long Island Sound at Old Saybrook. Dave says, "I put my feet in gear and my mind in neutral and averaged about twenty-five miles per day."

By mid-afternoon, May 21, Dave arrived at the mouth of the Connecticut, one of the most beautiful and unspoiled rivers in New England. He was met by Ed Brigham, director of NAS regional representatives, Old Dad and Miss Nancy, a host of chapter members and interested folks. Pete Seeger, the well-known environmentalist folksinger, was on hand to do a concert.

Along the way, Dave pointed out to journalists, business men and women, and interested citizens that while the Connecticut has some pollution problems, it is still beautiful and could and should be kept that way. He also let them know that National Audubon maintains seventy-three sanctuaries across the country for threatened plants, animals, and habitats—all of which cost money—and all donations are gladly received.

Meanwhile, back on the Hudson, Dave's involvement with environmental issues over the years has led Bob Binnewies and Ed Brigham, in our New York office, to the conclusion that David should broaden his interests to cover the whole state. We are sure Dave can do this and still keep an eye on Constitution Island.

He has kept such a good eye on the sanctuary, in fact, that *Reader's Digest* (whence cometh the money to manage the sanctuary) has seen fit to purchase additional nearby lands. These include some fifty acres of mature hardwood forest, ideal for nature trails, plus Indian Brook Gorge with its spectacular waterfalls and other features that show why they call it the scenic Hudson River.

David's contacts with nearby colleges and Audubon chapters continue to keep his schedule full of field trips and lectures sandwiched between his patrol of the sanctuary and other duties.

MAY 1979   In the past year, David Seymour has been up and down the Hudson. Last June he managed to paddle twenty-three first graders through the Constitution Island Marsh without dumping any of the little darlings in the drink. Various chapters of the Audubon Society also canoed the marsh.

The long-billed marsh wrens were more numerous in 1978 than at any time in the last eight years. This year the saucy little cattail hoppers were far less numerous. Such is the case with several species of dickey birds in the eastern United States, presumably as a result of the harshness of the last two winters.

Dave also gets around very well on dry land, and in the middle of July, off he goes to Williamstown, Massachusetts. There he is up at 5:30 A.M. for three consecutive mornings to lead bird walks. This exercise helps cement relations between members of the Massachusetts Audubon Society and NAS.

For several years, Dave has been the stem-winder for several environmental concerns in the Hudson Valley. Since that warden rustler, Eddie Brigham, stole him from the Sanctuary Department on a part-time basis, Dave's been regional repping round and about New York state. For example, Dutchess County is casting about for a site for the county garbage dump. A typical area under construction was a hilltop that drains into Swamp River, thence to Ten-Mile River, thence to the Housatonic. Dave persuaded the county and township politicos to consider recycling instead of stream pollution.

David also cooperates with the Natural Resources Defense Council,

Appalachian Trail Club, Hudson River Fishermen, the Sloop Clearwater, and other organizations concerned with keeping the Hudson alive. PCB's in the Hudson have rendered the fish unfit for human consumption. You can still catch a striper on hook and line, but somehow if you can't eat it, it's not the same—the thrill is gone.

Apparently also gone are the Blanding's turtles around Fishkill, which Dave knew as a wee lad, but which he and Eric Kiviat, of Bard College, can no longer find in these parts. Ward Stone, of the Delmar Wildlife Research Station, is another compadre of Dave's. He wades through a bushel of dead blackbirds that Dave brings in from Newburgh, New York. The *New York Times* has a picture of a field full of dead birds and one live Scotsman, and raises the question, "Whodunit and with what?" It turns out a farmer applies copious quantities of parathion, which is a no-no.

In the course of a year, it is not unusual for chemists, botanists, zoologists, pathologists, Audubon members, and even normal, average citizens to touch base with our manager of Constitution Marsh Island. He gets up to Syracuse for the Second Annual Loon Conference, which Audubon is sponsoring, to Cornell to keep Don McCrimmon at our Colonial Bird Register on the straight and narrow, gives programs at Vassar, the Rotary Club, at Dusty Dunstan's Regional Conference, and various Audubon chapters' meetings. All of which sounds very much like most everybody else in the Audubon wardening trade.

These Audubon chapters that manage sanctuaries, or volunteer their services on National Audubon Sanctuaries, or help new sanctuaries with the red tape of tax exemptions, legal problems, or environmental degradation also get a generous assist from Sagacious Seymour. A case in point is his warden's report for April 27 and 28, to wit: "From Garrison to Derby Hill (east shore of Lake Ontario). Here for Upper New York Audubon Council meeting combined with hawk watching. Excellent turnout of Audubon council members and one of the best days for hawk migration. Over 10,000 birds. Stayed overnight to discuss St. Lawrence River strategy in Mexico, New York."

Sí, Sí, Seymour.

MAY 1980 Pulling British chestnuts out of the fire is not exactly a favorite pastime for most Americans. But pulling Eurasian chestnuts out of his marsh ranks even lower in Dave Seymour's book. This exotic weed has spread up and down the Hudson, often growing in such dense stands as to eliminate more desirable aquatics.

In 1884 a clergyman, the Reverend John Herman Wibbe, is said to have planted it in Collins Lake; and in the 1920s, it spread into the Mohawk River, thence to the Hudson, and down to Constitution Island.

There are several herbicides recommended for control of water chestnut. None of them work. Dave Seymour gets down on his knees in his canoe, not to pray, but to pull water chestnuts up by the roots. In this manner, he says he can easily stay on top of the situation, although the Hudson brings him a new supply every year. 'Tis the same water chestnut you find in Chinese restaurants.

Some years ago, Dave put pressure on the Sonotone-Marathon Batteries Company, resulting in removal of over twenty-five tons of nickel and cadmium from Foundry Cove, next door to the sanctuary. Most of the vegetation, muskrats, and fish in Constitution Island Marsh now give negative readings for cadmium.

Last November 27 and 28, David, Bob Boyle, well-known author for *Sports Illustrated,* and Art Glowka of Natural Resources Defense Council were on a panel dealing with cooling towers for Con Ed's power plant at Indian Point. The federal Environmental Protection Agency conducted the hearings.

Dave says Con Ed will probably go along with cooling towers at Indian Point, where, in the past, there has been a very big fish kill. At other plants along the Hudson, Dave hopes Con Ed will reduce the water intake during critical periods in late winter when the fish are too sluggish to swim against the current.

The sly Scotsman has also been slipping up to the St. Lawrence to check some 310 great blue heron nests on Ironside Island and to confer with William Marshall, a glaciologist. When Marshall is not studying glaciers, he is concerned with acid rain in New England, oil spills along the St. Lawrence, and other issues that overlap Dave's concerns.

On February 5, the spry Scotsman accepts an invitation to join the Olympic team in a five-mile run, carrying the torch to Lake Placid for the Olympic Games.

In March he was off to Montezuma National Wildlife Refuge, where plans for a nearby landfill threaten to put the refuge out of business. Since it is usually unhealthy for federal refuge managers to oppose development plans too vigorously, Dave lined up a couple of Audubon chapters to remind the hearing officer that national wildlife refuges and city dumps don't go hand in hand.

At the eastern end of Lake Ontario, Derby Hill stands proudly above the town of Mexico, New York. Dave's excuse was that he had to take Ed Brigham to the Upstate Audubon Council meeting. The whole gang went hawk watching on Derby Hill and had the biggest day (for hawks) since records have been kept there: 15,640. Looks as though Derby Hill will soon rival Hawk Mountain, Pennsylvania, as the place to see hawks.

A New York state policeman stopped to see what was going on, got hooked on watching the watchers and the hook-beaked critters, parked his cruiser, paid his ten dollars, and joined the Derby Hill Hawk Watching Association.

There is money in birds.

MAY 1981 When David Seymour was hired in 1970 as warden for the Constitution Island Marsh Sanctuary, he looked up the Hudson, down the Hudson, and across the Hudson. He decided that his 267-acre marsh could not survive if the Hudson River died.

Across the river, Consolidated Edison planned to turn Storm King Mountain into a pumped storage plant. The outrageous cost in dollars could be passed on to customers. The cost in fish could not be measured; besides, fish don't vote or pay electric bills. Downstream, a nuclear energy plant was doing its thing. Upstream, General Electric was dumping PCB's in the Hudson. The state of New York declared Hudson River fish unfit for human consumption. This put the commercial fishermen out of business. But the Hudson River Fishermen's Association, with Dave as president, decided to fight back.

On December 5, 1980, their attorney outlined the settlement terms between a consortium of utilities and the fishermen, the Scenic Hudson Association, and the Natural Resources Defense Council (NRDC). Con Ed is dropping Storm King Mountain plans after seventeen bitter years in court; the utilities are putting up $12 million for Hudson River research and paying the NRDC and feisty fishermen $500,000 for their legal costs. Dave is somewhat satisfied but says the Hudson is still a long way from complete recovery, and protecting Constitution Island is not fait accompli.

While he was not pressuring the polluters, David managed to carry on in his usual manner. He led several field trips through the sanctuary for the New York Audubon Society; he showed special schoolteachers how to show their special students the world of warblers, turtles, frogs, and toads; he caught, tagged, and released snapping turtles. His warden's report for May 1980 says "almost no ovenbirds, very few veeries" but lots of catbirds and other dickey birds. The ovenbirds remained among the missing all season. We must check Bob Arbib's (editor, *American Birds*) blue list for more information on the "teacher-bird."

Dave has been cooperating with Bill Marshall in studies of acid rain, and on July 14 he met Bill at the Todd Sanctuary on the rockbound coast of Maine. Dave was just in time to help deliver 102 baby puffins to Eastern Egg Rock, some eight miles out to sea. Then he and Bill went about their business of looking for acid precipitation collecting sites.

On August 10, David drives down to a Dr. Abel's residence on Long Island. Abel is entertaining David's old friend from Okeechobee, Roderick Chandler, our NAS warden for Lake Okeechobee and Kissimmee Prairie. Dave and Rod make it up to the Miles Sanctuary, where Miss Nancy rustles up some catfish and cornbread, while Old Dad lectures the wardens on the virtues of clean living in a clean environment. Next morning Dave and Rod make it back to Long Island with their souls cleansed and their bellies full.

The observation is often made that National Audubon has as much chance of making peace with Massachusetts Audubon as the Jews have with the Palestinians. Nevertheless, Marshal Case manages to host a very successful NAS regional conference in the town of Brewster, September 26–28. David is on hand to escort the conferees from Brewster to Plymouth, thence out on the Atlantic to observe whales and pelagic birds. The early-morning downpour lets up, but the winds do not. Among the rolling waves, Dave sees a few whales, sea birds, and lots of seasick Auduboners. His report reads, "Seven hours of this will last seven years."

In mid-February, Dave and Anne decide that, during their vacation, there are places they'd druther be than on the banks of the Hudson. So betwixt February 15 and March 15, his daily report has only one word, "Vacation." Naturally, Old Dad is highly pleased to see that on the Sunday list he puts, "Day Off," so he is observing the Sabbath; with Jim Watt as secretary of interior, one can't be too careful!

On the other hand, warden reports come in from such places as Beidler Forest in South Carolina, Corkscrew Swamp and Kissimmee Prairie in Florida, and the Rainey in Louisiana describing hog barbecues, fish frys, crayfish etouffé, and blue goose gumbo. Wherever they went, it seems that Dave Seymour and wife, Anne, although from New York, managed to bring a taste of Old Milwaukee to the Southland.

In spite of all these peregrinations, that old slave-driver Dusty Dunstan (assistant director, Sanctuary Department) pressured Dave into completing his management plan for Constitution Island. When we warden-types work, we work hard; when we play, . . .

JANUARY 1982 David Seymour, the sly Scotsman who has lent a touch of class and color to the Sanctuary Department for eleven years, has announced his retirement, effective November 1, 1981.

Sagacious Seymour, manager of Constitution Island Marsh Sanctuary, played a leading role in stopping the dumping of cadmium into Foundry Cove on the edge of the sanctuary; he saved Storm King Mountain from becoming a pumped-storage plant; halted use of the Hudson as a dumping ground for PCB's, and stopped the wholesale slaughter of blackbirds with an illegal poison. Generally speaking, Dave helped keep the local citizenry aware of what was going on about them.

After David Seymour hit the Santa Fe Trail, his old compadre, Jim Rod, took over at Constitution Island. Jim is no stranger to the Hudson River, the sanctuary, or the Audubon Society. He did most of his undergraduate work at Iowa State University and finished his B.Sc. at Iona College in New York. He has four years of previous experience with National Audubon as assistant to the president.

Jim is an experienced writer, public speaker, and photographer. He is an expert herpetologist, which is a polite word for snake fancier, which we won't mention because Lonnie Legé takes a dim view of anyone who keeps snakes as pets. (Actually, Jim, Lonnie, and Berton are old buddies, since Jim was in on the great Audubon alligator program in Louisiana a few years ago.)

MAY 1983 If Satan is looking for idle hands, he will strike out at Constitution Island Marsh. On Valentine's Day, 1982, Jim Rod spent twelve hours painting and renovating the warden's residence on the adjacent Boscobel Restoration property in preparation for his upcoming occupancy of same. That went on for two solid months before he moved in on April 18.

On the diplomatic front, a problem arose on a couple of our Westchester County sanctuaries, which are managed by local chapters. Instead of a confrontation with contrary contiguous landowners, Ambassador Rod settled the boundary disputes and picked up a couple new members plus a fifty-dollar donation in the process.

As a cooperator in the New York State Breeding Bird Atlas (not to be confused with Cap'n Wimby's Bird Atlas), Jim was assigned the block that includes Constitution Island. He says a couple of his favorites, hooded and Canada warblers, appear to be breeding near the sanctuary. On the unexpected list, a white-tailed kite (a new record for the area) got the Waterman Bird Club all excited in May 1983. (Lonnie and Berton Legé had a pair of white-tails around Mouton Cove south of Abbeville, Louisiana, from December 26 to January 29, 1983.)

Canoe trips are now a regular feature at Beidler Forest in South Carolina, the Miles in Connecticut, and Constitution Island on the Hudson. Participants range in age from kindergarten through senior citizen, college students studying environmental law, the Natural Resources Defense Council board, garden clubs, bird clubs, the New York City Audubon Society, and Vassar College co-eds. On May 28, Jim had the Sawmill River Audubon Society canoeing in the morning and the Beacon Sloop Club in the afternoon. That set a record of fifty-three people in one day, which is a lot of paddling.

Since not everybody that wants to see the marsh close up can fit in a canoe, a boardwalk has long been considered. We have hesitated to build it because it would not function as a boardwalk does in the swamps of Florida and South Carolina. But it is one way of getting people in close contact with cattails, spatterdock, marsh wrens, and muskrats without undue disturbance of them. Besides, donors who are short on ecology like to see something tangible for their money.

To make a short story of a long boardwalk, Jim had raised the $2,500 for materials by last September, and construction was well under way before freeze-ups in December. Jim says the outstanding success of his fundraising efforts, for this and many other projects, is due to the very effective efforts of some old friends such as Gene Setzer, Bill Evarts, and Elvis Stahr. Of material help were ninety-one locust poles donated by Carl Thompson, a newcomer who was in the army at Fort Belvoir with a chap called Roger Tory Peterson, whom he remembers.

Another outstanding, long-standing supporter of the sanctuary and related programs is author-scientist-environmentalist Bob Boyle. Jim and Dave Seymour have worked with Bob for many years, taking water samples for acid rain studies, collecting and monitoring aquatic insect populations as indicators of environmental quality, and generally keeping tabs on such goodies as atomic energy plants, PCB's, and cadmium, and giving lectures around and about on the effects of same. Bob Boyle's environmental articles in *Sports Illustrated* are about the best we have ever read. It could be that Bob's example prompted Jim to begin his column in the *Putnam County News and Recorder* entitled, "Constitution Marsh

Patrol." (The editor appears surprised and pleased that so many people want to know so much about the goings-on in their own backyard.)

Officers of the West Point Military Academy, just across the Hudson River, have been most cooperative in supplying aerial photos of the marsh and making lab facilities available. Jim suspects his former boss and former secretary of the army, Elvis J. Stahr, is an effective catalyst in this happy situation.

Research by Jeannette Whipple, University of California, revealed that her striped bass population (originally stocked from the Hudson River over one hundred years ago) was not doing well. Bob Boyle, the Hudson River Fishermen's Association, and the Scenic Hudson Association, flew Whipple and a team of scientists over to study Hudson bass for a week. They used the lab at West Point for their work.

Speaking of fisheries research, Jim learns that the Hudson River Foundation has money available. He writes up a proposal in January 1983, which needs very little editing by Paulson, Duever, Sandy Sprunt, Carl Safina, Dusty Dunstan, and Old Dad. On March 24, 1983, he learns that his proposal has been accepted to the tune of $15,300. While he's out there slopping around the marsh, he might just as well be making like a scientist.

The exotic water chestnut often chokes Hudson River marshes. In July 1982, millions of water lily leaf beetles attacked the mat of water chestnuts along the south edge of the marsh. Within a few days, they had devoured all the leaves and killed the plants before the seed pods had matured. By September the tide had taken all the dead chestnut out of the cove, and the water was completely clear. Recalling Brigham Young and California gulls, Jim is considering a monument to *Galerucella pyrrhalta*. In this case, as an herbicide, a tiny beetle may be cheaper and better than 2-4-T.

JULY 1984   Jim Rod says his marsh may be unique in the Hudson Valley because you can find fresh, brackish, and salt water on less than three hundred acres. But three kinds of water quality generates at least thirty-three kinds of activities on his part. Surprisingly, they all seem to fall into place and get finished.

While slopping around in the marsh in May 1983 with noted author-lecturer-scientist Bob Boyle in quest of aquatic insects, they come up with a rare large stonefly, *Allonarcys biloba*. On July 10, an adult bald eagle— very rare in summer—gives the New York Audubon Society a field trip treat. With a young researcher from Rockefeller University, Jim finds about thirty pairs of swamp sparrows setting up housekeeping in the sanctuary.

On Saturday afternoons, instead of going fishing or birding or hunting, he lectures and leads field trips for St. Basil's Academy. Leading canoe trips is an old story for Norm Brunswig and Mike Dawson down at the Beidler in South Carolina, but those Four Hole Swampers ain't seen nothin' yet. In May and June, our roving river rat led twenty-one trips for about 350 canoeists. They ranged from kindergarten to senile citizens, high-school classes, environmental law school classes, Audubon chapters, and Boy and Girl Scouts. Paddlin' Madeline is a very popular form of outdoor recreation at Constitution Island Marsh, and Madeline keeps coming back for more. In fact, at year's end, over one thousand people had learned the difference between a canoe and a rowboat.

Jim's research on the populations and migrations of fish got under way in August 1983, with a grant from the Hudson River Foundation. He takes samples every two weeks, both day and night, on the ebbing tide, using a fyke net, two bag seines, and several minnow traps. Each fish must be counted, identified, measured, and returned to the water. A few additional chores included taking air and water temperatures, measuring water depths, testing the pH, dissolved oxygen, and conductivity during each sampling period. And all these records must be legible and kept from falling in the drink.

Sounds easy? Maybe so, except for night work and a net full of snapping turtles. Jim's report says, "If you can imagine standing in a small boat at 2:00 A.M. with nothing but two bobbing head lamps for illumination, with one arm shoulder-deep in the dripping meshes of a fyke net, trying to find the tail of a 30-pound snapper while avoiding the jaws of three others and the attentions of several crabs, and the other arm trying to support this 150-pound tangle of fish, eels, crabs, turtles, and net, so you can see what you're grabbing, you have some idea of what fish counting can be like. Scientists call this research. Normal people have other names for it."

In addition to such playful pursuits, James assists the nearby Audubon chapters, the town fathers, West Point Academy, the local game warden, and various outdoor groups interested in keeping life interesting. They persuade the highway department not to cut several giant hemlocks and oak trees in Indian Brook Gorge where the bridge crosses the gorge. The cadmium that was dumped in Foundry Cove in World War II is about to receive strict attention from the Environmental Protection Agency. Tankers belonging to a well-known oil company have been coming upriver with a ballast of salt water that is discharged and the tankers refilled with fresh water that is hauled to Aruba. The Hudson River Fishermen's Association allowed as how free fresh water was not good business, and the judge agreed to the tune of $500,000 awarded to the fishermen. Metro North was persuaded to quit dumping drums of toxic chemicals along the railroad tracks. West Point is beginning to cooperate and control vandalism and trespass on their own Constitution Island.

On February 3, 1984, an otter is a new record for the sanctuary. Among Jim's miscellaneous notes for September, we find such entries as, "New game warden and I were called to deal with a deer that a dog had chased through a plate glass window into a St. Basil's classroom—full of children—then into marsh. Deer had a broken leg."

"Livetrapped and relocated nearly a dozen skunks and several possums for local residents, rescued a snapping turtle from an outlet pipe, handled many wildlife calls ranging from dead cat to birds."

With guidance, counsel, and generous assistance from Bill Evarts, Gene Setzer, and Elvis Stahr, our farm boy from Iowa seems to find the funds to stay in business. He must be doing something right.

SEPTEMBER 1985 In the summer of 1984, Jim Rod spent one day per week with researchers, collecting muskrats, wood ducks, marsh wrens, red-winged blackbirds, fish, frogs, crabs, and insects for heavy metal analysis. They collected 1,200 samples of water and sediment that were analyzed for cadmium, nickel, and cobalt. Bottom sediments near the outfall pipe measured 160,000 parts per million, which came from a former battery factory that had dumped its toxic waste into the marsh.

What did James do those other six days of the week? Well, the breeding season wound down in late summer—for birds, that is—and Jim's records showed seventy species breeding on the marsh and in adjacent woods, all of which are now entered in the New York Breeding Bird Atlas. On August 22, he did his last fish sampling with data for one year, sampled every two weeks, day and night. He has the vital statistics on 7,747 fish of thirty-four species, eighteen families. Fortunately, his wife, Dee, is a statistician. So, by the time Jim gave his report to the Hudson River Foundation at the American Museum of Natural History, it was full of chi-squares, analysis of variance, and all that good stuff.

Every Sunday afternoon, he lectured on the front lawn of the Boscobel Restoration, on the bluff overlooking Constitution Island Marsh, thus giving some two hundred people the good word about rivers and marshes according to Saint James. CBS did a half-hour documentary on the Hudson River, including river rats such as Jim, Bob Boyle, and Pete Seeger.

Such goings-on must come in handy around budget time in view of $15,246 from the Open Space Institute, $15,000 from *Reader's Digest*, $2,500 from Marsh and McClennan, plus a winning smile from Jane Pelson (NAS Development Department). Turn that Iowa farm boy loose on the Hudson, and he'll catch more dollars than most folks catch fish.

Comes last October and the opening of duck season, and Jim teams up with the local game warden, and they go about harassing duck hunters who are harassing ducks on the sanctuary. In November about 500 black ducks, 225 mallards, and a smattering of pintails, woodies, and greenwings clutter up the marsh. Jim says protecting all those black ducks should make brownie points with the chairman of the board, Donal O'Brien, with whom the black duck is a favorite.

A snapping turtle that he collected for cadmium analysis had a carapace length of 19.5 inches, which beats the world record by 1.5 inches. Another entry in his report says, "Met for two hours with the head of EPA, William Ruckelshaus, in Garrison at meeting arranged for Hudson Valley environmental leaders by Congressman Hamilton Fish. Bob Boyle pressed him hard on acid precipitation, and I asked him about the continuing use of dicofol (Kelthane), which contains up to 13 percent DDT as an impurity." It is reported that some enterprising souls are now asking who's gonna protect the Environmental Protection Agency from Audubon wardens?

In cooperation with the World Wildlife Fund, Museum of Hudson Highlands, and Hudson River Fishermen's Association, Jim is studying the possibility of reintroducing eagles, ospreys, and peregrines in the region. Six eagles wintered over on or near the sanctuary in 1983 and 1984, but only three in 1984–1985.

Jim feels quite optimistic about his chances of receiving a grant from the Hudson River Foundation to do research on muskrats in the sanctuary. He will assess the effects of cadmium on breeding females and get an accurate population index. Then, if cadmium is removed from the marsh, he can do a before-and-after cadmium study.

It is generally conceded by struggling young authors such as Durward Allen, Joe Linduska, and Ed Zern that John Madson is one of the best in the business. Since John is also an Ioweegian and a boyhood hero of Jim's, it is most gratifying to take John and Dycie Madson and *Audubon* editor

Les Line and wife, Lois, around the marsh and up the river on the boat *Riverkeeper* on May 4, 1985. When the Corps issue a permit to build a super highway that would have sounded the death knell for striped bass and the overall productivity of the Hudson River, the Environmental Protection Agency and the U.S. Fish and Wildlife Service threw in the towel. Not so the Hudson River Fishermen's Association. They put up $25,000, took the case back to court, and the federal judge allowed as how the Corps had done wrong. On September 30, 1985, the Westway boondoggle died, and the Hudson got a new lease on life. It takes a heap o' humpin' to make Constitution Marsh a home for marsh wrens.

NOVEMBER 1986 Jim Rod is another lad whose extreme versatility makes him just an ordinary sanctuary manager. His regular newspaper columns supplement his lectures, slide shows, canoe trips, and scientific papers on the flora and fauna of Constitution Island. Not content with weekly canoe trips through the marsh, Jim and Dee lead a boat trip in Alaska in June 1986. This proves to be a very successful fund raiser, thanks to Michael McIntosh and his good ship *Observer*.

John Adams regularly brings his environmental law classes from New York University to the sanctuary, where the students can see conservation in action. On April 11, 1986, Jim caught a forty-four-pound snapping turtle to show them. His affinity for reptiles is becoming widely known. A farmer in Garrison who shot a timber rattler notified Jim immediately. Since the snake was beyond rehabilitation, Jim gave it to the Museum of Natural History. It was the southernmost confirmed record in the state.

On April 5, 1986, Jim accompanied Randy Stechert from the state's Endangered Species Unit on a visit to a known timber rattler den north of Cold Spring. The owner happens to be very protective of the den and won't let state personnel on his property unless accompanied by that Audubon sanctuary manager. The things we do for snakes and science! Timber rattlers are now protected in New York, and Old Dad suspects how that came about.

On August 14, 1985, Governor Mario Cuomo presented the Hudson River Foundation a check for $1.5 million. This was the state's share of the settlement with Exxon over the case of river pollution and the transfer of hundreds of millions of gallons of fresh water from the Hudson to a refinery in Aruba. On hand for the ceremony was NAS president Peter Berle, who had firsthand knowledge of the case. The Hudson River Foundation will make very good use of the money in an effort to restore, research, and protect the river.

For example, Jim's research proposal, entitled "An Ecological Study of the Muskrat in Constitution Marsh" was submitted to the foundation and approved in January 1986. All of the sanctuary is an EPA Superfund study site. Jim had previously finished and published the results of his exhaustive study of the populations and migrations of fish, which was also underwritten by the foundation.

Among the other wild critters coming to Jim's attention was a brood of black ducks in May 1985, the first confirmed breeding record for this sanctuary. Also that year, there were more least bitterns than usual. The severe drought enabled the salt water front to reach the sanctuary by late spring and then up to Poughkeepsie by late summer. This makes for a good influx of bluefish, menhaden, and blue crabs.

A very good acorn crop around the periphery of the marsh was much appreciated by wood ducks, mallards, and black ducks. In April 1986, the ospreys returned; Atlantic snow geese were going north; green herons arrived along with blue-winged warblers, chipping sparrows, house wrens, and four Virginia rails. In September a photographer from the *Today* show came by. Then in November, on *Today,* Jim was shown handling muskrats on the sanctuary.

MARCH 1988   In January 1987, Jim Rod says several flocks of redpolls in the marsh and environs were his first record for them. Also present were an adult and an immature bald eagle, a couple of kingfishers too far north for comfort, and a snowy owl who had come down for southern comfort.

During the March migration of flat-faced fowl, black ducks numbered about one hundred; mallards, about thirty. An occasional black-mallard hybrid reminded Jim that mallards seem to be displacing blacks in the Atlantic Flyway. He believes at least one pair of blacks nested at Constitution Island. On April 25, 1987, Jim saw a duck hawk (sometimes called peregrine) reduce the red-winged blackbird population by one bird. His team came in second with sixty-four species on May 9 for the Putnam Highlands Birdathon. On September 2, seventy-five broadwing hawks circle the sanctuary. Jim assisted researcher Bryan Swift in *Analysis of Avian Breeding Habitats in Hudson River Tidal Marshes,* and his assistance was gratefully acknowledged in the publication.

During the duck hunting season, about 1,200 blacks, 700 mallards, 200 woodies, and 200 Canada geese frustrated the wildfowlers by staying in the sanctuary. On the Christmas Bird Count January 2, 1988, a great egret was either the latest fall or earliest spring record, along with three Virginia rails and two bald eagles.

Unfortunately, environmental degradation threatens both birds and bird-watchers. Because cadmium, a very toxic heavy metal, was dumped in one corner of the marsh by a former battery factory, Jim continued to study the effects on muskrats, turtles, and vegetation. Livers, kidneys, and femurs go to the Hazleton Lab for analysis. Jim hopes to get a permit to collect ten deer from the land adjacent to the marsh to compare cadmium levels in the livers with those from deer killed by hunters several miles from Foundry Cove. Venison liver from the Foundry Cove region could be hazardous to your health. Admittedly, there is a serious overpopulation of deer in Putnam County because ignorant deer hunters and deer lovers have refused to allow a doe season in recent years. But Jim says there should be a better way to control deer numbers than poisoning them with cadmium. Because of his involvement, it is quite likely that several parties who discharged cadmium into this Hudson River marsh may eventually suffer pains in their pocketbooks.

Jim is keenly aware that Audubon president Peter Berle is oft quoted as saying the Audubon Society "can make a difference." Some fifty years ago, the protective arm of Croton Point reached a mile out into the Hudson, and Croton Marsh nestled within its elbow. Here the river boiled with life. Fish, crabs, and shrimp by the millions attracted fish-eating birds, fish-eating humans, eagles, songbirds, and bird-watchers. Among the latter was a youngster from the Bronx County Bird Club named Roger Tory Peterson. 'Tis said he got the idea for his first field guide while birding here in 1930.

But the Westchester County officials viewed Croton Marsh as an ideal site—made to order—for the county garbage dump. Before long, Croton Point cradled a growing heap of noxious refuse—ugly to gaze upon, offensive to the nose. For fifty years the stench and mountain of garbage grew and grew. The county had conveniently ignored the Federal Refuse Act of 1899, which simply said that no one could pollute navigable waters of the United States. The Hudson River Fishermen, of which Jim and his predecessor David Seymour were prominent members, decided the old law was still in effect. The u.s. attorney agreed, so in 1975 the county agreed to close the dump and restore it. But ten years went by in which the county did nothing except keep the dump open and ignore the marsh. The u.s. attorney agrees that this is contempt of court and appoints James as his surrogate. James is expected to inspect, photograph, and report on certain operations at the dump.

As a result of Jim's attention to his assignment, on December 8, 1987, Westchester County signed a remarkable document. They will hire a leachate consultant, a marsh restoration consultant, and prepare plans for control of leachate, final closure of the dump, and the restoration of Croton Marsh. If the county again fails to pay attention to the judge, they will be fined a minimum of $10,000 per day. An Audubon sanctuary manager, with help from Audubon staff and members, can make a difference.

JUNE 1990 Jim Rod says, "Ever since National Audubon assumed management of the marsh in 1970, we have made do without any kind of building. We were happy to have the use of Ann and Howard Fawcett's property for access to the sanctuary and a place to launch our canoes for education programs. In fact, without the generous cooperation of the Fawcetts all these years, we wouldn't have been able to run our program."

'Tis said that all things come to those who wait. Be that as it may, to every sanctuary that has a building to be repaired or built, Papa Joe Edmondson, our ace building construction and maintenance man, comes to get it done. So in mid-July 1989, Joe and wife, Char, arrive to supervise the Sanctuary Wardens Attack Team. The latter includes Dave Kuhl from Corkscrew Swamp in Florida and Steve McHenry from Hunt Hill in Wisconsin. Jesse Jaycox, a senior at Unity College in Maine, was hired June 1 as summer intern. In addition to completing his research on nesting female snapping turtles, Jesse proved to be right handy with hammer and saw.

Jim says he will take competent help from whatever source, including youthful offenders who are assigned to community service as punishment for their indiscretions. So when the SWAT arrived, all piers and foundations were in place, thanks to willing and some not-so-willing hands. From that point on, it was onward and upward as far as the visitors center was concerned.

On September 10, 1989, Char and Joe headed for the Todd Sanctuary on the Maine Coast, leaving a closed-in building with doors and windows in place, stained siding all the way around, and a sure enough shingled roof. The roofing job was aided and abetted by Mike Dudek and two of his summer interns from the Miles Sanctuary in Connecticut.

With the outside pretty well finished, all the plumbing, wiring, and sheetrocking could proceed apace. And so it did throughout the fall and winter months. And so, on June 9, 1990, there was something new under the sun. The visitor center opened its doors with about 150 people to witness the ceremony. Featured was Papa Joe christening the new building. As pink champagne cascaded down the brown shingles, the roof leaked nary a drop.

WINTER 1991   Since the new visitor center was dedicated on June 9, 1990, Jim Rod has met not only himself coming and going but more visitors, students of all ages, movie makers from PBS, movie actors such as Kevin Kline and Phoebe Cates, and scientists from the Environmental Protection Agency (EPA awarded Jim their Environmental Quality Award for his outstanding activities on the environmental front), nearby universities, West Point Academy, Costa Rica, Hudson River Foundation, Audubon chapters—several thousand folks who realize that economic and environmental health are one and the same.

Hundreds of people took guided canoe trips through the marsh; hundreds more were on guided walks. Fortunately, Jim says he had excellent help from Stacey Ebbs of Dickinson College, Chris Melazzo from Cornell University, plus Eric Lind on a Hudson River Foundation grant. West Point's Environmental Department provided four interns for five weeks in July–August 1991. Says Jim, "This allowed a seven-day a week operation of the visitor center and an expanded canoe tour and an education program."

A hummingbird and butterfly garden with perennials donated by Mr. and Mrs. Frank Cabot was planted near the visitor center with gratifying results. Four hummers were steady customers.

Other wildlife notes include catching our first black-nosed dace in Indian Brook, first records for marbled salamander and eastern fence lizard, several deer summering in the marsh, including very young fawns, and six bald eagles wintering in the area.

Of course, no sanctuary can escape the inexorable pressure from developers and polluters. The *Amerada Hess* spilled 163,800 gallons of kerosene in the Hudson. Fortunately, the Coast Guard's floating booms kept it out of Constitution Marsh. The Nelsonville Planning Board thinks eighty-seven condominiums on twenty acres next to a tributary to the marsh would be a great asset. Jim spells that differently in his testimony.

Another "goodie" would discharge ten thousand gallons per day of treated sewage into another tributary with a small tidal marsh at the mouth. Jim showed both adult and fingerling brown trout to the state biologists.

Two weeks later, they upgraded the stream to TS (trout stream). That should kill the sewage plant plans. Other schemes we hope to lay to rest serve to remind us that in the struggle to keep the environment fit for people (and some less destructive forms of life) sanctuary managers are in the front lines.

DECEMBER 1994 Jim Rod says he hopes certain events that happened in 1994 for the first time have happened for the last time. His report for October reads thusly: "*Three hundred Homo sapiens* in visitor center, on trails, and boardwalk in four-hour period Saturday, October 8, greatly exceeded carrying capacity of sanctuary."

The flood of visitors was caused by an unsolicited, unwanted write-up in a major New York newspaper that told people what they could see and do at the sanctuary. Unable to find space in our parking lot, they blocked Indian Brook Road with seventy-five cars, which caused a traffic jam and exasperated travelers in general. Standing room only on the boardwalk did provide a firsthand study of human nature but did not enhance study of other animals such as egrets, grebes, and muskrats. By noon that day, the sanctuary was closed.

Monday was Columbus Day and many visitors, taking advantage of the long weekend, had planned to visit Constitution Island Marsh. Naturally, they had an unpleasant surprise coming. To Jim's very pleasant surprise, however, only two visitors out of several hundred got irate and vowed to "tell Peter Berle about this!"

Now we all know Jim is an accomplished writer, educator, and naturalist, all of which brings visitors to the marsh and visitor center. As a diplomat, however, he has few, if any, equals. For three weeks, Jim and Eric Lind handed out written information explaining and apologizing for the closure. Those turned away showed their disappointment by donating about $2,500 to keep the show on the road, or should we say, off the road.

You ain't seen nuthin' yet. A letter from a second-grade teacher tells of one seven-year-old who was on a canoe trip and lecture last year. Upon learning the sanctuary and boardwalk were closed for repairs, this budding biologist put on a bake sale and proceeds of $450 went to Constitution Marsh!

The boardwalk and nature trails reopened November 6, and the visitor center willl open on time next spring. As the poet from Stratford-on-Avon said, "Sweet are the uses of adversity."

Another Hudson River event took place on November 6, 1994. It happened to be the fiftieth birthday of one James P. Rod. And across the river, at a place called West Point, the would-be army officers stood at attention as a special flag was raised in honor of the sanctuary manager across the way. Also, a plaque was printed saying what the Constitution Marsh and manager had done for the wildlife in the area.

Speaking of wildlife, a horned grebe showed up on April 1, 1994, in Indian Brook, our first record in ten years. The brook was open even though the marsh was still frozen over until April 7. An adult bald eagle hung around until June, which is unusually late. Both an adult and immature were present throughout August and September, along with two ospreys.

Speaking of eagles, incoming Governor George Pataki (also a Garrison resident) is a friend of Jim's and of the national emblem. The great promoters have been pushing for a $5 million visitor center on Iona Island in Palisade Park, which is a state-designated bald eagle sanctuary. Naturally Jim has opposed the developers for some time, and the governor emphatically says Iona Island will remain an eagle sanctuary, and the visitor center will go elsewhere.

Throughout the summer, from one to three peregrine falcons played over the marsh, giving the dickey birds some anxious moments. Jim believes the falcons are from a nest on Breakneck Ridge just two miles north of the marsh. This represents the first known nonbridge nesting in the Hudson Valley since 1962. National Audubon strongly supports Tom Cade's efforts to restore these duck hawks, and it appears to be a success story. Jack Dunstan has good evidence of successful nesting around Borestone Mountain Sanctuary in Maine.

The butterfly-hummingbird garden played host to thirty-four species of butterflies, including several new records.

On June 19, 1994, a harbor seal came up the Hudson. Jim has seen six or eight in twelve years. On August 18, other mammals of more than usual interest included James Earl Jones, Peter Berle, Donal and Katie O'Brien, Bill and Nancy Ross, Lowell and Franny Johnson, and some New York office staff. They made a swallow-watching canoe trip and a catered dinner. Rainy weather, according to Jim, dampened the numbers of swallows coming to roost, but not the spirits of the NAS president, board members, and staff.

The staff Birdathon raised $7,100, a new record, including a $2,000 gift from the contractor who is cleaning up the cadmium in Foundry Cove.

The chapter Birdathon netted $3,500 for the sanctuary, and the Favrot Fund, in addition to donating three new Mad River canoes and a video camera, sent a check for $5,000 to help with year-end budget. Somebody thinks we are doing something right at Constitution Island Marsh.

MARCH 1997 "Sweet are the uses of adversity, which, like the toad, ugly and venomous wears yet a precious jewel in his head. And this our life exempt from public haunt, finds tongues in trees, books in the running brooks, sermons in stones, and good in everything."

Unlike Shakespeare's toad, the various industries along the Hudson were seldom called ugly. But venomous? About twenty years ago, General Electric disposed of PCB's that killed the fish and put Hudson River commercial fishermen out of business. The conservation commissioner, seeking a penalty from GE, found himself out of a job. His successor thought twice before taking on polluters.

Starting in 1952, for about thirty years, the Marathon Battery Company discharged hazardous waste including nickel, cobalt, and the deadly cadmium into Foundry Cove, near the Constitution Marsh. Heavy metals accumulated in plants, animals, and soils surrounding the property.

The site was placed on EPA's National Priorities List in 1983. Enforcement efforts resulted in two settlement agreements under which former owners and operators of the battery plant conducted a cleanup at an estimated cost of $90 million.

The Scenic Hudson Land Trust of Poughkeepsie, under a landmark agreement with the federal government, has been allowed to acquire and preserve Foundry Cove for public use. This will preserve the property and provide public access for educational and recreational purposes.

And guess who's been providing access, education, and recreation in the area since 1978, when that sagacious Scotsman David Seymour became the first manager of Constitution Island Marsh Sanctuary?

Scenic Hudson purchased the property on November 12, 1996, through the generosity of the Lila Acheson and DeWitt Wallace Fund (*Reader's Digest*) for the Hudson Highlands.

In Old Dad's humble opinion, Jim Rod has a right to be elated and proud. He reported in February 1997, "Aside from the delisting of Constitution Marsh and Foundry Cove from the Superfund list, the biggest news is our second visitor center, built here at headquarters entirely at the expense of one of the former owners of the battery plant. It is fully heated, giving us a warm winter place to work like everyone else in Audubon.

The visitor center at Constitution Island Sanctuary.
(Photo: James P. Rod)

"This came about because in 1988 EPA accepted my recommendation in the final Record of Decision for the cleanup that the polluters establish a visitor center on the site for the public and visiting scientists during the cleanup and beyond.

"They devoted an office trailer to the project but late in 1995 realized that after the cleanup they had no place at Foundry Cove to continue the center (something I had thought of in 1988), and they came to Audubon and asked if they could build us a new center here to our specifications, especially since we seemed to have most of the visitors already. I was already ready with my blueprints, and the new facility is now a reality. In addition, they are giving Audubon $1,000 per year for thirty years to pay the electric bill and minor maintenance. There may be no free lunch, but there is a free building.

"We also have the contract with the polluters to conduct all the biological monitoring for the next five years, including sampling wood ducks, Canada geese, swallows, marsh wrens, benthic worms, fish, crayfish, vegetation, and muskrats for cadmium. This will bring in another $25,000, plus they have bought all the sampling equipment for us, which looks mighty nice in our new building.

"Other recent good news is the acquisition of all eighty-five acres of the Foundry Cove property by Scenic Hudson. As I expected, they have asked us to manage it for them, and when the call came, I had already drafted the agreement. This will give us a new canoe access as noted in some of the enclosures. I was also successful in writing a grant application with the new executive director of Boscobel for three interpretive panels to be installed this spring at their overlook above the marsh. One panel will be devoted to Constitution Marsh and will introduce their 35,000 annual visitors to Audubon without clogging up our small parking lot. Boscobel is also building a loop half-mile nature trail that will lead their visitors, who tour the restored mansion, to the edge of our marsh on their property."

When last you visited this sanctuary, you may have had to park out on the road because of the overflow of visitors. Not so today.

In schools throughout this region, you will find Jim and Eric Lind teaching children how to live in, without destroying, their own environment, just as we've been doing here and at every other National Audubon Society sanctuary for several decades.

Getting back to "As You Like It," the former site of Marathon Battery now wears yet a precious jewel in its head. "And this our life . . . finds tongues in trees, books in the running brooks . . ."

JULY 1998 It comes as no surprise that our loss of Jim Rod, one of our most versatile wildlife managers, is felt nationwide. We can and will establish an appropriate memorial in Jim's memory. But his effect on the wildlife and citizens of Garrison, New York, and the entire Hudson River Valley will stand as a tribute forever.

❧ 9 ❧

CORKSCREW SWAMP

SANCTUARY

Naples, Florida

JUNE 1996   What wings are to a wood stork, the boardwalk is to this sanctuary. But manager Ed Carlson says this new boardwalk is the longest, best, and last one he will ever work on. Meanwhile, Ed often reflects upon the many men who have built and repaired our boardwalk over the past forty years.

The original cypress strand was about twenty-five miles long. By 1953, it had been reduced to three miles in Collier County's Corkscrew Swamp. There was a swelling tide of sentiment to save this remnant of the world's last strand of virgin cypress.

To make a long story short (see *The Audubon Ark* by Frank Graham Jr. for details), National Audubon was the catalyst that brought the owners of the strand, the Lee Tidewater Cypress Company and Collier Enterprises, together with those conservationists determined to save not only the trees but the largest rookery of wood storks left in Florida, if not the world. This group had an abiding love and respect for the flora and fauna of Corkscrew Swamp. They also had the ability to put their money where they did their bird-watching, and so our management of Corkscrew had its start.

In 1955 Alexander Sprunt IV, long before he replaced Bob Allen as director of research, was sent to Corkscrew to help build our very first boardwalk. Going from the sandy pine ridge, where the visitor center is located, across the wet prairie to the edge of the pond cypress was easy going. But in the first lettuce lake, things got a bit damp. The swamp-stompers could stand up to drink. Young Alexander, being of giraffish proportions, had no trouble gulping air instead of water. But Manager Hank Bennett was wading on tip-toe most of the time.

For more than forty years, a female alligator—possibly the same one—has claimed title to a tiny island on the edge of this lettuce lake. She kept an eye on the lads. Today, her annual brood of crocodilian reptiles provides entertainment for visitors on the boardwalk, as well as an occasional tidbit for hungry adult gators. Even the wood stork (a.k.a. preacher bird, flinthead, pond scoggin) is not above snapping up a baby gator now and then.

Fortunately, Grandma Gator didn't seem to object to those foolhardy humans slopping around in her domain. Sam Whidden and brother, long-time residents of Corkscrew and vicinity, were members of the construction crew. In view of the Whiddens' prowess as gator hunters (the meat'll do to eat and hide'll do to wear), Sandy Sprunt allows as how the old girl was prudent in keeping her distance.

In 1958 attendance had reached the point where two-way traffic on the short boardwalk left much to be desired. So the walk was extended on south through the cypress swamp for about a mile, where it came to a dead end.

In 1969 Sandy and Ed improved business for the ribbon clerks in Naples by purchasing enough to flag a new route about one and one-half miles long, from the south end of the walk back to the visitor center.

We also ran a spur out into the wet prairie on the west side of the cypress strand, where an observation platform was erected.

Driving piling in a swamp, where the nearest machinery of any kind is miles away, presents problems of a sort. But have you heard of Cajun ingenuity? Berton Legé, from Abbeville, Louisiana, is a charter member of Audubon's Sanctuary Wardens Attack Team (SWAT for short). He climbs up this big wooden post, jumps up and down on it, and gets it down to a level where a sledge hammer can be used. Another SWAT member observes, "As for common sense, I dunno. But he's sure got a real sense of balance!"

The late Phil Owens, manager of Corkscrew back in the 1960s, told of a couple of visitors who had come straight from Disney World. They spotted a typically immobile barred owl on a limb above the boardwalk. Says the man, "Well, I never thought the Audubon Society would use stuffed animals in a so-called wilderness!" Says the hootie owl, with a blink of his eye, "Who-cooks-for-you-all?" Whereupon the wife began to chide her husband, who declared, "Well, using tame birds is damn near as bad!"

Phil assured them the owl was wild. Which brings up the somewhat indeterminate subject of wilderness values—a welcome change from the family values that Republicans and Democrats love to fight about.

Upon construction of the first boardwalk out to the north lettuce lake and the adoption of an open but controlled visitor policy, Manager Hank Bennett quit in protest. Hank maintained that a wilderness invaded by people was a wilderness in name only.

While Hank's idealistic viewpoint is understandable, the human race is not inclined to preserve an ecosystem it has never seen nor a spiritual value it has never felt. That being the case, the policy of our Sanctuary Department has been to let the majestic cypress trees, the wood storks, plus other birds, mammals, and reptiles speak for themselves. So far at least, our naturalists along the boardwalk have not found it necessary to ask visitors to refrain from loud talking while moving at a leisurely pace

Following the boardwalk into the heart of the swamp and deeper water, the last remnant of virgin bald cypress swamp in the United States is found.
(Photo: John M. Anderson)

along the walk. Somehow or other, the virgin cypress swamp gets its message across with a minimum of prompting from us.

Consequently, we believe the wilderness value of Corkscrew Swamp is relatively intact. On the other hand, change is the only constant feature in the world. The rate of change is increasing, and we must adapt to change, just as other animals have been doing since the beginning of time.

Old Dad recalls the early 1970s when in March we might get 400 visitors in a single day! With some trepidation, we wondered if visitation would ever go much beyond that, and, if so, could we handle it? Ed Carlson's reports for 1996 provide a timely, albeit somewhat sobering answer. For March 1996, he reports, "We experienced the highest attendance levels ever. Attendance approached or exceeded 1,000 visitors on a regular basis. Both the Living Machine (our waste water treatment system) and the boardwalk handled the flow of people perfectly. However, the parking lot and nature store were overwhelmed." His total attendance for the month was 23,845.

As late as 1978, our visitor accommodation consisted of one drinking fountain in the chickee (a chickee, a Seminole word, has a board floor, a thatched roof, and is open on four sides). Our chickee, just inside the gate, served as visitor information center and ticket office. An outside building for ladies and gentlemen (separate but equal) completed the layout.

Chances are the state health department didn't know or care about us, and the state didn't bother to tax our income from the admission fee of one dollar per person. Times have changed. You cannot cater to the public without permits to do so. Applying for a permit marks the beginning of a tangle of red tape that keeps many a state officeholder busy and can require months or even years to untangle. (It took us six years to get the necessary permits to repair a levee at the Paul J. Rainey in Louisiana.)

In addition to permits, you don't provide drinking water and rest rooms for the public without many tests to prove the water imbibed by visitors is pure and the water excreted by visitors does not contaminate the water in the swamp. Corkscrew built the first Living Machine treatment system, one that uses sunlight, bacteria, green plants, and animals to restore and reuse rest room waste water.

While providing for the creature comforts of visitors is a necessity, our main purpose is to instill in them an appreciation of an ecosystem that is natural, wild, and free. To do this, we need a boardwalk that can support over a thousand visitors per day, a guide book that tells what you're looking at when you stop at station number *X,* plus a few naturalists who can answer questions and point out the cottonmouth moccasin on the log, the warbler flitting overhead, the otters playing tag, possibly the black bear cubs, even a Florida panther track. Of course, our bread-and-butter bird is the wood stork. In a successful nesting year, they draw visitors from every state plus many foreign countries.

Before the Army Corps of Engineers made the Everglades safe for sugar cane growers, it used to rain about every day from May to November. Then a dry spell would set in, and the ponds and roadside ditches would shrink down, thus concentrating tons and tons of fish, just as the wood storks were catching and carrying fish to their hungry, homely nestlings. Before World War II, the Corkscrew rookery usually produced up to four thousand young storks per year.

Admittedly, we are not professional meteorologists, but we are painfully aware that the age-old rainfall pattern has undergone radical change. The finger of suspicion points to drainage of the vast Everglades as the cause.

Unfortunately, there is no doubt that the altered climate has upset the nesting regime. Falling ground-water levels trigger nest building and egg laying, but heavy rains at the wrong time cause desertion of nests and young. Admittedly, this provides the black vultures a bonanza, but we can hardly point with pride to a flock of well-fed black vultures.

In January 1995, manager Ed Carlson reported, "Water levels are the highest ever recorded for this time of year and continue to thwart wading bird nesting." In February rainfall was normal for the month, causing water levels to decline and wood storks to think about making little storks out of big ones. Further decline in March triggered nest building and egg laying; in April and May drier conditions allowed the young to survive. But in June the colony was decimated by heavy rains. An aerial survey showed the number of fledglings would number about two hundred instead of two thousand as in May. Rain and more rain forced us to close the boardwalk for the first time in our forty-year history on April 25, 1995. We were able to reopen on September 10.

Fortunately, 1996 was a different story. Ed reported February weather as extremely storky, and they responded in kind. In spite of light frost in February, total rainfall was less than one inch, reminiscent of the good old days. We counted 540 nests with between 2 and 3 young per nest; 560 nests fledged about 1,400 in May.

No matter how the wood storks fare, attention must be paid to maintenance of the boardwalk. Ed says, "We've known for several years that

Fledgling wood storks.
(Photo: National Audubon Society)

the boardwalk must be replaced. . . . it has finally come to the end of its natural life span and can no longer be patched or repaired."

He experimented with various building materials, constructed over two hundred feet, using several types of recycled plastic and chemically treated wood. All were relatively new products and left him with more questions than answers.

Ed recalled that boardwalks at Coney Island and Ocean City had a solid history of durability without fiberglass, ultraviolet stabilizers, or toxic chemicals, using a tropical hardwood in use by Incas, Mayas, and Aztecs for thousands of years.

Upon learning more about this unique wood, he betook himself to Brazil. There a wood products company named CEMEX had purchased 44,000 acres of rain forest from someone about to clear-cut it, a practice all too common there and reminiscent of what we did to our magnificent forests in pioneer days. CEMEX is reforesting the cleared areas and sustainably harvesting the rest. They map the forest and determine species distribution and growth rate. The number of trees harvested and time interval between cutting is adjusted so that more wood is grown than harvested. This means an average of two to three trees per acre harvested every twenty-five years. Rare species are totally protected, and no cutting occurs adjacent to streams.

In the too-good-to-be-true department, thousands upon thousands of visitors to Corkscrew Swamp will see and walk upon the wood from CEMEX. Some features of the new boardwalk that opened July 1, 1996: no toxic preservatives; will probably last one hundred years; five feet wide for handicapped access (one foot wider makes a tremendous difference); one-half mile longer; routed through more beautiful and interesting areas; all stairways replaced with ramps; a gated segment totally devoted to special programs for schools; more shelters and benches; and cross connections for an optional short walk.

The job was completed on time, even though 1995 was the wettest in one hundred years. We had never closed the old walk because of flooding, but closed it twice in 1995. Ed says, "We went through fifty eager construction workers to find fifteen who would stay with the job. We used boats, scaffolding, hip waders, and alligator repellent to get the job done. Although the work was grueling and sometimes dangerous, we had no significant injuries or setbacks. I am proud of the way the entire staff pulled together."

In spite of being inundated with work and water, our staff made more than the usual unusual wildlife sightings. Assistant manager Andrew Mackie and intern Jason Seitz found seventeen species of fish in our parking lot! A couple of black bear cubs kept the cameras snapping. In addition to storks, from the boardwalk white ibises, green herons, little blue herons, great blue herons, black-crowned and yellow-crowned night herons, and an occasional tri-colored heron, plus limpkins, could be seen. The north marsh is often cluttered with flocks of over two hundred white ibises, one hundred glossy ibises, and up to forty roseate spoonbills. We have reason to suspect the endangered Everglade kites may nest there. The swallow-tailed kites return in late February.

In April, when Albert Alligator is making amorous noises and advances on Alberta, birders are trying to focus on Cape May and black-throated green and worm-eating warblers. Baltimore orioles are now called northern orioles, but some H. L. Mencken fans don't go along with the taxonomists. By any other name, that flash of orange would look as neat. While painted buntings are colorful and common, short-tailed hawks give the life-lister a real lift. One was recorded in January and early February of 1996. In the same month, a young Florida panther was seen by intern Chris Bergh in the back country of the sanctuary.

It goes without saying, but we'll say it anyway: Corkscrew Swamp Sanctuary is a wildlife spectacle without parallel. But as every sanctuary manager knows, you can't confine yourself to the sanctuary and expect it to withstand the inexorable pressure from real estate developers as the human population continues to expand. Throughout Audubon endeavors, education has gone hand in hand with sound wildlife management. At any Audubon wildlife sanctuary, you find students from preschool to "senile" citizens, from toddlers to dawdlers, and Corkscrew Swamp is no exception. Nearby schools and colleges schedule field trips, and our ecologists travel far and wide giving illustrated lectures about the role of wildlife in human affairs.

Ed plays a prominent role in the agency known as the Corkscrew Region Ecological Wetlands, or CREW for short. Urban expansion in Collier County threatens every square foot of open space. CREW continues to purchase land from willing sellers in order to save the remaining wetlands and wildlife.

But in southwest Florida, the drainage canals and structures built by humans are by no means the only threat to our native plants and animals. Exotics pose a nationwide threat, especially in south Florida.

On February 6, 1995, Shannon Ludwig of Madison, Wisconsin, was finally selected from an impressive list of applicants for the resource manager position. Shannon has a good background in prescribed burning, exotic plant control, and water monitoring. In view of his past experience, it is not surprising that, with some help from interns, he managed to kill 5,514 melaleuca trees, 960 Brazilian pepper bushes, and 100 Java plums in fifty-three and one-half hours! He also sprayed herbicide on about one acre of water hyacinth in the north marsh and on numerous patches of invading sedges in the lettuce lakes in the cypress swamp. Ed says this is some of the most aggressive and efficient exotic control work ever done here.

While the major leagues have little trouble selecting their most valuable player, Ed says the MVP at Corkscrew Sanctuary is a different story. Without David Kuhl, the maintenance supervisor, the land, buildings, and every kind of equipment could cease to function. Whereas in 1960, we had no office as such, in 1998, in all of southwest Florida, no office and gift shop handles more business than Kay Kuhl and Lori Piper do.

Ed also believes our intern program is a win-win situation. At various Audubon sanctuaries, we announce openings for interns to spend a season or possibly a full year, depending on circumstances. The vast majority of interns are college or graduate students interested in wildlife management, in becoming naturalists at a state, federal, or private wildlife area, or simply in enhancing their teaching skills. On occasion, interns become full-time Audubon staff members.

Here at Corkscrew, the interns learn how this unique ecosystem functions and gain valuable experience in handling and/or dealing with the general public. In return, they contribute immeasurably to sound management of wildlife and people.

LAKE OKEECHOBEE

SANCTUARY

Okeechobee, Florida

At least fifty years before several endangered species became known as such, our sanctuary managers kept them in the endangered category rather than in the extinct or extirpated. For example, Guy Bradley did it for the egrets; Emily Payne, our manager for South Bird and Pelican Islands, with Dave Blankinship did it for the few remaining pairs of brown pelicans left in Texas; and our Research Department exposed DDT just before DDT got rid of our national emblem.

Let's take the case of the Everglade kite. Early in the twentieth century, it was common in the Everglades. The *New York Times* for August 25, 1964, however, reported that fewer than twenty birds existed. When the Army Corps of Engineers made the Everglades safe for sugar cane growers, and our benevolent government protected them from Cuban competition, the "River of Grass" became more like a trickle, and the apple snails that make up the kites' entire diet were in trouble.

A lot of south Florida hunters believed that because the kites had hooked beaks and sharp claws, they must be bad news for ducks, rabbits, and quail. It is quite likely the kites could have survived the shotguns, but as the Everglades dwindled, so did the number of Everglade kite nests and eggs.

In the early 1930s, Marvin Chandler became sanctuary warden for all of Lake Okeechobee plus thousands of acres on the Kissimmee Prairie. Being a native of the area, Marvin was able to persuade the would-be guardians of the ducks, rabbits, and quail that Everglade kites ate nothing but snails. Up on the prairie, he vastly improved the chances that other species of that restricted section of the Florida peninsula, such as the burrowing owl, chuck-will's-widow, caracara, and limpkin would live long enough to reproduce, and their eggs would stay in the nest instead of in some egg collector's display. At the time, egg collecting was very big in this region.

In those days in this neck of the woods, bird hunters were not above rustling a few cattle to supplement their diet and pocketbooks. Let's just say that if Louis L'Amour had not invented the Sackett family, who came from the Tennessee mountains and ventured across the western prairie bringing law and order to the wilderness, he could have relied more on fact and less on fiction had he followed our first warden around Lake Okeechobee.

Glenn Chandler carried on where his Uncle Marvin had left off. When Glenn retired, his brother Rod Chandler took over. Where Uncle Marvin got around by canoe, horseback, and on foot, Rod could rely on an airboat, outboard, Jeep, and occasionally an airplane.

Rod did much original research on the kites. In 1973 he had twenty-eight nests under observation and saw twenty-three young fledged. Whenever the Army Corps of Engineers rapidly lower the level of the lake, the vegetation supporting kite nests loses support and the nests capsize. Rod devised a basket that saved many a kite nest. He learned and published much about the life history of this endangered species. Educating and making allies of the local duck hunters has paid dividends in Everglade kite numbers, but undoing the damage caused by draining the Everglades requires a much greater educational effort, aimed at a much wider audience. The Everglades campaign may have been late in getting started, but we're sure Rod's Uncle Marvin would be grateful to see it in operation.

Admittedly, the Everglade kite is not completely out of danger, but thanks largely to efforts of the Chandlers in patrolling the area and educating the duck hunters, it may be removed from the endangered species list in the near future.

On the education front, our latest Lake Okeechobee warden, Barry "Chop" Legé, is a welcome addition. Chop, although a volunteer, is the third member of the Legé family to wear the Audubon Sanctuary uniform. Big brother Lonnie managed the Paul J. Rainey in Louisiana for over thirty years, and brother Berton is still there.

We can't restore the Everglade kite without restoring the Everglades for which the bird is, or was, named. (Yes, yes, we know the name changers now call it snail kite.) Widespread appreciation of the plants and animals in our Lake Okeechobee Sanctuary must precede restoration of them.

That being the case, our latest Okeechobee warden has already made a name for himself. When a Cajun from the Louisiana marsh falls in with Florida Crackers who have loved and lived all their lives with the native plants and animals of Lake Okeechobee, 'tis like adding a wee bit of dry vermouth to a double shot of vodka. Widely acclaimed, in other words!

In addition to identifying the birds encountered on the boat tour, Chop lectures on the ecology of the entire region, from the Kissimmee River (which the engineers are trying to restore) to the outlet of the "River of Grass" into Florida Bay.

In addition to old standbys such as Corkscrew Swamp and Disneyland, Chop's attraction, known as Swampland Tours, is on the latest ecotourism maps. His comments on the efforts to restore the natural resources of the region even came to the attention of the Environmental Protection Agency, from which came complimentary recognition.

As Louis L'Amour would say, "You just can't stop a man who knows he's right and keeps right on a-coming."

❧ 11 ❧

SABAL PALM GROVE

SANCTUARY

Brownsville, Texas

Once upon a time, a subtropical plant community dominated by palms covered about forty thousand acres along the lower reaches of the Rio Grande. The palms extended up the river eighty or more miles and southward into Mexico to San Luis Potosí and Veracruz.

Because most Texans and Mexicans consider a virgin palm forest and native brush a waste that could be converted into citrus and cotton, which in turn can be converted into pesos and dollars, the Texas sabal palm is an endangered species.

In 1940 the grove still contained more than 100 acres of palms. The pressure continued until 1971, when Audubon, with a grant from Exxon, bought the grove, by then reduced to a pitiful 32 acres. The sanctuary contained 172 acres, most of it former cropland. Converting these old fields to native shrubs and eventually to sabal palms is a process that requires a lot of time, dollars, and sweat.

MARCH 1985 But it is very gratifying to stroll through this area today and see *Sabal texana* seedlings, along with Texas ebony and anaqua successfully competing with weeds and grass. In April 1984, manager Lloyd Bletsch continued mowing strips and planting palms and native shrubs. By May 1, he had put out 21,303 palm seeds to supplement the seedlings transplanted since 1972 by Dave Blankinship, area manager for Audubon Texas coastal sanctuaries, and Ernest Ortiz, our warden for Sabal Palm Grove Sanctuary.

In 1983, with friendly persuasion from our Development Department, Atlantic Richfield made possible a new visitor center and nature trail. The March 1985 issue of *Texas Highways* features the Sabal Palm Grove with writing and pictures of *Audubon* magazine quality.

The botanists, beetle chasers, and snake hunters have long been aware that this sanctuary contained species they could not find elsewhere. And the birders go batty over least grebes, ringed kingfishers, black-bellied tree ducks, chachalacas, white-tipped doves, kiskadees, green jays, Altamira orioles, and olive sparrows. The fourth in a long line of Alexander Sprunts saw his first buff-bellied hummingbird in the Palm Grove, which put him well over the six hundred mark on his life list. Speckled racers, cat-eyed snakes, and indigos were often sighted in 1984, along with Mexican tree frogs.

On April 9, 1984, Lloyd counted a minimum of 2,300 broadwinged hawks and a few Swainson's in the grove in fifty minutes. He observed, "It's good to know the broadwings come through this close to the coast and use the sanctuary."

Bobcats are fairly common on the sanctuary, but the possibility of seeing an ocelot, jaguarundi, or maybe even a margay cat, along with the lesser yellow bat, keeps the mammalogists wanting to get in the palm grove. Botanists come to see Palmer's bloodleaf and David's milkberry, two species that may no longer survive in Texas outside the palm grove.

As a former schoolteacher, Lloyd made a habit of spending his summers in Mexico, Alaska, the Canadian Rockies, Great Smokies, or some place that did not look at all like south Texas. So he writes Old Dad, "I'm not getting any younger, and it's now or never to get out and see the country. It's the one advantage of being unattached. You have an impressive crew. I'll miss the inspiration."

Lloyd also pointed out that recent publicity has put the sanctuary on the map, even though it is " . . . in an area of very little environmental awareness. The past environmental record of south Texas is poor. . . . a phenomenal growth rate (population expected to double in twenty years) makes current environmental action critical. Less than 1 percent of the land remains in its natural state. Public and private groups have very little set aside for wildlife. . . . projected growth makes it vital that NAS maintain a presence now to establish local support for the sanctuary. Community involvement and contacts by sanctuary staff are vital to this process."

Lloyd grew up in the Brownsville area. He has worked for the National Park Service and the U.S. Fish and Wildlife Service and is convinced the feds cannot carry out their hopes of acquiring a "wildlife corridor" along the Rio Grande without Audubon's help. We are presently looking after their adjacent 365 acres of abandoned cropland and plan to help them restore the native vegetation.

And so Lloyd yielded to his itchy foot as of June 1. But the seedling palms, anaqua, baby bobcats, downy least grebes, and altricial young hummingbirds kept on growing. Everything kept growing except the once-mighty Rio Grande. It became less and less grande. Because the same thing that has happened to the Platte, the Colorado, and the Arkansas has happened to the Rio Grande. The sewer-laden little stream that meanders past the sanctuary is often too salty to pump into the resaca.

When it comes to pumping, quality and quantity of water is but part of the problem. Our location right on the Mexican border encourages midnight requisitions by our neighbors across the river. In September our visitor center was visited, and it cost us a lawnmower, typewriter, pump, and power brush-cutter. Fortunately, they were insured.

On November 1, 1984, Douglas Davis took over as manager. His first on-site inspection, with Dave Blankinship, found the ebony seeds Lloyd had planted "doing exceptionally well." A heavy September rain had filled the resaca and given the palm seedlings and other native plants a new lease on life.

Doug is a botanist par excellence. His high-school biology teacher's name was Anna May Davis, who wrote her master's thesis on the Sabal Palm Grove in 1942. As Doug says, "Her memory and work live on." Nearby universities are showing considerable interest in working in this unique outdoor laboratory.

In January 1985, Doug and Ernest Ortiz planted seedlings of 165 hackberries, 32 Texas wild olives, and 10 coral beans. The sabal palms and other native shrubs are spreading and thriving. Serious birders, botanists, researchers, winter Texans, and photographers kept Doug busy. Now that the palm grove has been "discovered" by scientists, American tourists, and Texan neighbors, you might say we have a bear by the tail and can't let go. It would be more appropriate to say we have a very rare jewel in our hands and can't afford to lose it.

On November 7, 1985, after finishing his research on the exotic Nilgai antelope on the King Ranch, Steve Schulze took over Sabal Palm. Steve talks the language of Mexican cowboys, millionaire ranchers, birders, entomologists, botanists, and tourists that visit the Sabal Palm Grove Sanctuary.

Almost immediately, Steve learned that not all visitors from Central America wear feathers or feed on insects or vegetation. On December 10, fifteen visitors wearing long black hair camped on the banks of the Rio Grande. At other times, visitors are seen leaving the sanctuary who never came through the gate or visitor center. Mostly they say they are from Nicaragua or El Salvador.

On Washington's Birthday, three tractors were stolen from our neighbor and driven across the Rio Grande into Mexico. Says Steve, "It is doubtful that they will ever be recovered. Ernest Ortiz's vigilance seems to be paying off as our tools and supplies remain untouched." (That requires almost a twenty-four-hour vigil.)

Last winter Mr. Santa Claus, alias our controller Jim Cunningham, bought a new pump to pump water out of the Rio Grande into the old oxbow lake (resaca) to keep the least grebes, shorebirds, and various species of flat-faced fowl happy. And a new pickup, of which Steve reports, "You can even drive in the rain without getting wet." This is in contrast to our old 1977 Chevy Suburban, whose speedometer had turned over twice while its transmission turned over hardly at all.

Unfortunately, the quality and quantity of water in the Rio Grande are so low that pumping into the resaca has to be properly timed. Steve and Ernest also use some water to irrigate seedling palms, anacuas, granjenos, and Texas ebonies, seeds of which are collected, germinated, and transplanted. In the great rush to grow government agencies and surplus crops, most of these native trees and brush were eliminated. One day the entire sanctuary and probably some adjacent land now in crops may look as it did before progress came to the Lower Rio Grande Valley.

Fortunately, not all visitors are of the human type. On December 6, 1985, two parrots were circling and screaming over headquarters. Steve reports, "Unfortunately, the distance was too great for further identification, and the birds left almost immediately." Could be a pair of thick-billed parrots were way off course, or escapees from the zoo were having a fling. December 18 was a red-letter day with a cinnamon teal and peregrine falcon making the scene. A white-fronted goose, on January 14, 1986, was a new record. Wintering ducks included wigeon, green-winged teal, blue-wings, gadwalls, mottled ducks, pintails, shovelers, ring-necks, scaups, canvasbacks, wood ducks, plus pied-billed grebes, coots, and gallinules, which are now called common moorhens although moors in Texas are mighty scarce. By February 12, four pairs of least grebes were nesting; a young great-horned owl was learning the hooked-beak-and-talon trade. Scissor-tailed flycatchers arrived on March 3 along with seven black-bellied tree ducks.

A bobcat continues to entertain visitors and collect a tame duck or two from the yard of Señor Ernesto Ortiz. Ernest is wondering how many ducks equal the price of one bobcat pelt. On February 19, a long-tailed weasel approached within ten inches of Steve's foot as he stood motionless on the trail. Says Steve, "I've got to wash those shoes." Another weasel ran back and forth along the window ledge as Steve was registering three very impressed visitors.

In the bright colors department, on December 10, 1985, Steve was collecting palm seeds and came across a beautiful ten-inch coral snake. And in January, a six and one-half foot indigo snake was seen frequently. The shed skin of this gorgeous blue reptile, on display in the visitor center, drew lots of attention. (Lonnie Legé, at the Rainey, has special adjectives for Texans who call snakes "beautiful.")

It is in entomology, however, that Sabal Palm continues to be the onliest place in the United States where scientists make new discoveries. Professor Lois O'Brien of Florida A&M University writes Old Dad a glowing report on a fulgorid tree-hopper. She says, ". . . very interesting that it is the first record for the United States for a species described from Surinam." She has several records from Mexico and believes the insect crossed the Rio Grande under its own power.

During the first twenty years, our most numerous and enthusiastic visitors were scientists impressed by the many plant and animal species that were found very seldom, if ever, outside the Sabal Palm Grove Sanctuary. Our files are replete with letters from those visitors who expressed their deep appreciation.

To mention just a few such finds: Dan Heffern finds a click beetle in 1984 new to the United States. A golden-crowned warbler made the Rare Bird Alert. The 1989 Christmas Bird Count hit 161 species, including a black-throated gray warbler for the third consecutive year and a pair of Mexican crows.

By 1988, when Rose Farmer took charge of the sanctuary, she realized that no matter how enthusiastic they might be, visiting scientists could not teach the natives how the Lower Rio Grande Valley with its unique ecology affected their own welfare.

In November 1991, Rose wrote a scholarly summary of the situation facing our sanctuary program. She says, "The Rio Grande Valley and Brownsville are about 85 percent Hispanic. Probably 95 percent of the residents of Brownsville never heard of Audubon, don't know the sanctuary exists, know virtually nothing about the environment in their area, and are unaware of local environmental problems that threaten the future quality of their lives.

"Local environmental groups are not reaching out to these populations. Our Frontera Audubon Society and Sierra Club are more than 95 percent Anglo. Staffs of the USFWS refuges in the Valley are almost entirely Anglo from outside the Valley. Very few Hispanics visit the sanctuary except with school groups, and all our publications are in English. We are all trying to expand our cultural and language outreach to reach the local population.

"This project would be a local beginning to a nationwide problem of including minorities in the environmental movement. . . . to solve serious local problems such as water pollution, water supply problems due to increasing development, and toxic wastes dumped in the river a much larger percentage of the local population must become concerned.

"The sanctuary regularly has visitors from all over the United States, plus foreign countries, but few from Brownsville. Mostly, it serves the needs of visiting bird-watchers. Unless we continue to do more for the Valley's residents to make the sanctuary more relevant to their lives, we will fail in the long run."

Rose concludes that all environmental issues are population issues; whether they be deforestation, pesticides, soil erosion, endangered species, or whatever, they are all caused or worsened by people, usually too many people in one place at one time.

If you visit the Sabal Palm Grove Sanctuary in 1999, you will find a community outreach program that embodies all of the concerns expressed by Rose back in November 1991. The positive effects of this program are an outstanding success story that deserves all the credit and attention that we can provide.

Fortunately for all concerned, Karen Chapman, with her fluent Spanish and vast experience on both sides of the border, was able to carry on and expand our efforts. Together, she and Rose are teaching students on both sides of the border.

Rose Farmer moved on, and Karen took over in 1996. There can be little doubt that when Rose left for higher ground, she left our endangered plant community in good hands. A headline in the *Brownsville Herald* reads, "Brownsville Pupils Discover Effects of Man on Nature." The article says that Adalberto Betancourt, eight, had no problems understanding that people should be very careful not to destroy certain natural habitats. Adalberto was one of about fifty El Jardin Elementary School students who heard that rare and radiant maiden whom the teachers name not "the lost Lenore" but Karen Chapman. Edgar Allan Poe's raven, Nevermore, does not come near the Sabal Palm, but his cousin, the white-necked raven, does.

Although greed and ecological illiteracy are still the driving forces behind policies determining the use of air, land, and water in the Lower Rio Grande Valley, the Sabal Palm Grove Sanctuary is steadily chipping away at this mountain.

Not only is our influence gradually expanding, the staff, additional land, visitor center, and equipment to manage the sanctuary present a marked contrast to the lonely grove of Mexican sabal palms we acquired about thirty years ago. That somebody is doing something right is reflected in the $50,000 grant from the Jesse Ball duPont Foundation, $10,000 from the Kleberg Foundation, and $10,000 from the Wray Foundation.

Consequently, Karen has hired Jimmy Paz, a former volunteer, and our pump and canal systems that enable us to manage our oxbow lake are much improved. A new alarm system and security guard has reduced the loss of equipment due to midnight requisitions by personnel from across "the reever."

By the time Adalberto is of voting age, let's hope the pitiful trickle that now flows past the Sabal Palm Grove will be restored to a volume more than adequate to sustain our nesting least grebes, to say nothing of thirsty people in Brownsville.

In March 1998, Karen Chapman received an offer from the great state of Texas that she couldn't refuse. Whereupon, Jimmy Paz became manager.

On April 26, 1998, the president of National Audubon, a birdy fellow named John Flicker, accompanied by Catriona Glazebrook, executive director, Texas State Office, NAS, were on hand to dedicate a new sanctuary trail. Since Old Dad and Miss Nancy were "birding" nearby federal refuges, they attended the ceremony.

The enthusiasm of the crowd, nearly all of them natives including many Latinos, showed that the Brownsville community is vitally interested in this endangered plant community of Mexican sabal palms. Obviously, Jimmy Paz did not have to make "paz" with the birds, reptiles, and mammals for which he is responsible.

❧ 12 ❧

STARR RANCH

SANCTUARY

Trabuco Canyon, California

It has been said that Starr Ranch is a living laboratory that represents what southern California would be like if there were no people. The sanctuary is named for Eugene Starr, who donated 4,000 acres of his 10,000-acre cattle ranch in 1973. Orange County purchased 5,000 acres of the ranch, which is now Caspers Wilderness Park, adjacent to the sanctuary. Fortunately, Starr Ranch Sanctuary, Caspers Wilderness Park, and Cleveland National Forest form a corridor for wildlife in an otherwise solid mass of towns and condominiums. When National Audubon acquired the sanctuary, it was bordered on the west by several square miles of open ranchland. Today the condominiums come right to our gate.

The following excerpts from our newsletter, *Places to Hide and Seek,* reveal some Starr Ranch History.

JANUARY 1975 In June 1973, the new Starr Ranch Audubon Sanctuary was dedicated, and Norm McIntosh was hired as warden. Hoot Mon! Another Scot on a sanctuary. Although bagpipes and heather are lacking, there are wild music, wildflowers, and wild canyons aplenty on the Starr Ranch. Mac has over three thousand acres of undeveloped and unspoiled sycamore canyons, groves of live oaks, and rolling hills covered with chaparral to look after.

The sanctuary is situated on the coastal side of the Santa Ana Mountains, southeast of Los Angeles in Orange County. The terrain provides several kinds of habitat that sustain widely different plant and animal communities. The high desertlike plateaus support cactus and sagebrush, while the canyons support live oaks, sycamores, and other broadleaved species. The variety of birds, mammals, reptiles, and insects is bound to keep Mac from getting bored.

Many of our sanctuaries are closed most of the time in order to keep disturbance of wildlife at a minimum, and some, such as Corkscrew, are occasionally closed because of fire hazard. At the Starr Ranch, however, an extreme fire hazard exists year-round and visitors are governed accordingly. They are admitted only on certain days of each month and are not allowed to smoke, even in their cars.

There's an old axiom among ecologists that environmental extremes are more important than the means. If so, the plants and animals on Starr Ranch are up against some powerful, limiting factors. During the hot, dry summers, the streams quit their babbling, and many disappear. Comes the cool, wet winter, and the canyons may flood. During January 1974, Mac experienced everything from beautiful sunshine of the Florida variety to heavy rains and winds that blew down several oaks that he made into

A mountain lion in the manager's front yard, indicative of the sanctuary's wildlife value.
(Photo: Peter DeSimone)

firewood. The so-called Santa Ana winds are a regular January feature that usually dries out the countryside.

The abundance of mule deer and rabbits on the sanctuary is enough to make the mountain lions, bobcats, and coyotes fat and lazy. Mac saw his first lion on July 6, 1974, which was the only valid record for the big cats on any of our sanctuaries that year. They do occur in or around the Corkscrew in Florida and also the Rainey in Louisiana. Coyotes and a long list of other hairy critters of the four-legged type are being inventoried through the courtesy of the El Dorado chapter of Audubon. We also have inventories under way on raptors, plus studies of the gray fox and various plants by personnel from nearby universities.

We have grown accustomed to having our sanctuaries threatened by drainage, stream channelization, dredge and fill operations, housing developments, highways, and what the big-city boys call "progress." So far, however, Mac and board member Agee Shelton have been very successful in combating the people pollution around the Starr. Having the Cleveland National Forest on our north and east boundaries is a big help, plus good relations with the county parks people on another side.

Had the Starr Ranch not been made an Audubon Sanctuary, however, there would be condominiums instead of cougars in the canyons by now.

During the 1976 hunting season, Norm McIntosh was busy saving his mule deer to fatten up the cougars, bobcats, and coyotes on the Starr Ranch. He figures one muley got dragged across the line by a two-legged predator, but if he can hold the poachers to that level, considering the many miles of boundary he has to patrol, that's doing pretty well.

It's not that we can't spare the deer or that the big cats don't need help in keeping the herd within the carrying capacity of the sanctuary. If we get an overpopulation of deer, however, we will seek open cooperation from the state wildlife department instead of hunters who can't read signs.

Although deer, cougars, white-tailed kites, great-horned owls, and other species may dominate the scene, the mountains and valleys on the sanctuary offer such a diversity that the botanists, birders, mammalogists, and snake hunters know the sanctuary well.

Over a dozen college classes, and as many chapter field trips, plus individual researchers keep Mac and wife, Beverly, busy. Bev is one of the sharpest ornithologists in the region, so Mac makes sure she is around whenever those breathless, wide-eyed bird listers whisper, "What is that?"

Last February, Mac was caught off the sanctuary (good excuse, had to

Mule deer consider Starr Ranch a safe haven.
(Photo: Peter DeSimone)

take son Robert to the doctor) when the rains came and made the dirt roads impassable. He got in about six days later. Then comes the annual drought in summer; by August he has his fingers crossed and fire breaks plowed around all the buildings.

Mac still has to contend with developers who want to build a small airport in nearby Dove Canyon, strip mine the gravel or lower the water table in San Juan Creek, widen the road through an adjacent county park, and so on. Whether in California or Carolina, threats to the sanctuaries will probably always be with us.

Mac was not boxed up in Bell Canyon for the whole year, however. He managed to get over to the Audubon regional conference at Asilomar and up to the Western Bird Banders Association meeting in Fort Collins, Colorado, and to Western Interpreters' Conference at Lake Tahoe.

Being a retired training officer in the Seabees, Mac is dickering with the public project officer of the local reserve unit. He hopes to get them to practice their road maintenance exercises on some fifteen miles of roads in the sanctuary. 'Twill be a good trick if he can do it, giving the Seabees something worthwhile to do and such a blessing to his budget.

All good things must end, and so it was with management of the Starr Ranch by Norm McIntosh. Mac retired on June 30, 1977. In his four years at the ranch, he kept poachers, vandals, and developers at arm's length but cozied up to nearby Audubon chapters, college faculty, students, and park rangers. We wish Mac continued success following his retirement from Audubon.

And so Jeff Froke now has the honor of first place for last warden hired. After graduating from Humboldt College, where he majored in wildlife management, Jeff worked for the California State Parks for three years, then spent one whole month with the U.S. Fish and Wildlife Service. All this rich experience convinced him that managing an Audubon sanctuary would be more rewarding than being stalled with the state or fed up with the feds.

He had been on the job only four days when John Borneman, from the California Condor Sanctuary, descended on him to give an orientation course in the potential trials, tribulations, and triumphs of a sanctuary manager. And, according to Jeff's report, "John did a find job of mowing the lawn!" And we thought all he could do was sing. (He was formerly a soloist with Fred Waring.)

Old Dad allows as how Audubon wardens don't make much money, but they get a lot of "perks." Which is short for perquisites, which is short for the privilege of having a mule deer herd, a mountain lion, a hootie owl, and a common bushtit in your backyard.

As far as the weather is concerned, the Starr Ranch perks alternate with quirks. Santa Claus about got grounded and drownded when winds from fifty to ninety miles per hour roared down Bell Canyon for about ten days. Over eleven inches of rain washed the old year out, along with what we used to call roads. A portion of the main road had to be rerouted around a fallen oak tree that was too big to cut or move.

With his mass transit system completely inoperative, Jeff took up jogging and hiking along the four-mile trail to get groceries and mail. Within an hour after a gully-washer had let up, Jeff came across lion tracks that had been made since the rain. A rain that lets you see cougar tracks that are still smoking can't be all bad.

His arrival at Starr Ranch coincided with the necessity of replacing the water and sewage systems and the reconstruction of the former foreman's house. Presumably all this falls in our category of general maintenance and/or other. It takes a heap o' plumbin' to make a house a home.

For those of you who drink water, Old Dad hopes and trusts there is little need to point out that it can cause problems. With his regular supply shut off, Jeff was unloading drinking water bottles on November 27, when he tore several muscles in his back. Old Dad calls your attention to Timothy I 5:23, which reads as follows: "Drink no longer water, but use a little wine for thy stomach's sake and thine often infirmities."

In spite of these vicissitudes, Jeff and his wife, Martha, have managed to visit several nearby chapters, such as the Sea and Sage, Pomona Valley, South Coast, El Dorado, and others. Jeff was on two Christmas Bird counts and the annual Jack Smith Bird Walk that celebrates a locally popular newspaper columnist. In return for this, the sanctuary received good publicity in the *Los Angeles Times*.

In other words, Jeff got a lot done in his first six months, and according to what he tells Old Dad, he loved every minute of it and so did Martha. See what we mean by perks?

JANUARY 1979 Jeff Froke says his committee in charge of weather turned in a sterling performance in 1978. The New Year blew in on fifty to ninety mile per hour winds, and he had over twenty-one inches of rain by mid-February. But he observed in his warden's report, "We are not suffering major and life-taking floods and mudslides like much of southern California is today." Apparently a canyon whose walls are covered with sage scrub and chaparral has an advantage over one which is wall to wall houses.

Nevertheless, the gravel roads were criss-crossed with gullies into which a four-wheel drive could rest on the frame with four wheels spinning in the air. By February 13, Jeff had already turned away over one hundred would-be field trippers. A beekeeper offered to repair some damaged roads in exchange for a permit to place beehives on the sanctuary. With the spread of insecticides and asphalt, our sanctuaries play a role in the lives of honeybees that T. Gilbert Pearson, Audubon's first president, probably didn't anticipate.

Heavy rains and flooding continued into March, and some landslides and flooding occurred throughout the sanctuary. But in this land of extremes, the plants and animals that can't tolerate the conditions that prevail have long since left the stage. According to Jeff, hiking into the highlands revealed super wildflower blooms and widespread bird-nesting activity, including golden eagles! Back at the ranch, he put up an experimental set of love nests around the sanctuary buildings and within minutes the house wrens were playing house. And mountain lions, spotted owls, varied thrushes, ringtailed cats, and white-tailed kites continued to clutter up the place in spite of the weather.

In his spare time, Jeff served on an advisory committee on controlled burning and wildlife planning in the Cleveland National Forest adjacent to the sanctuary; met with Orange County school officials regarding outdoor education and possible roles for the sanctuary; took a "vacation" in western Mexico for two weeks of research on lilac-crowned parrots (supported by an NAS grant); prepared an exhibit for the county fair; attended the Audubon Camp of the West, where he got contaminated by Jay Reed's enthusiasm, which may affect planning of educational programs at Starr Ranch; gave evening workshops on zoological museum techniques at UCLA; finished his Starr Ranch Master Plan; and negotiated with developers who consider land with less than four houses per acre as unholy.

In December, Jeff calls Old Dad for authorization to purchase a new four-wheel drive. Old Dad says, "Since you never do nothin', you don't need no vehicle." But he got one, after due deliberation plus some great help from a southern California board member, Agee Shelton, by name.

JANUARY 1980 Those who have to classify everything and everybody—it is this, he is that, or the other thing—will go crazy trying to put Jeff Froke in one pigeonhole. His warden reports show that he teaches biology, does research, gives radio programs about Audubon, writes articles, inspires chapters, arrests poachers, repairs the plumbing, pours concrete, and in general carries on as Audubon wardens do.

At an Audubon sanctuary, nothing's ever simple. This includes just getting to and from most of them, and Starr Ranch is no exception. An adjacent developer thinks a small airport would be good for wildlife. Jeff doesn't think so. Developer says, "If that's your attitude, you can't cross my land." That means going the long way around over some very interesting roads. Our board of directors, meeting in San Diego last February, planned a trip to the sanctuary. Jeff's report says they didn't make it because of "wet, slippery, partly absent roads." Have you been over a partly absent road lately?

By September things had dried up a bit. Jeff says, "Temperatures above one hundred degrees occurred on twenty-four days of this month, causing extremely high fire danger in our foothills." In Caspers Park, south of the sanctuary, 775 acres burned. The fire threatened to move up Bell Canyon into the sanctuary, closing his only access route. The fire didn't make it, so next day Jeff and his assistant, Dave Henderson, were out setting up permanent photo-study points for future studies of plant succession following fire. Although fire was affecting the landscape long before men started messing it up, and we use it as a management tool on many sanctuaries, we still have much to learn about its long-range effect on plants, animals, soil, air, and water. It seems obvious, however, that in contrast to man-made structures, native wild plants and animals suffer no devastating lasting effects.

On Sunday, May 5, the *Los Angeles Times* had an excellent article on the sanctuary. The photos were good, the reporting accurate, and the extensive quotes from Jeff and his predecessor, Norm McIntosh, were very convincing.

In contrast to the situation around northwestern Connecticut, the chicken hawks and hootie owls in Bell and Crow Canyons had a banner year. Data gathered last spring by Art Gingert, Pete DeSimone, and Mike Root, based at the Miles Sanctuary near Sharon, Connecticut, show a decline in productivity of goshawks, red-shoulders, Cooper's, barn owls, and great horned owls. This may reflect the severe Connecticut winter, which reduced small mammal populations.

In contrast, Jeff banded an early record white-tailed kite's brood in February, and the parents had time for another go at it. Pete Bloom, the leading raptor-captor in Orange County, wound up his banding program with the conclusion that the sanctuary's density of red-shouldered hawks and barn owls exceeded any comparable area in the state. Apparently, two and even three broods were common among white-tailed kites and barn owls in the area last year.

In August, according to Jeff's records, the big pussy cats terrified three deer and one carpenter. Dave Everitt hears a crash in the brush and turns to see a mule deer charging at him. Before he can get out of the way, a cougar drags the deer down from behind. Pussy cat and prey are now twenty-five feet from Dave. Next thing we know, Dave is in Jeff's living room, one thousand yards away. As Jeff writes, "He's a good carpenter and never claimed to be a dedicated field biologist."

JANUARY 1981 Last year was fairly normal for Jeff Froke. In January the rains, floods, and roads were so bad the stork could not get in, so Jeff and Martha went out. And on January 29, Benjamin Bray Froke was hatched in Arcadia. And the next day it rained.

The top storm of the season dropped six and one-half inches on Starr Ranch, which made a commuter out of Jeff. But he says back-packing four and one-half miles from Coto de Caza beats strap-hanging from the Pennsylvania Station over to 950 Third Avenue.

Besides accommodating various blessings from heaven, Jeff manages to carry on his own research involving raptors, teach a couple birdy courses at the University of California, give numerous programs for Audubon chapters, coordinate the field activities of various researchers and classes at the Starr, and cosponsor an International Symposium on Air Pollution and Forest Ecosystems. The postconference tour of Starr Ranch and the Audubon concept of privately protected wildlife sanctuaries was "most interesting" to visiting Yugoslavian and East German scientists.

In April, Jeff and Martha play hosts to the second annual Starr Ranch Rodent Trappers and Frog Grabbers Beer Tasting convention. This will soon become a classic among those who study the lives and times of mice, squirrels, frogs, toads, and related species.

In June, Jeff takes a busman's holiday, and his report reads, "Camped with John and Mary Ann Ogden at the Red Rock condor nest area and spent an enjoyable and provocative day watching condors and talking about future directions of Audubon's wildlife research and management." (There simply is no accounting for the way Audubon wardens spend their spare time.)

Heavy rains in the previous three winters displaced a lot of humans, but the cumulative effect on Starr Ranch wildlife appeared beneficial. Postbreeding season studies showed that last year was highly productive. California quail and black phoebes double- and triple-brooded; mule deer produced twins for the third consecutive season; and coyotes were more numerous and widespread than in former years. The Department of Fish and Game helped Jeff track and census mountain lions, and they found evidence of at least three big cats on the ranch.

But in the changing world of birds, some business groups are singing the blues. When the swallows don't come back to Capistrano, neither do the tourists. Jeff speaks to the Kiwanis Club on the economic and social values of birds. The absence of swallows gives local business people a pain in the region of their pocketbooks. In addition to making Jeff an honorary member, they are considering a grant to Audubon to investigate ways to bring the swallows back to Capistrano.

On Tuesday, November 25, it had not rained for nearly 180 days; relative humidity was 3 percent. One of eleven wildfires that burned 80,000 acres in five nearby counties came roaring up Bell Canyon, backed by thirty mile per hour Santa Ana winds with gusts up to eighty-five. By mid-afternoon on Wednesday, about 90 percent of the grasslands and brushlands on the sanctuary were burned. Woodland flames in Crow and Fox Canyons and adjacent Cleveland National Forest persisted for about ten days.

When Jeff reported the fire on Tuesday, he was told that firemen feared the deep and narrow Bell Canyon as a "death trap" and that saving our buildings was out of the question. But on Thursday afternoon, with the fire about 200 yards from headquarters, the Forest Service arrived with five engines. They hooked up to Jeff's new 43,000 gallon water tank (which paid for itself then and there) and saved the houses, office, main garage, and citrus orchard. We lost several barns, outbuildings, well pumps, and utility lines. Jeff says they set up a priority list of buildings to be saved—some of which were already burning—and in ten minutes the old pros from Stanislaus National Forest had laid out a brilliant system of backfires and safety zones and made a gallant stand.

By December 2, Jeff reported, "Wildlife losses appear to have been moderate. Most animals probably escaped by running, flying, or crawling to safer canyons or deep underground burrows. . . . a wide assortment of small mammals and birds apparently died from suffocation. More impressive . . . was the large number of animals that became disoriented . . . many deer, bobcats, badgers, and woodrats wandering in the daylight, apparently confused by the sudden lack of cover."

But the chaparral had evolved with fire as a major environmental factor. Starr Ranch foothills would have naturally burned about every eight to twelve years, but they had been protected from fire since 1912, which was about as ecologically sound as some irrigation schemes in Nebraska. Anyway, research plans to document the postfire succession were under way before the flames actually reached the sanctuary. Jeff has completed his aerial photography and is predicting that species diversity and abundance will be higher in ten years than they were in 1980.

JANUARY 1982   Jeff reports that 1981 was just ordinary as far as Audubon sanctuaries go. On February 4, a mountain lion killed a deer just twenty-five feet from his kitchen window. The lion ate half of the venison and stashed the rest, which was discovered by eight coyotes who fed on it for a week.

The bird-trapping and banding business continued at a frantic but highly productive pace last spring. In an effort to monitor population recovery, following the fall fire, several ground traps and mist nets were operated in a thirty-acre plot, for which Jeff now has seven years of data. They banded as many as 127 birds per day with USFWS and color bands and kept that up two to three days per week for ten weeks.

Since so many of the hole nesters lost their domiciles in the fire, our volunteer helpers are now studying the hammer-and-chisel workings of the woodpecker tribe. As Jeff explains, "My goal here is to encourage the growth of the volunteer observers who will operate under the supervision of the formal researchers while contributing data and physical support to those studies. With close coordination and supervision, we may be able to operate effectively with twenty to twenty-five individuals in the field."

Jeff says that because many of our raptors are of known age and origin, the sanctuary was asked to furnish blood for analysis of pesticide levels to compare with peregrine falcons being studied by Bob Riseborough of California Fish and Game.

A relic population of Bell's vireos inhabits a nearby stretch of riparian woodland that a developer wants to make into a golf course. As you might suspect, our rabble-rousing environmental extremist is quietly contacting the Orange County board of Supervisors and pointing out that golf courses can go anywhere, but Bell's vireo has no place to go.

Jeff and Martha not only look after Starr Ranch, but Martha trains the volunteers who work in the adjacent Caspers Wilderness Park. The volunteers point out the wonders of the park, the wonders of the National Audubon Society, and they just happen to have a goodly supply of membership blanks.

Those who believe that growth can go on forever live in great anguish because there are no houses in the canyons of Starr Ranch to be crushed in mudslides and floods. Therefore, Jeff must constantly battle the forces of righteousness who want to (1) build a major airport on the sanctuary by filling in Bell Canyon; (2) build a rifle and pistol range in Caspers Wilderness Park adjacent to Starr Ranch; and (3) build a riding and hiking trail through the sanctuary. He combats the first by being appointed to the new Orange County Airport Site Selection Advisory Committee and the second by testifying before the Orange County Harbors, Beaches, and Parks Commission in favor of a rifle range but *not* in a wilderness park full of people and wild critters. His was literally the lone voice crying in the wilderness, but he won anyway. Afterward, according to his report, "It was a long, lonely walk in a dark parking lot to this warden's pickup truck." He handles the third by lectures round and about showing Starr Ranch just as it is.

Gary Arballo joined the staff in March as temporary maintenance and construction man to help rebuild after the fire. Gary, at eighteen, is a veteran cowboy and a nephew of the oldest surviving Starr Ranch cowhand, Reyes Serrano. Reyes is among the last of the Juaneon Indian tribe. So with Gary, Ernest Ortiz, the Legés, the Chandlers, Jerry Cutlip, and Miss Nancy, the Indians in the Sanctuary Department might rise again, since all the above have some Indian genes.

Jeff's program on Audubon and Starr Ranch for the local historical society brought unexpected rewards. He met the county's oldest living ornithologist, Don Meadows, who showed him an egg collection and photographs taken in Bell Canyon in the 1910s and 1920s. And Carl McKenzie, a former resident and cowhand on Starr Ranch, gave *Jeff* a tour of the sanctuary and showed him several rich Indian archeological sites and the spot where he had shot "an old she-lion." He donated the cat's hide to the ranch and promised to turn over the chaps (riding britches) that Tom Mix gave Gene Starr years ago.

Comes July 1982, and the temperature exceeds one hundred degrees on nine different days. But that didn't stop Jeff from putting on his game warden hat and working with the Department of Fish and Game at night. They staked out an area about two miles south of Starr Ranch in which a ring of mountain lion poachers was hoping to bag a big pussy cat. So far, both lions and hunters are at large.

In October the Sanctuary Wardens Attack Team consisting of Dusty Dunstan, assistant director of the Sanctuary Department; Pete DeSimone, assistant manager of the Miles Sanctuary in Connecticut; and Lonnie Legé, manager of the Rainey Sanctuary in Louisiana, arrived. In sixteen days, the SWAT remodeled, rewired, and recovered what is known as the Tortuga House, which is now an efficient laboratory building. Jeff's detailed records show Audubon saving about $30,000 by using this motley crew.

Our neighbor, in keeping with what is going on in southern California, has great plans for three thousand modular homes on about four hundred acres. In addition, he is considering a four-lane public highway through his easement in Bell Canyon, through the middle of Starr Ranch and adjacent Caspers Park. Our sanctuary manager, an expert on things natural, wild, and free, will spend much of 1983 dealing with those to whom growth in population, air pollution, noise level, and monoculture is a sacred charge. Since this is Orange County, stronghold of the John Birch

Society, where conservation and communism are considered equally meritorious, it could be an interesting year.

MARCH 1984 Jeff Froke says people in Orange County are better fed than those in Calcutta or New Delhi, but as for elbow room, the Californios are not much better off. Our neighbor still has great plans for three thousand modular homes on about four hundred acres plus a four-lane highway through his easement in Bell Canyon. Holding about four thousand acres of Starr Ranch open for mule deer, white-tailed hawks, and mountain lions is, in his opinion, a criminal act perpetrated by communists.

But old Jeff is a sly one. As a member of the Orange County Open Space Committee and as special adviser to county planners, he was influential in establishing a county-wide plan for the private and public acquisition of critical wildlife habitat areas. These range in size from a few acres to more than ten thousand acres. In 1983 more than four thousand acres of wild land on developing properties adjacent to the sanctuary were dedicated as "Permanent Open."

Behind every successful man, there stands an astonished woman, but in Martha Froke's case, Old Dad finds her more astonishing than astonished. In February 1983, heavy rains washed out the Bell Canyon road, blocking all traffic until after summer plowing. Flash floods in canyons were frequent throughout the year. Rainfall was three and one-half times normal for the year, but sun and Santa Ana winds also made for hot dry spells. In September the thermometer hit 114 degrees and stayed 110 degrees for a week. And in January 1984, Santa Ana winds with gusts up to one hundred miles per hour dried out the vegetation, and the nearby Mojeska fire burned about one thousand five hundred acres. In a recent survey by *Dog's Life Magazine,* these, and other environmental factors such as ticks and rattlesnakes, were included in "Ten Reasons Why Women Leave Home." But instead of flying the coop, we find Martha raising funds to keep the sanctuary going! She writes up grant proposals, talks sweet and purty to visiting dignitaries, and keeps Jeff attentive to his duties.

New records for 1983 included a varied thrush and a prairie falcon. On March 19, Jeff is asked to be present at San Juan Capistrano. It is St. Joseph's Day at the mission, the day the swallows are supposed to come back to Capistrano. In preparation, Jeff reads up on the natural and unnatural history of cliff swallows in Cap'n Wimby's Bird Atlas. Gene Autry was supposed to be an added attraction. Gene didn't show, and neither did the swallows, but ten thousand people did. Jeff was interviewed by the Ted Turner broadcasting system, and he told 'em all about cliff swallow nests and how some folks do not like those hollow mud balls under the eaves. This explains why swallows do not return to some of their former habitats.

In spite of the versatility and energy displayed by Martha and Jeff, there is never a time at Starr Ranch that doesn't call for more personnel than we have on hand. This situation was enormously relieved on August 23, 1983, by the arrival of Pete and Sandy DeSimone. Jeff's report says, "Although Pete's official starting date is September 1, much was accomplished by him before the end of August." Old Dad watched Pete for a few years back at the Miles Sanctuary and is not at all surprised that "much was accomplished" in his first week at Starr Ranch. Pete is one of the best raptor biologists in the Northeast, and Sandy is a first-class botanist and teacher. If the late Eugene Starr could return this winter, we think he would be proud and pleased.

As Jeff says, the mountain lion is a proud vestige of North America. Here in southern California, the Starr Ranch and surrounding area is one of its last strongholds. But the population is increasingly disrupted and reduced as nearby private ranches sprout 2,500 or more houses per square mile, and every vestige of wild land is replaced by condominiums. Lions frequently encounter people on the wild edge of the sanctuary and nearby parks and national forest.

Management to enhance the people-lion relationship and to minimize dangerous conflicts in and around the sanctuary has long been our goal, but we've been seriously handicapped by a lack of information on local populations, their ecology, and movements. In absence of same, lions are apt to be "managed" by superstition, fear, and political pressure.

Jeff has been seeking grant money for lion research for a year or two. Now suddenly his request is receiving a lot of attention due to the sad death of a five-year-old girl, killed by a mountain lion in adjacent Caspers Park on March 24, 1986. It now appears that Chevron and two or three local government agencies are about to underwrite the research. It is further evidence that wild creatures that require a lot of room or specialized habitat are often in the way of this headlong human race.

Meanwhile, Jeff, Martha, Pete, and Sandy continue to demonstrate to developers, politicians, scientists, and resource managers what the voice of reason is all about. The contribution by Jeff and Martha Froke to the wildlife and human resources in southern California and elsewhere is something to be admired. It is not surprising, therefore, that this comes to the attention of various institutions around the country. To make a long story short, we bid Jeff and Martha a fond adieu in 1988 when he became director of the Roger Tory Peterson Institute in Jamestown, New York, leaving Starr Ranch in the equally capable hands of Pete and Sandra DeSimone.

DECEMBER 1989 From time to time, Pete DeSimone thinks about the Dutch boy who, according to legend, stuck his finger in the dike and held back the flood. But Pete says holding back the North Sea is one thing; holding back real estate developers in Orange County is something else. When we acquired the ranch in 1973, miles of open space lay between the gate and the nearest town. Today the flood of condominiums has rolled up against our fence.

In addition to the inexorable human pressures, a complex of buildings, machines, roads, fences, exotic plants, and computers keeps the manager occupied. No matter how versatile and energetic a manager may be, there are only twenty-four hours in a day. That is, until Papa Joe Edmondson and wife, Char, show up, and suddenly it's like having seventy-two hours per day as far as maintenance, repairs, remodeling, and office work are concerned.

Papa Joe has long been in charge of the Sanctuary Department's buildings from Maine to California. And when it comes to record keeping, be it personnel, financial, or general, Char is our Number One Good Lookee.

While Pete and Joe are making like engineers and building contractors, Char makes for the office. She gets four years of breeding-bird data (over four thousand records) organized, printed, and mailed, plus the myriad duties of temporary secretary and office manager.

The Laguna Hills Audubon Society, the Sea and Sage Audubon Society, Pomona Audubon Society, Rotary Clubs, business clubs, and nearby schools and colleges call on Pete for programs. Meanwhile, back at the ranch, there are graduate students in need of guidance and helpful hints as to research, hootie owls to band, and the annual Leslie Love trail ride with sixty equestrians. Sandra DeSimone's plant physiology class stays overnight while experimenting on the xylem water and relative osmosis potential from plants from different plant communities.

We now have three sanctuaries—Rookery Bay in Florida, Research Ranch in Arizona, and Starr Ranch in California—doing work on various races of scrub jays. Dave Bontrager has been banding ash-throated fly-catchers, two of which have been wearing bands for ten years. In September 1989, about seventy-five people were on hand to watch Pete Bloom capture and band a few barn owls. During May 1989, the crew caught and collared four female mountain lions.

Speaking of lions, Sandy saw one standing in the road and looking into the sanctuary office on May 18. And on June 26 at 5:45 A.M., Pete hears a rustling outside the bedroom window. Says he to Sandy, "That's either a deer or a lion." Since it is definitely not a deer, he grabs his binocs and goes out for a better look. He reports, "When our eyes met, it charged, and I had to kill it with my bare hands . . . Actually, our eyes did meet, and we looked at each other for about thirty seconds before the lion turned away. . . . my look was long enough to see it was not wearing a radio collar." So he informs his colleagues, who are hoping to snare and collar the cougar. On October 9, they snared and collared a male, the only male in a group of twelve that are collared. By that time, many of the collared females had kittens. By radio telemetry, we are gradually learning more about the lives and times of the big cats.

Also in the feline friends department is a bobcat that frequently hunts gophers outside the workshop; and, although it is wild, it tolerates two-legged mammals within fifty feet or less.

February at Starr Ranch usually finds wintering Oregon juncos and red-breasted sapsuckers still around, roadrunners doing their booming territorial calls, golden eagles displaying around their nest, and orange-crowned warblers singing.

A quote from Pete's report typifies the problems we face with nearby developers. "The Dove Canyon Company had surreptitiously tried to remove some twelve-feet high earthen berms from a tract map. These berms had been designed to block noise and light from affecting the golden eagles nesting in Bell Canyon. I was able to organize the efforts that eventually resulted in a return to the original plan. The berms will be built."

With the winter rains come heavy loads of silt flowing from the development into the sanctuary. Pete must maintain constant contact with the Orange County officials to keep the Dove Canyon and Coto de Caza projects in compliance with the rules. Nary a month goes by in which he does not have three or four meetings with the companies, their attorneys, their engineers, and the environmental watchdogs. He says, "I have found some of the people involved with this project have a tendency to sit on the side of the fence that is most comfortable at the moment. I find this very tiresome as well as incredibly deceitful."

Another outfit wants to drill a water well on our property and threatens to tap into our aquifer from an off-site location if we decide not to let them drill in the sanctuary. Pete says that whatever they do it won't be during the golden eagle nesting season if he can help it.

Then comes meetings with the Airport Site Coalition that is to choose a site for another airport in southern California. A field of fourteen sites is narrowed to four, of which number one is in the adjacent Cleveland National Forest. This would have a major impact on Starr Ranch, so Pete has another fight on his hands.

On the bright side, the San Joaquin Marsh is one of three remaining fresh water marshes in Orange County. It was formerly saved and managed by six duck club members. The city of Irvine now prohibits duck hunting, so the duck club is folding and withdrawing the $50,000 they spent annually. Pete helps organize a meeting with the city, a business firm, the California Fish and Game Department, and other interested parties. The city has now allocated $110,000 for the next two years, while long-term management plans are hammered out.

An earthquake of 4.7 on the Richter scale on April 7, 1989, and another of 4.3 on June 12 shook buildings and composures but did no other damage.

Being a woodsman of the first order, whenever trees blow down across roads, Pete makes and sells firewood for about $2,000 per year. He says it's "found money," since he would have to remove the wood anyway. And for hardship duty, he censused the deer on the public hunting range of the Cleveland Forest. He counted X mule deer and made it X minus one, a fine four-point buck.

Our congratulations to Sandy DeSimone for completing her M.Sc. this year.

JUNE 1992 He can operate anything from a bulldozer to computer with consummate skill. He's one of our foremost raptor biologists, an excellent botanist, birder, photographer, and speaker, picks a mean guitar and mandolin, and is an expert marksman. Talk about versatile! That being the case, we might expect to find Pete DeSimone spending all his time in the beautiful hills and valleys of Starr Ranch. Alas! It ain't necessarily so.

Orange County, home of the John Birch Society, a stronghold of "growth and development," still has a few (very few) acres of coastal sage scrub or chapparal. It's the last stronghold of the California gnatcatcher, so both the ecosystem and the bird are endangered, although not officially listed as such. At the north end of Mission Viejo, a development company is drooling over 210 acres, the last bit of rural land in the county. A grading permit is required by the city council before work can begin, but the city says what's going on there is not development or grading, it is "weed abatement."

In the middle of Caspers Park Wilderness Area, the Santa Margarita Company plans a big development known as Las Flores. Pete and local Auduboners met with the company and county officials. Pete reports, "In essence, they couldn't believe we were suing them because of the illegal way they processed the project and the complete lack of consideration of major impacts such as traffic and water quality. They were constantly asking 'what do you *really* want out of this?' Our response was we wanted them to obey the law. They could not grasp the concept."

Several other developments with similar disastrous effects on the environment keep Pete and local Audubon chapters such as Sea and Sage, South Coast Audubon, and Whittier Audubon fighting on several fronts against staggering odds. The city, county, and state governments and the courts just can't understand how anyone could be opposed to progress. Attempts at compromise call for meetings with developers. One such meeting drew this conclusion from Pete: "It really was a waste of time. The development community is not willing to realistically compromise on anything if it cuts into their profits."

While not otherwise engaged, Pete entertains Krista Johanssen and son, from Sweden; Krista is a bird bander. Pete lectures to undergraduates at UCLA on the California Environmental Quality Act and to chapter and other activist groups and assists researchers working on scrub jays, mountain lions, raptors, and such.

In the interesting wildlife department: four pairs of golden eagles in and near Starr Ranch, an Oregon junco nest (may be a record for Orange County), and a very rare but very dead coastal patch-nosed snake in the road. Intern David Choate contributes valuable data to the lion crew by doing twenty-four-hour tracking sessions. The crew has sixteen lions radio-collared.

Instead of listing the California gnatcatcher as endangered, which would have meant saving the remnant of coastal sage scrub, the state Fish and Game Department gave in to the developer against the wishes of over six hundred people at the hearing. NRDC may sue the state.

Charlotte Williamson, an intern from Marple, England, arrived in September, as did David Choate from Chicago. Randy Snodgrass and Tom Horton, from our Washington, D.C., office, dropped by to discuss Starr Ranch's role in the campaign to reauthorize the Endangered Species Act.

In his spare time, Pete made a couple quick trips to Michigan to repair osprey nesting platforms at Fletcher Pond and to meet with Dusty Dunstan, Sergei Postupulski, Tom and Pat Fraser, and Steve Stackpole, who underwrites the project.

Pete also managed to assist Wayne Mones, development division, in contacting potential big donors. Mission accomplished.

JULY 1993   If we offered a prize for the manager with the most irons in the fire, several managers would be tied with Pete DeSimone, but none would surpass him. He can and does run anything from computers to bulldozers with consummate skill, can and does repair any kind of engine, is an expert at carpentry, plumbing, and wiring, and observes, records, and manages wildlife on four thousand acres in the foothills of the Santa Ana Mountains in southeastern Orange County, while letting the developers know he's there.

Because of the unique combination of climate, soils, and drainage, vegetative types such as coastal sage scrub, which is the California gnatcatcher's only habitat, are as endangered as whooping cranes and gray wolves.

When we acquired Starr Ranch, about twenty years ago, the area between sanctuary and coast was mostly ranchland. Today condominiums come smack up to our gate, which has developers casting greedy eyes at all that land "going to waste; just standing there idle." Not only is Starr Ranch under such scrutiny, so is every acre of open space in southern California.

The state wildlife boss does not have enough political clout to list the gnatcatcher nor the coastal sage scrub as endangered. If he did so, developers would undoubtedly usher him out of office. As Gary Pearson, Rich Madson, and Bruce Barbour learned years ago in North Dakota, what is ecologically right is often politically wrong.

It's not surprising, therefore, that in the nearby Caspers Park Wilderness Area (that's really what they call it) the Santa Margarita Company plans a big development. Will the state wildlife department try to stop them? This is state land, so the USFWS and the EPA are out of the picture. So who is taking them to court? You guessed her, Chester! While Pete is the catalyst for political and legal action by National Audubon and local chapters, he does not ignore practical wildlife management, research, and education. The Sea and Sage chapter leases the six-hundred-acre San Joaquin Marsh, with Pete's advice on management and Melanie Ingall's taking the lead on educational aspects of the program.

Roy Taylor, from jolly old England, continued his breeding bird survey with much enthusiasm. A Lewis's woodpecker hung around during March. Roy and another biologist located twenty-three pairs of California gnatcatchers on the ranch, which may represent 1–2 percent of the world population. Roy found more breeding rufous-crowned sparrows than expected, good numbers of grasshopper sparrows and cactus wrens, and also located a few raptor nests that Pete Bloom, the raptor specialist, hadn't found. Roy left on May 10, 1992.

On June 10, 1992, Kevin Pilz arrived from Massachusetts to begin a study of barn owl feeding behavior by observing two nest boxes from a blind. When he left on August 29, Pete reported, "He did an excellent job for a youth that turned twenty while he was here. He prepared two excellent papers and was a pleasure to have around."

Interns on Audubon sanctuaries have, in general, been invaluable. Old Dad well remembers when young Pete DeSimone showed up at the Emily Winthrop Miles about fifteen years ago. The Homeland Foundation endorses our intern programs with an annual $5,000 donation. For 1992 they raised it to $7,800.

Pete did a local television interview on the Natural Communities Conservation Program, which was launched at a state hearing to list the California gnatcatcher as endangered. Pete says, "It is a noble effort, but floundering badly. It was also a blatant attempt by the state to circumvent the listing. I gave them an earful."

South Coast Audubon cohosted a forum on endangered species for local developers and agency people. Pete says, "We attempted to give them our viewpoint on our turf. It was well attended and productive." Randy Snodgrass, John McCaull, and a couple attorneys of the good kind were there.

In the interesting wildlife department (is there any other kind?) a four-week-old spotted fawn with doe on September 14, 1992, was in first place for latest date of birth on record. A road-killed mountain lion was brought in by a local officer. Pete helped measure and skin the 138-pound male, one of many such tragedies in overcrowded Orange County.

Jan Beyea, from our New York Office, came by to discuss research possibilities. Dusty Dunstan came by to discuss management. Nippon TV (Japan) came by for an interview on the gnatcatcher and development. Carl Safina, our marine fisheries expert, came by for some kind of mischief. The Transportation Corridor Agency bought part of an ecological reserve (complete with nesting gnatcatchers) and plans to build a toll road through it. And so, along with the Sea and Sage Chapter, we have an expert wildlife manager—who knows the outdoors better than Daniel Boone or Kit Carson—spending much of his precious time in court.

On the other hand, in March 1993, he gets about 150 miles south of the border as part of a "Wildlife Discussions" group trying to integrate southern Californian and Mexican concepts of land use and habitat preservation. In that same month, Pete spent ten days as an Audubon tour guide in Baja California. Sanctuary managers do get around.

JULY 1997 Back in the Dirty Thirties when the Okies crawled out of the Dust Bowl and headed for California, those that made it to Orange County found jobs picking oranges. But today an orange picker would find mighty slim pickins because land that sprouts two thousand five hundred condominiums per square mile has precious little room for orange groves.

And if commercial crops are feeling the squeeze, what about wild plants and animals? Pete DeSimone can sympathize with that legendary Dutch boy who stuck his finger in the dike and held back a flood. When we acquired Starr Ranch in 1973, miles of open space lay between our gate and the nearest town. Today the flood of condominiums has rolled up against our gate and developers look with greedy eyes at "All that perfectly good space just going to waste. And all because some damn-fool birdwatchers are up in arms about some brush and weeds called coastal sage scrub and some dickey bird called California gnatcatcher. All coastal sage scrub should be scrubbed, and we can take care of gnats with aerial spray. We don't need gnatcatchers!"

Pete's report for June 1997 says, "The biggest news I can pass on at the moment is that you can now refer to us as Dr. and Pete DeSimone. Yup, Sandy finished her Ph.D. in ecology in May. Both her master's and doctoral research were done on Starr Ranch in the coastal sage scrub. Also, throughout this academic endeavor, she never got a *B:* we're talkin' 4.0 student, my friends."

He goes on to say, "Sandy's working part time for me overseeing all the research projects at Starr (twelve at the moment, represented by nine colleges and universities). She's also responsible for our interns and their projects; we have a pretty steady flow of two interns every three months. And she organized and runs a docent/volunteer program to help with the increase in our public events and provide researchers with assistants."

To the consternation of developers (and, no doubt, the John Birch Society), Pete is heavily involved in California land use planning efforts that are driven by the Endangered Species Act.

One time-consuming project involves polluted water entering the sanctuary. A development known as Dove Canyon started on about eight hundred adjacent acres in 1987, and they're still building the remainder of some 1,200 homes. The whole project drains into our Bell Canyon. Early agreements were supposed to provide for ponds that collected and monitored run off. This never happened; the original developer went broke. Before he could leave the scene, we sued him and all the new builders that came in to finish the project. We based our suit on the cost to put in a system to collect the run off and pump it to a treatment plant. Pete says, "This came to about $735,000, which we got. But now the real good part."

Working with the local water district, Pete learned they were eager to get access to this water. When Dove Canyon began construction, water was going for $200 per acre foot. It is now around $1,000 per acre foot, and reclaimed water about $600 per acre foot. Pete may be able to turn the settlement into cash for Starr Ranch use. A finger in the dike? More like Hoover Dam across the Colorado River.

Through it all, this versatile manager finds time to observe the activities of a female mountain lion and two yearlings living near headquarters, as well as a checklist of birds that would make our late patron saint, Roger Tory Peterson, take notice.

This sanctuary has made and is making a significant difference to the present and future natural resources of southern California.

❧ 13 ❧

EDWARD BRIGHAM ALKALI

LAKE SANCTUARY

Jamestown, North Dakota

About twenty miles northeast of Jamestown, North Dakota, the combination of North Dakota winters, arid summers, and rolling topography
had kept the plows and cows off the remnant of virgin prairie that bordered Alkali Lake. But by the mid-1970s, developers were drooling over
the possibility of buying the unbroken prairie and subdividing it for summer cottages.

But a few ranchers, plus members of the Enpro chapter of the National
Audubon Society in Jamestown, wanted to see swans floating on the lake
in the fall instead of water skiers, to hear grebes calling in the spring instead of roaring outboards, to find deer trails and coyote tracks along the
lake instead of beer cans.

Every species of waterfowl that nests in North Dakota nests here. Cottonwood trees that three men can barely reach around shelter deer, foxes,
horned owls, and other denizens of this prairie-woodland-lake zone. As
Aldo Leopold once observed, the right to find a pasque flower is a right
as inalienable as free speech. There are pasque flowers aplenty on this prairie sanctuary where their place in the sun and our right to find them is
assured for years to come.

In 1976 Audubon purchased 442 acres bordering the southwest side of
the lake. We hoped to eventually acquire and restore much of the rolling
prairie that was eroding rapidly.

JANUARY 1977 Our newest sanctuary is managed by our newest manager, Gary Pearson. A veterinarian with a keen interest in wildlife diseases, Gary worked on the outbreak of viral enteritis on Lake Andes National Wildlife Refuge three years ago and managed to keep the mallard mortality well below what it could have been.

Although his professional reputation couldn't be better, his opposition to some of the worst environmental pork barrel projects in North Dakota history incurred the wrath of old Senator Milton Young. Uncle Miltie told the U.S. Fish and Wildlife Service to "get that Pearson fellow out of North Dakota." When it comes to political power, the Refuge Division of the Fish and Wildlife Service is not in the same league with Senator Young.

Gary's refusal to be transferred resulted in his availability as an Audubon sanctuary manager. Old Dad was only too glad to take advantage of Gary's devotion to sound wildlife management. The Department of Interior's loss was National Audubon's gain. Thanks to the determined efforts of Gary, Audubon chapters in Jamestown, and Rich Madson, our regional representative, the massive irrigation project called Garrison Diversion, undertaken and promoted by the U.S. Bureau of Reclamation, was never completed, although we lost a few valuable marshes and prairie habitat before bringing the dragline shovels and bulldozers to a halt.

MARCH 1978 Myron Swenson grew up in Iowa, the land of big bluestem, blue-winged teal, black prairie soil, and tall corn. By the time he was born, the U.S. Department of Agriculture was busily draining every marsh and prairie slough wherein a teal or a muskrat might build a nest. Consequently, corn has replaced cattail over most of the Iowa prairie, and the white-tailed deer has given way to John Deere.

In spite of that, the prairie is in Myron's blood, and at Alkali Lake, he is working hard to save a remnant that has never been plowed, around a lake that provides nesting habitat for every species of duck in North Dakota. For the past year or so, Myron has been buying and selling prairie farms and has done so well at it that Old Dad was afraid we would be unable to lure him back into the fold. His secret of success is no secret: buy low and sell high.

This experience is very valuable at Alkali Lake just now, since there are still a couple of parcels needed to keep the summer cottages off the lakeshore. But alas! There is no such thing as buying low when it comes to prairie lands nowadays. In spite of North Dakota blizzards, droughts, depressed wheat markets, and the farmers' strike, land on which there is any possibility of grazing a cow or raising a crop has doubled in price in recent years.

Therefore, even though he knows prairie farms and farmers and how to deal with them, our newest warden faces a tremendous assignment in our effort to sew up the lakeshore and thereby save the lake. So far there are no motor boats or fishermen cluttering up the lake, which explains why you can see broods of canvasbacks, ruddy ducks, and redheads scattered about on a summer evening. This could change overnight if the wrong buyer gets in ahead of us and decides to subdivide the unbroken prairie on the lakefront.

Gary Pearson, our former Alkali Lake warden, decided he had to give his profession of veterinary medicine first priority—even over saving Alkali Lake—and so he resigned as of December 31, 1977. We hired Myron "High Pockets" Swenson, who claims he is no high-binder, even though his belt buckle may be almost four feet off the ground. He and Gary are old friends and keep in touch on all wildlife matters in general.

In addition to the deer, ducks, geese, and swans around the lake, the area is a very important sandhill crane staging ground. Last year the U.S. Fish and Wildlife Service was about to grant North Dakota a twelve-day season on cranes starting September 1. The reason given was that cranes were eating the farmers' wheat. The season had previously opened October 1, when the mighty nimrods were chasing ducks, geese, deer, and pheasants, and most of the cranes were gone. Old Dad recommended cutting the season back to five days, since they could wind up with a lot of hunters and a lot of cranes in the same area at the same time. This recommendation was adopted, but hunters still killed about five thousand cranes. This made the farmers and hunters and state Game Department very happy, but sandhill crane biologists reacted differently.

As is so often the case with Audubon wardens, Myron's greatest asset is his wife, Charlotte. She is from Jamestown, so she tolerates not only old High Pockets but she takes the North Dakota winters and dust storms in stride. What's more important, she understands us—the minority that believes the right to find a pasque flower is a right as inalienable as free speech.

MARCH 1979 As the sun went down over Alkali Lake on October 17, 1978, members of various Audubon chapters in North Dakota turned their attention from canoeing, birding, and botanizing to beef and bourbon. Myron Swenson's house on wheels, which he had driven out to the sanctuary, provided all the comforts of home while the pintails, wigeon, ruddies, and a red fox, two deer, and two pairs of great horned owls provided good reasons for being away from home. The brisk October wind was better meant for duck hunting than canoeing, but on that particular day on that particular lake, shotguns were out and canoes were in. So Old Dad kept his trigger finger wrapped around a paddle and pretended he was Edward M. Brigham III explaining to the populace how pasque flowers, pintails, and prairie lakes help soothe the pain in the pocketbook caused by the Garrison Diversion, the Starkweather, and the Oahe projects. (Ed Brigham is in charge of all regional representatives, but he pays much attention to North Dakota.)

After seven years, thousands of dollars, and countless frustrations endured by our staff, it appears that the Garrison project is on its last legs. If so (remember, old BuRec projects never die; they wait until their opponents do), it's time we get on with acquiring any available unbroken prairie bordering Alkali Lake and restoring the productivity of that which has been abused. The Northern Prairie Wildlife Research Station at Jamestown has some of the country's best range ecologists on its staff, who happen to be members of the Enpro chapter of National Audubon. They are eager to help with restoration of the native prairie.

We also believe that what the nature center division, under the capable leadership of Duryea Morton, has accomplished in other regions is entirely feasible for schools in the far, frozen north. Fighting boondoggles and applying gentle persuasion to suspicious Scandihoovian prairie farmers can be very time-consuming. We've also found that land acquisition can be very expensive, since it takes so many American dollars to equal the buying power of German marks and Japanese yen when it comes to the unbroken prairie.

Even if we can't wrap up the entire prairie perimeter of Alkali Lake, we can still demonstrate to keen young minds that on arid, submarginal lands a regime of *moderate* grazing and restoration of native prairie grasses can provide an income without destroying the land.

MARCH 1980 There is something to be said, and a lot that can't be, about a country full of Swedes. Last July, Paul Jensen replaced Myron Swenson as warden-biologist for our northernmost sanctuary, and the savannah sparrows, ground squirrels, and Scandihoovians had no trouble adjusting to the change. Paul, a high school science teacher from over

Fargo way, says he likes natural science and likes to teach, but he thinks a lake out on the prairie makes a better classroom than a building.

He started the summer like a good chemist should by analyzing the water of Alkali Lake. He finds the water not as strongly alkaline as we had expected, but more on the brackish or salty side. Paul had so much fun with his chemistry set that John Peterka, from North Dakota State University, got into the act and corroborated Paul's results.

Our Mr. Jensen then switched to botany and started recording and photographing vegetation on those areas that have never been plowed. His warden's report for August 8 says, "I was truly amazed at the diversity of prairie flowers on the east portion of the land we own. Spent several hours keying out plants I didn't know. Am making plans to camp out next week for the biological inventory." (A young bachelor can get away with this.)

On nearby Spiritwood Lake, many a summer cottage was built barely above water level in recent years. Comes the inevitable high-water period, and the cottage owners are in deep trouble. As a rule, engineers and county commissioners are easily persuaded to drain water from one group of victims and dump it on another. Just five years ago, the draglines were all set to dig a drainage canal from Spiritwood Lake into Alkali. Rich Madson and a group of farmers bordering Alkali took a dim view of this, and the project was stalled by order of the judge.

Last summer Spiritwood came up again, and our new warden had his chance to see Rich Madson and our attorney, plus affected landowners, in action. The County Water Management Board decided that this new drainage scheme was no better than the old one. Consequently, our sanctuary land bordering Alkali Lake is still producing bluestem and pasque flowers instead of sago pondweed.

Since we purchased some 442 acres about three years ago, we have reduced the grazing pressure and begun a gradual restoration of native prairie vegetation. In return for our efforts, we now have at least fourteen sharp-tailed grouse on the sanctuary where none existed for several years before its establishment.

Paul went back to school teaching last September, but will join us, probably on a permanent basis, come summer. Meanwhile, Gary Pearson patrolled the area during the fall hunting season. (Comes January to North Dakota and the sanctuary is pretty well patrolled by Old Man Winter.)

In his December 10 report, Gary said, "Another new species . . . is one we anticipated: a coyote was reported near the lake, and I have found coyote tracks. Of course, our 440 acres are not enough to assure survival of coyotes, but the appearance of one demonstrates the high wildlife value of the area. In addition to the sizable deer population, several red foxes, common raptors, passerines, and waterfowl, . . . at least thirty whistling swans were using the lake on November 7. On November 18, a bald eagle and a prairie falcon were sighted."

One of the key reasons for acquiring Alkali Lake was its diversity of prairie habitats and wildlife. The 16,000-acre Arrowwood National Wildlife Refuge northwest of Alkali Lake contains these same habitats and species, but we know of no other area, of the size National Audubon could hope to acquire, where native prairie, bald eagles, prairie falcons, coyotes, beaver, whistling swans, and white pelicans occur on the same lake. As Gary says, "It is truly exciting to speculate on the potential of the area if it could be managed as a complete wildlife sanctuary unit. It still might not be too late to include greater prairie chickens!"

MARCH 1981 For Paul Jensen, getting his feet wet as the new manager of Alkali Lake was like playing hookey from school. To a high school biology teacher, the sanctuary offers certain features not found in the laboratory. These include pasque flowers, big bluestem, Juneberries, white-tails, red-tails, and sharp-tails, plus every species of duck that nests in North Dakota.

On the 442 acres we already own, the gradual restoration of food and cover, plus the elimination of fall plowing and overgrazing, have been accompanied by a sharp-tailed grouse population of zero in 1977, fourteen in 1979, and twenty-two in 1980. In spring the ring-necked pheasants are strutting, crowing, fighting, and fertilizing in a manner satisfactory to bird-watchers and assuring the food supply of hootie owls, red foxes, and two-legged foxes.

The nearby Chase Lake National Wildlife Refuge boasts the world's largest concentration of nesting white pelicans. The yearling birds apparently learn the pelican trade in summer at Alkali and Arrowwood Lakes. In the case of pelicans, no one knows just when youth's sweet-scented manuscript doth close. Probably at age three or four, they take up pelican propagation over on Chase National Wildlife Refuge. In any case, Alkali Lake is very important in the formative years of big white satchel-mouths.

As is generally known, the most beautiful, most important, and most delectable birds in the world are the flat-faced fowl. (Old Dad is a waterfowl biologist. You'd never guess it, would you?) Broods of canvasbacks, redheads, mallards, pintails, gadwalls, wigeon, blue-wings, and green-wings learn to swim and fly at Alkali. When it forgets to rain, as it often does on the prairie, and the sun and wind dry up the thousands of small sloughs and potholes, then permanent lakes, such as Alkali, enable a nucleus of breeding ducks to survive the crisis. Such was the case last summer, and we sadly fear 1981 will be a repeat performance.

In recent years, we've had one bald eagle feeding on fish and fowl in the fall. Last year we had two, and they hung around until Old Man Winter persuaded them to leave the local folk in charge of things.

Because it was too dry to risk prescribed burning last summer, Gary Pearson suggested we knock back the grass cover by deliberately overgrazing a field for one month. Our friend, Jim Szarkowski, an adjacent landowner, put eighty-two head of cattle on the Attleson pasture for $420. This made controller Brian Bedell happy and—almost equally important—come spring of 1981 the lack of cover gave the desirable grasses a place in the sun. Otherwise, Kentucky bluegrass, which Tim Williams welcomes on the Buckley, would get a head start on Andropogon, Panicum, and Bouteloua. Getting what you want, where, and when you want it is the Audubon warden's secret of success.

Paul returned to the classroom last September, and Mark Allbrecht set up camp on the sanctuary during the deer and duck seasons. As is often the case, our protection of the deer herd is too effective for the critters' own good. In three years, the winter herd has gone from about twenty, to forty, to one hundred. Obviously we have a harvestable surplus that we want to shield from snow drifts, starvation, and other tools of the Grim Reaper. Rick Ashley says that Schlitz Audubon Center, near Milwaukee, does not want any deer. Durward Allen's timber wolves would rather stay on Isle Royale, so they are no help. Old Dad thinks the twanging of about five bowstrings for five days would sound good by the shores of Gitche Gumee.

Rich Madson has been making like a developer wanting to buy up the last rim of unbroken prairie around an unspoiled lake. The difference is that if Rich succeeds there will be canvasback nests instead of condominiums around the shore. We hope that when Paul Jensen returns in June, to become full-time manager, his canoe in the middle of Alkali Lake will be surrounded by nothing but Audubon sanctuary.

MARCH 1983 Leo Kirsch has long been known as one of the country's best range ecologists. His past experience as a national wildlife refuge manager and director of Woodworth Station of the Northern Prairie Wildlife Research Center and author of several papers on prairie restoration, the effects of grazing and prescribed burning on prairie wildlife, comes in very handy at Alkali Lake. Leo came on board as of July 1, 1982, a colorful character on a colorful sanctuary.

We have a leafy spurge problem at Alkali. Officially classified as a noxious weed, we must control it or the state will do it for us. Leo says he's never seen leafy spurge knocked out by spray alone. But a combination of herbicide plus fire may rid the sanctuary of an undesirable alien.

Assembling the necessary experienced manpower on a day when prairie winds are favorable for burning is not easy. Last fall we had to rely on hand spraying with herbicides a couple times, but this summer of 1983, *Euphorbia escula* is going to catch hell.

On August 10, Leo made a cursory inventory of the vegetation. He identified sixty-four natives and seven exotics. Relic stands of eighteen native grass species were noted. He suspects other native grasses were present but were missed during this rather hasty survey. More than forty species of forbs were identified. Leo says he is "confident that more were missed than were identified."

From his experience with mixed grass prairies in similar condition, he believes Alkali Lake may be restored rather rapidly by prescribed burning. His preliminary management plan outlines a program that has the potential to make the sanctuary a showcase we can be proud of.

Negotiating with landowners around Alkali Lake would have been a valuable experience for Secretary of State George Schultz before he tried to get the Middle East to come to terms. Nevertheless, the confidence the local farmers have in Leo is beginning to pay off handsomely. Parcels of unbroken prairie, other parcels that should never have been plowed, croplands that can be restored, and wetlands that have their own special values have been added to the sanctuary. Our objective is to acquire the entire lakeshore, so the canvasbacks and redheads won't have to compete with water-skiers. Our objective is now clearly in view.

MAY 1984 Because Leo Kirsch is an excellent range ecologist, it's not surprising that as part-time manager of Alkali Lake he can hardly find time to hunt prairie chickens, snipe, canvasbacks, deer, and other pursuits that compensate, in part, for North Dakota winters. Leo's report says, "At Christmas time, frigid arctic cold broke records—temperatures between thirty and forty below zero for most of ten nights. Wind chill temperatures of one hundred below were recorded, and minus sixty and minus seventy wind chills were common."

In March 1983, Leo gave a paper entitled "Historic Ecological Records of Great Plains Grasslands" at a symposium in Bismarck. He was on an advisory team at Crescent Lake National Wildlife Refuge in Nebraska, working on a grassland management plan. In Colorado he was asked to inspect prairie chicken areas and draw up research and management plans, helped draw up plans for restoration and management of prairie chickens in North Dakota, helped design the Habitat Evaluation Program for gadwall, blue-winged teal, and sharp-tailed grouse, and did a bit of editing for the *Wildlife Society Bulletin*.

In spite of such carryings on, our Alkali Lake sanctuary was not neglected. About 190 acres of native prairie that former owners had badly mistreated were prescribe burned to control exotic plants and restore the native ones. Our new boundaries were posted with new steel signs and posts. About 250 acres of land with a new house, grain bin, and pole barn were purchased. The services of our new legal eagle, Gene Ruane, were invaluable in that transaction, as well as in negotiations with other landowners. While pressure from cattlemen is putting more cows on many federal refuges, the reverse is true at Alkali Lake, and a trespass grazing problem has been solved.

On October 24, Leo counted about six thousand snow geese on the sanctuary. They stayed about two weeks, feeding on harvested fields both on and off the area. The goose hunters had lots of fun trying, but Leo says the harvest was not high. The birds finally headed for the Paul J. Rainey in Louisiana, where the climate is more hospitable.

About 30 white-tailed deer spent the summer on the sanctuary. On February 14, 1984, an aerial census came up with 106. No depredation complaints have been registered, but some neighboring farmers are apprehensive about the size of the herd.

Leo established four photo stations on the burned prairie, and pretreatment photos were taken. In the past, National Audubon has played the leading role in saving plume birds, Everglade kites, whooping cranes, bald eagles, and Mexican sabal palms from extinction. It is fairly easy to get folks worked up about glamour-pusses such as whooping cranes and grizzly bears. But nobody cries when habitat dies. After pounding rains last July, some of our newly acquired lands, mistreated by former owners, were devastated by erosion. For someone who loves the prairie, this is just cause for homicide. But since capital punishment of those who murder plant communities is frowned upon, the next best thing is to begin the steady but sure process of prairie restoration. We will set up a schedule of areas to be restored each year for many years. We hope we can handle from one hundred to two hundred acres annually.

On April 1, 1984, Bruce Barbour and his wife, Carmen Luna, arrive from California condor country. At last we have a full-time manager for this chunk of northern lake and prairie. Although Bruce and Carmen have been in the Research Department for a few years, the association with characters such as Sandy Sprunt and John Ogden has done no permanent damage. But going to Florida, to southern California, to North Dakota — well, now — no one but an Audubon warden could survive it or even try it. Comes next December and Carmen (who started out in Puerto Rico) may be calling Marie Strom, on the Rowe sanctuary in Nebraska, about games people play when it's fifty below.

Sandy and John say both Bruce and Carmen are very versatile, competent researchers. Dusty Dunstan came by to explain what's expected of Audubon wardens. The Northern Prairie Wildlife Research Station is nearby, and we will continue some joint projects with it. Bruce is primarily a waterfowl biologist (Is there any other kind?) and is looking forward to a sanctuary all cluttered up with nesting ducks plus all those geese, swans, and cranes that come by in spring and fall. Bruce happens to be a decoy carver, both working decoys and decorative. He also has a respectable collection of fowling pieces. Now what on earth is a waterfowl man gonna do with such stuff in North Dakota?

JULY 1984   Bruce Barbour and Carmen Luna arrived at Alkali Lake on April 1. Although T. S. Eliot says, "April is the cruelest month, breeding lilacs out of the dead land, mixing memory and desire . . .," the lesser Canada geese, giant Canada geese, snow geese, swans, upland sandpipers, and Lapland longspurs kept coming and going. Canvasbacks, redheads, mallards, pintails, wood ducks, and other flat-faced fowl started nesting. Bruce and Carmen say they never enjoyed such cruelty so much.

But when you take an abandoned prairie farm with its barns, machine sheds, beat-up pastures, and eroded croplands and convert them into an Audubon sanctuary by restoring the native grasses and providing suitable habitat for the native fauna, you don't have much time for contemplating the scene allowed for your demesne.

Carmen is a talented artist; Bruce, an experienced research biologist. Summer 1984 saw Carmen painting the porch and applying hammer and saw to improve the landscape. With truck, tractor, front-end loader, and other delicate tools, Bruce was determined to demonstrate that the same equipment that destroyed the prairie could be used to restore it.

In May cliff swallows and barn swallows delayed certain repairs to the barn. Spreading gravel on the driveway had to wait until the colony of bank swallows got out of the gravel pit. But there was plenty to do without busting up the birdies' lifestyles.

Birding for pure dee-light would not look good on a warden's monthly report. On the other hand, every management plan calls for a checklist of birds, mammals, reptiles, and plants, so while Bruce keeps his hand on the throttle, and Carmen keeps hers on the brush, they both keep their eyes, ears, and notebooks open. It's hardship duty, but someone's gotta do it.

And from their duck blind on Alkali Lake, they shot many a duck in beautiful breeding plumage, with camera that is. Carmen's photo of a wood duck won second prize in a Jamestown photo contest; all of which will liven up the lectures in the months ahead. Many a lone drake defended his territory on the sanctuary in May, indicating the presence of an incubating hen nearby. Unfortunately, when most of the land in North Dakota is black and bare, with clouds of dust following the tractors, about the only animal protein a hungry fox, skunk, or coon can find is around the marsh. Instead of hatching eight or ten pale green eggs, many a mallard hen winds up greasing the chin of Brer Fox. The Northern Prairie Wildlife Research Center says only five percent nesting success is about average for puddle ducks in North Dakota nowadays.

On June 19, Bruce spent a day on Arrowwood National Wildlife Refuge helping find duck nests and recording their fate. It being late in the season, blue-winged teal and gadwalls were the most common nesters. In one experimental area of eighty acres, surrounded by an electric fence and small-mesh hardware cloth, about 95 percent of the nests hatched, while the other areas with no protection had virtually zero success.

Mallards, pintails, canvasbacks, and redheads are in trouble. Prairie-nesters in the u.s. have lost over half of their nesting marshes, and Canada is rapidly following our example. Recent droughts and heavy harvest by hunters compound the problem. Bruce figures that his flat-faced friends have troubles enough without such prominent place on a raccoon's bill of fare.

Down on Green Island, Texas, Friday Fluman convinces the coons that wading out to the island is a mistake. Alkali Lake has not only coons but beaucoup foxes, striped skunks, and ground squirrels—all of them very fond of ducks, ducklings, and eggs. Bruce has plans for a few islands to be built in the lake, and last winter he hauled several bales of flax straw out on the ice, which serve as nesting islands in spring. Nest boxes for wood ducks are sprouting around the lakeshore. As a result of such goings on, Alkali Lake was one of the most productive waterfowl areas in North Dakota this summer.

Bruce says that ducks and diplomacy go together. Farmers are just naturally suspicious of outsiders who'd druther raise ducks and deer than cows and corn. But Bruce and Carmen have made much headway on this problem, seeing as how Terry Schwartz is willing to come over with tractor and pull our manager out of a snowbank in the middle of the night at twenty below. And another neighbor is going to try these new-fangled ideas of no-till farming and leaving food and cover for wildlife.

This summer our control-burned areas are already looking healthier than surrounding farms, and our neighbors take note of same. So do the upland sandpipers.

For October 16 to 25, 1984, Bruce reports, "Worked with Joe Edmondson and Steve McHenry, cutting and framing garage doors, electrical wiring in the pole barn, garage, and red barn for lights and outlets for power tools and engine block heaters, putting up a storm door, water spigot on side of house, etc." Our SWAT team, under Papa Joe's supervision, does get around. (Steve takes care of Hunt Hill in Wisconsin.)

On May 22–24, 1985, Old Dad and Eddie Brigham are on hand to help Leo Kirsch with prescribed burning plus inventory of nesting waterfowl, upland sandpipers, sharp-tailed grouse, and Famous Grouse.

SEPTEMBER 1986 We assume there was a time when geese were more important than girls to Bruce Barbour. And in those days, the giant Canada goose (*Branta canadensis maxima*) was considered extinct by most experts. In fact, they were completely extirpated in the Dakotas by the early 1900s. Then in 1962–1963, Harold Hanson, well-known ornithologist from the Illinois Natural History Survey, found a small population breeding in southern Manitoba and wintering in Rochester, Minnesota. Since then, the big honkers have been restored throughout much of their former range.

Because Alkali Lake and Anseriformes were meant for each other, Bruce allows as how giant Canadas should follow the example of eight species of ducks that nest there. With the help of North Dakota biologists and neighbors, a front-end loader, tractor, snowplow, and two feet of ice, he manages to get eleven bales of flax straw out on the frozen lake.

And when a brighter iris changes on the burnish'd dove, the ice melts, the bales settle to the bottom in shallow water, and the giant Canadas think these islands of life were meant for them. By May 11, 1986, three pairs of geese were incubating. As the weeks went by and summer came on, about sixty broods of various ducks were using the lake.

Bruce and Carmen were not so intent on waterfowl that they failed to add black-billed magpie to the sanctuary list on November 13, 1985. On New Year's Day, Carmen saw two coyotes, one red fox, and eleven sharp-tailed grouse, and the magpie had found the bird feeder.

On January 9, 1986, the trees in the shelter belt north of their house sheltered forty Bohemian waxwings. On February 24, a chinook wind blew in, driving the mercury into the seventies, and all the wintering snow buntings headed for Canada. On March 29, the first pasque flower bloomed, and the white-fronted geese came back from Louisiana. In early April, the place was cluttered up with big flocks of ruddy ducks, canvasbacks, bluebills, snow geese, tundra swans, and winged vermin such as bald eagles, sharp-shinned hawks, roughlegs, and so on. (Vermin, a term of endearment so often used by poultry farmers.)

April 15 brings a blizzard and Karl Bednarik, from the Lake Erie marshes, to review Bruce's management program. A day or so after the storm, Karl reports that we have the right man and woman in the right place doing the right thing. Karl also says Bruce could use a few more hours in the day, some extra hands, and more of the prairie wetlands around the lake that we do not own. Karl was one of a team of professional wildlife managers hired to review our entire sanctuary program.

On May 3, a yellow rail provided a new record, and we trust board member Howard Brokaw will take due note of same. The last we knew, this birder, with six hundred plus species on his list, had not seen one.

Golden plovers arrived May 12. On May 22, three pairs of bluebirds arrived, a Canada goose brought off her brood of goslings, while another giant Canada was incubating a nest of mallard eggs! Bruce doesn't know just how or when this came about. Anyway, on June 7 the old gander and goose were proudly protecting a brood of eight mallards. Says Bruce, "It's a wise duckling that knows its own father."

Now it may be biologically sound to reduce an overpopulation of deer through starvation, but from the public relations standpoint, it just isn't done. So a combination of weekly trips to Wimbledon for free grain provided by the State Fish and Wildlife Department, plus a limited bow hunting season (eleven permits) and a limited gun season (twenty-two permits) pacifies the local citizenry but reduces the herd by only six deer. Sub-zero temperatures, six feet of snow, and high winds make the deer-slayer abandon the forest in favor of Old Forester. Deer, oh dear.

Bruce says Governor Sinner is not about to let money from the Garrison Diversion agreement be used to acquire wetlands if he can help it. Nor is the Bureau of Reclamation going to sit idly by while their dreams of reservoirs, canals, and irrigation of already productive farmland come to a rude awakening. Consequently, Bruce in North Dakota must make like Ken Strom in Nebraska, who must fight politicians to save the Rowe Sanctuary on the Platte River. Hundreds of miles to drive, meetings to attend, letters to write, programs to give. While the promoters fight over the flow of water and federal funds, every severe wind or rain moves more topsoil from the rolling hills into the wetlands.

"Don't try to tell me how to farm, sonny. I wore out two farms before you was even born."

JANUARY 1988 Ecologists have long known that there are millions of acres of prairie in North Dakota that never should have been plowed. But no one is more painfully aware of this sad truth than Bruce Barbour. A case in point is the heavy rain in May 1986 on which Bruce reported, "Deep gullies and mud deposition in those wetlands surrounded by tilled land was everywhere in evidence. On the sanctuary, much nutrient, pesticide, fertilizer, and topsoil-laden water entered the lake at the north end from the Hoggarth brothers' tilled hillsides. Also two smaller wetlands south of the lake were partly silted in by topsoil from adjacent tilled croplands." If we paid farmers to deliberately get rid of their topsoil, they could hardly do it any faster.

Water conditions were good throughout North and South Dakota in 1986. If there had been ample nesting cover and normal predator pressure, production of flat-faced fowl, coots, and marsh wrens would have been excellent. But there is very little cover except on lands too wet to plow. Here the ducks must nest and here the skunks, foxes, and raccoons hunt for groceries. Consequently, waterfowl biologists refer to North Dakota as "the black hole." About 95 percent of all duck nests are destroyed, which is one reason pintail, mallard, and blue-winged teal numbers are the lowest in thirty-one years.

While most privately owned land in North Dakota is eroding at a frightening rate, the native vegetation is largely eliminated, and the black soil is lying bare and exposed to the wind in fall and winter, there is one outstanding exception; and that is the Edward M. Brigham Alkali Lake Sanctuary.

On October 5, 1987, a very impressive ceremony took place when the sanctuary was dedicated to the memory of Ed Brigham. Eddie loved the prairie and especially Alkali Lake as much as we loved him. There are those in and around Jamestown, plus members of Audubon and Audubon staff, who will work a little harder knowing there is a lake on the prairie known as the Edward M. Brigham Sanctuary.

As we learned at the Research Ranch in Arizona, any deviation from the accepted local land abuse is looked upon as the works of the evil one. It would not do for Bruce to try to tell his neighbors what soil erosion costs in dollars and ducks. On the other hand, if he quietly goes about planting dense nesting cover on the eroding hills, planting trees as windbreaks, erecting nest baskets and tubs for mallards and Canada geese, and plugging the drainage ditches, the response by flat-faced fowl is easy to see. Waterfowl hunters, bird-watchers, biology teachers, and tired housewives find there is something sort of comforting in seeing a brood of fuzzy ducklings. They even notice that land does not wash away on the Ed Brigham Sanctuary.

But when it comes to bringing a suspicious neighbor around to your way of thinking, nothing does it like bluebirds. (Art Gingert, manager of the Miles in Sharon, Connecticut, learned this years ago.) One neighbor, whose farm is strategically located, has what Lonnie Legé, from Louisiana, calls "l'esprit constipé." He and his family want nothing to do with Audubon; he figures they all come from New York, and that's all he needs to know.

Then one day in May, the missus sees a male bluebird in full sunlight messing around one of those boxes on the fence. And beyond the fence, she can see broods of canvasbacks, redheads, and mallards. It's amazing the effect of a male bluebird on a female human. So she calls up our audible-boy-bird-watcher for information about nest boxes for bluebirds, mallards, and geese. Bruce manages to supply same and eventually is able to discuss a conservation easement on the family farm. The lad works in mysterious ways.

When it's January in Jamestown, most of the mallards, blessed with a migratory urge, find themselves in Arkansas. Bruce may not possess an instinct to migrate, but he has a wife who was raised in Puerto Rico. Being a dutiful son-in-law, he and Carmen spent their January vacation with her parents. It was definitely not hardship duty.

As proof that elevated nest baskets, hay bales, and nest boxes frustrate the foxes, twenty-two Canada geese fledged on the Ed Brigham in 1987, along with dozens of broods of dabbling and diving ducks. Red-tailed, Swainson's, and ferruginous hawks fared well. Sharp-tailed grouse, upland sandpipers, ring-necked pheasants, and gray partridges nested successfully in the restored native prairie and a mixture of grasses known as dense nesting cover. In just four years, 274 acres of cropland have been converted to wildlife habitat, the remnants of native prairie is being rejuvenated by removal of cattle and periodic rotational burning, four wetlands have been restored, and a handful of North Dakota farmers don't hate the word "conservation" as much as they did.

NOVEMBER 1988 Bruce Barbour takes note of Gene Knoder's Mohave rattlesnakes and masked bobwhites on the Research Ranch in Arizona near the Mexican border and Pete DeSimone's mountain lions and condominiums on the Starr Ranch on the Pacific Coast. But for blizzards, dust storms, hard-headed farmers, and flat-faced fowl, the greatest display is up Canada way.

While soil erosion, wetland drainage, and other man-made disasters continue to ravage North Dakota, the diversity of wildlife and the stability and fertility of the soil on the sanctuary have steadily increased since Bruce and Carmen took over on April 1, 1984. We now have about nine hundred acres of highly erodible former cropland that have been planted to soil-binding grasses. The latter are either native prairie grasses, such as bluestem, Indian grass, and switch grass, or a mixture known as dense nesting cover. In any of these grasses, the probability that a nest will be destroyed by a predator is reduced from 99 percent to about 30 percent or less.

In August–September 1988, a choice parcel of 263 acres of adjacent native prairie, wetland, and some cropland was purchased. Some of this cropland will be seeded to native grasses next year. Selected units of our native prairie were prescribe burned, which benefits native grasses and prevents encroachment of exotics such as Kentucky bluegrass. In the past, ditches to drain prairie sloughs were subsidized by taxpayers. Fortunately, it is not impractical to plug the ditches or dig up buried drain tiles, although the engineering must be done right. In 1988 Bruce completed three projects for a total of eight so far.

When a vertical bank is graded, it is degraded as far as a colony of bank swallows is concerned. The colony at Ed Brigham Alkali Lake is back in business, thanks to restoration of the bank.

The lion far outweighed the lamb in March 1988. Bruce reports, "The twenty-seventh was the worst with forty-five mile per hour winds and incredible amounts of blowing topsoil—in places and at times visibility was below one-half mile—a blizzard of dirt." But that dirt did not come from the sanctuary.

But the March weather could not stop the arrival of hawks, ducks, swans, snow and Canada geese, bluebirds, doves, and shorebirds. The wildlife has responded very well to management. A few examples: giant Canada geese fledged 27 goslings from the flax straw bales. Wood ducks and hooded mergansers hatched over 240 ducklings in the nest boxes. Purple martins nested successfully for the first time in the new apartment houses.

Especially gratifying was a dancing ground established by thirteen sharp-tailed grouse on newly established dense nesting cover. The dancing resulted in several broods seen throughout the summer. As our native grasslands and seeded grasslands increase both in quality and quantity, they are accompanied by increases in nesting upland sandpipers, gray partridges, pheasants, many species of native sparrows, and ducks. Badgers, coyotes, rabbits, and small mammals are also on the increase.

For reasons not yet fully explained, predation by coyotes on nesting ducks is considerably less than is the case with the red fox. Fortunately, coyotes do not look with favor on the presence of foxes, all of which increases the hatching rate of our flat-faced fowl. So whenever Bruce and Carmen hear coyotes rendering a few hymns and vespers 'neath the prairie moon they listen with approval.

The Jamestown Cub Scouts are exposed to carpentry and wildlife management at the sanctuary. They construct bluebird boxes, and in late March they are on hand to help Bruce put them up. Admittedly, some boxes needed a bit of remodeling by volunteer Kathy Kraft. Nevertheless, bluebird boxes number 60 through 65 were erected on our own and neighbors' fence lines. A photograph and caption appeared in the *Jamestown Sun* about the program. Bruce reported the arrival of one male bluebird on March 31, 1988, at the south end of the sanctuary. Next day this hardy individual was singing at headquarters, although there was still some ice in Alkali Lake. Black-capped chickadees and house wrens also took up residence in appropriate boxes, as did sparrow hawks and screech owls.

By May 1988, Bruce reported, "The entire prairie pothole region is in severe drought condition, the driest since dust bowl days in the 1930s. . . .

ducks are exhibiting a very lackluster breeding attempt. Many females are not even attempting to nest. Molting male mallards were seen in flocks in late May–early June." These drakes were going into the eclipse molt about a month early, which is bad news.

In spite of the drought, some new species were added to the sanctuary list in May, including a broad-winged hawk, a snowy egret, Say's phoebe (territorial), and two American avocets.

As in the case of all sanctuary managers, Bruce was called upon to give several lectures and lead field trips for visitors, including two from France and Denmark.

The restored grasslands, once well established, can withstand severe drought. The 212 acres of dense nesting cover planted last summer will probably have to be replanted because of the hottest, driest year on record. But the 239 acres planted in 1987 and 35 planted in 1986 appear to be in excellent condition. In those plantings, for the first time in years, we have nesting bobolinks, northern harriers, and dickcissels.

Should the Sanctuary Department ever decide on an award for "Most Patient Wife," Carmen might come in first, albeit in a crowded field. For May 1988, Bruce reports "Because of extremely high winds and blowing topsoil and Russian thistle (tumbleweed), considerable time and aggravation was spent cleaning wind-blown dirt from the house, porches, shop, garage, and pole barn. Thistles piled almost to residence roof, completely filling the space between house and shelter belt. With the front-end loader, thistles were pushed into seven large piles and burned."

By September, snow geese and lesser Canada geese were coming in along with tundra swans, canvasbacks, and other flat-faced fowl.

On October 12, 1988, a lone whooping crane is sighted in Kidder County, northwest of the sanctuary. A mink with a thirteen-lined ground squirrel in its mouth adds to the general interest and inventory on the sanctuary. And, in his spare time, Bruce went over to Arrowwood National Wildlife Refuge and helped trap and band about three hundred wood ducks.

DECEMBER 1989 For over forty years, the federal government, through the Army Corps of Engineers, the Soil Conservation Service, and Bureau of Reclamation has worked feverishly at draining prairie wetlands. Tax incentives to plow up virgin prairie and subsidized payment for surplus grain kept North Dakota farmers happy and voting for more of the same.

Bruce Barbour says Hosea was right: "For they have sown the wind, and they shall reap the whirlwind." In 1988 and 1989, the drought, wind, and occasional rains washed and blew the topsoil off the hillsides into roadside ditches, marshes, and lakes. Bruce says he can't turn the entire state around, but at least he can show those who are interested that their land can produce all kinds of flat-faced fowl, sharp-tailed grouse, upland plovers, gray partridges, bluebirds, chickadees, swallows, deer, rabbits, and such. If they are so inclined, they can graze—but not overgraze—cattle and still keep the topsoil on the hillside.

When it was thirty below with a wind chill of eighty below, Bruce hoped for heavy snow followed by heavy spring rains. He got a fair amount in March, but the dry soil absorbed it like a sponge, leaving very little to fill the prairie potholes. May 1989 was windy with much blowing soil, but good rains fell during the last week. On the sanctuary, both the native prairie and Bruce's seeded grasslands responded well with good nesting cover developing rapidly.

Unlike 1988, when most ducks didn't even try to nest, they were actively seeking suitable nest sites by late May. Unfortunately, except on the sanctuary and state and federal refuges, there was no nesting cover around the ponds. It had been plowed under in 1988 and may take two or three years to recover.

On Uncle Sam's birthday, the morning hit 101 degrees, and the next day, 108 degrees. Both were record highs for those dates. This was the second hottest July on record; only 1936 was even warmer. On September 17, 1989, it hit 92 degrees to tie the record, followed six days later by the first frost. Bruce says he can't control the weather, but he can modify its effects on wild plants and animals.

In the drought of 1988, farmers in North Dakota flexed their political muscles and were allowed to hay every green sprig of grass and graze cattle on land that had never been grazed before except by buffalo. So in the spring of 1989, Ed Brigham sanctuary has about the only nesting cover for miles around. To increase the carrying capacity for wildlife, Bruce plants dense nesting cover on selected areas and continues to convert former cropland to grass, which controls erosion. By August 1989, a total of 595 acres had been converted to good cover.

Ditches, which in times past had destroyed habitat for waterfowl, are plugged, and ponds are restored. The u.s. Fish and Wildlife Service assists with these projects and actually pays Audubon fifty dollars per restored wetland! The North Dakota Wildlife Department also cooperated. Perhaps the most valuable assistance comes from Ducks Unlimited, which did the surveying and engineering for building dams and creating ponds. And in spite of the inevitable red tape in dealing with the USDA, Bruce gets cooperation from the SCS, ASCS, and gets 450 acres of sanctuary land in the Conservation Reserve Program. Imagine those ag departments spending money to restore marshes, not destroy them!

But as all sanctuary managers know, you can't spend all your time working with wild plants and animals if you want the land to be treated with love and respect. You must cultivate some missionaries. Which explains why Bruce donates a few nest boxes to legislators and school-teachers, keeps local activists informed, lectures to service clubs, does a barbecue for those who volunteer labor and equipment, erects a photo-observation blind by the grouse dancing grounds, loans Audubon videos to various locals, and frequently leads field trips. Judging from the way the wild critters and humans are responding, his overall program has made a difference.

NOVEMBER 1991 In chemistry a catalytic agent speeds up a process without being used by it. In North Dakota waterfowl and wetland management, the Ed Brigham Alkali Lake Sanctuary is a catalyst; Bruce Barbour, the master chemist. When you see the USFWS, Ducks Unlimited, and National Audubon creating an island in Alkali Lake, you're seeing something new under the sun.

The once-fabulous duck-producing wetlands of North Dakota have largely been converted to subsidized surplus wheat and barley. The plight of the flat-faced fowl is exacerbated by recent years of severe drought. The majority of farmers, the governor, and state legislators look upon non-agricultural use of water and prairie grasses as downright sacrilegious. There is ample evidence that this attitude borders on hatred for those who think otherwise.

On the other hand, a growing number of people appreciate the value of wetlands and wildlife. They are beginning to take pride in the sanctuary and to highly approve of the cooperation between Audubon, DU, and state and federal agencies.

After seeing and hearing about the sanctuary wildlife management, residents of nearby Spiritwood Lake have built and put up wood duck boxes, one hundred bluebird-tree swallow boxes, and flax straw bales for nesting geese.

In May there were ten avocet nests, a new record for the sanctuary, on the island created by DU for waterfowl and shorebirds. In fifty-nine wood duck boxes, there were sixteen duck nests with 176 young and nine hooded mergansers with 108 eggs that hatched, making 1991 the record year for duck and goose production. In March a saw-whet owl (another new record) took up residence in a duck box and stayed about a month.

OCTOBER 1994 While the people pressure on Starr Ranch and Sabal Palm Grove is such that, in the long run, survival of the native plants and animals cannot be taken for granted, Bruce Barbour finds a different situation around Alkali Lake. There are far fewer people per square mile, but there has been a dangerous threat to the prairie and prairie wetlands since the first Europeans arrived.

A prairie slough, if not drained, will produce ducks but not wheat or sunflowers. For many decades, the Soil Conservation Service vied with the Bureau of Reclamation to see which could get the most money to drain the most marshes. Draining thousands of small reservoirs that held the rain where it fell contributed to the floods in the Mississippi Valley. Even the engineers are probably aware of this but won't admit it.

Perhaps nowhere in North America have love and respect for the land been so slow to develop as in North Dakota. If you associate long enough with enough North Dakota farmers, you will detect an attitude bordering on fear and hatred of the prairie, as though the prairie grasses and wetlands are an enemy, a threat to the health, happiness, and pocketbook of the landowner. Exposing fertile hillsides to wind and water erosion, draining every prairie pothole, and bitterly criticizing the "environmental extremists" is considered sacred duty by many North Dakota farmers.

The U.S. Fish and Wildlife Service, hoping to buy or lease prairie wetlands for waterfowl production areas, has been stopped in its tracks by the collective power of the farmers. To the pleasant surprise of all concerned, Edward T. Schafer, current governor of North Dakota, does not fit the mold. He is a businessman, not a politician. He can and does approve of setting aside wetlands and supports the Conservation Reserve Program, which pays farmers to leave highly erodible land alone. Bruce commends and encourages the governor.

Fortunately for native plants and animals, pressure from the one mammal that destroys its own environment and outstrips its food supply is kept relatively low in North Dakota. The winter of 1993–1994 offers an explanation. "Ground blizzards" of blowing snow often bring visibility down to zero, while the temperature is often far below zero with a frequent wind chill factor of minus seventy-five degrees. Rural mail delivery cannot get through for days at a time because of snow drifts higher than a car, which means Bruce has ample time to keep abreast of the scientific literature. But nothing is forever. One week, March winds bring a promise of spring, with a holdover of winter the following week. Snow melt fills all of the small restored wetlands on the Ed Brigham Alkali Lake Sanctuary, which makes for the best waterfowl production in over a decade.

Maintaining this wildlife oasis in a hostile environment wins the praise of locals and many contributors. Notable among the latter are $140,000 from the Warren Compton estate, plus $16,750 from Michael Roach in memory of his aunt. We must be doing something right at Ed Brigham Alkali Lake.

JULY 1997 Having overcome Germany in World War II, the u.s. Bureau of Reclamation, the so-called Soil Conservation Service, and the Army Corps of Engineers declared war on the millions of prairie potholes and native vegetation. It is relatively easy to get people worked up over saving species with feathers, fins, and fur, but very few cry when habitats die.

Bruce and Carmen Barbour have listened and acted accordingly when respected range ecologist Harold Duebbert said, "Any time you're ready to restore the prairie grasses that never should have been plowed in the first place, we have learned how to do it."

Bruce worked with the late Leo Kirsch in prescribed burning and prairie grass management. And thanks to their determination, our leafy spurge problem has been brought under control, and we want to keep it that way. Bruce had restored eight wetlands by 1988, and about seventy small basins on the sanctuary will eventually be restored and filled with water.

When Bruce and Carmen joined the u.s. Fish and Wildlife Service in 1997, we can truthfully say they left the Edward Alkali Lake better than they found it. There are a growing number of North Dakotans who appreciate the value of wetlands and wildlife, including the current governor, and hundreds of restored small wetlands and nest structures that provide safe habitat for various flat-faced fowl. What more can we say?

❧ 14 ☙

FRANCIS BEIDLER

FOREST SANCTUARY

Harleyville, South Carolina

The original Four Hole Swamp in South Carolina, located about forty miles northwest of Charleston, covered about forty thousand to fifty thousand acres. In this swamp, the legendary Francis Marion, a.k.a. the Swamp Fox, and his guerrilla troop known as Marion's Brigade are said to have frustrated and defeated the British several times during the Revolutionary War.

The dominant tree species were cypress and tupelo gum. By the mid-1900s, almost the entire forest had been logged off; in some cases even the second-growth had been cut.

Fortunately, in the heart of the Low Country, about 3,900 acres of this virgin forest belonged to Francis Beidler of Chicago, an unconventional lumberman of his time, who wanted to preserve this remnant of what-used-to-be. On December 31, 1969, the National Audubon Society, with some financial help from The Nature Conservancy, acquired the property from the Beidler estate.

This tract of virgin cypress-tupelo forest is the last and largest in the nation. As is still true of every unique wilderness area, the Four Hole Swamp was under threat. In those days the Soil Conservation Service was busy turning wetlands into farmland. Straightening or "channelizing" streams was their frequent and perhaps most costly practice. The water quality of the channelized river was usually adversely affected.

To measure the effect of a project upstream from Beidler, we tested the chemistry and aquatic flora and fauna of the sanctuary streams. Our data are highly essential in bringing wetland destruction to a halt. We will continue to monitor the limnology of Four Hole Swamp for the foreseeable future.

Old Dad interviewed several professional wildlife managers and finally selected Norman Brunswig, who had earned his master of science in wildlife biology from the University of Georgia. On September 1, 1973, Norm became manager of Beidler forest Sanctuary.

Norm proceeded to cruise the timber in the sanctuary, determining the species of trees, their size and value, surveying and marking the boundaries, getting acquainted with our neighbors, and hiring a competent staff. The following from *Places to Hide and Seek* will bring you up to date.

JULY 1976 Norm Brunswig never gets to say, "Ho hum! Day in, day out, these same four walls!" He has about three thousand five hundred acres in which to dodge cottonmouth moccasins, copperheads, and an occasional canebrake rattler. According to our number one snake hunter, Jim Rod at Constitution Island in New York, the canebrake is the same species (*Crotalus horridus*) that Art Gingert has on the Emily Winthrop Miles in Connecticut, but the South Carolina climate and moonshine make the canebrake act meaner than the Yankee variety. Norm is also on the lookout for the race of the pygmy rattler that is bright brick red in contrast to the gray-brown curlicues in Corkscrew Swamp in Florida. Norm doesn't keep his eyes on the ground, however, since within the sanctuary he has the world's largest tract (about one thousand five hundred acres) of virgin tupelo-cypress to look after.

One fine day in May, Elvis Stahr, president of Audubon, Carlyle Blakeney, NAS regional representative, and Old Dad, along with three trustees of the Whittell Estate dropped in to thread their way by canoe through the winding shallow channels and hike the route of the boardwalk that we will start building this fall. Since one of the trustees, Jack Harper, is an ardent birder, Norm made sure the prothonotary warblers did their stuff. When it was lunchtime, special thanks were given to Norm's wife, Beverly, and to the Schlitz Brewery for seeing to it that we survived the Four Hole Swamp.

The Holly Hill Lumber Company has claimed title to a tract of virgin timber within the sanctuary boundary, and our legal eagles have decided it would be costly and risky to settle the issue in court. The lumber company has offered to give us half the disputed land and sell us the other half, and we've accepted.

When Norm is not making like a forester cruising timber or like a lawyer looking up deeds in the courthouse, he takes regular water samples and runs the limnological tests at the South Carolina Wildlife and Marine Lab. This is to check on the effects of a channelization project by the Soil Conservation Service in the Horse Range Swamp upstream. Tom Logan, assistant sanctuary director, who's had considerable experience checking water quality in Oklahoma, put his knowledge of statistics to work on Norm's data. He allows as how the final results will probably show that the channelization project kept a few bulldozer and dragline operators busy and drained a swamp that should not have been drained, but is too far upstream to have effects on the Four Hole that we can measure. We shall see.

Meanwhile, Norm has been working with Russ Hall of Mansfield College, Pennsylvania, who is making a record of what we have and how many in the reptile and amphibian department. A botanical survey by Dr. Porcher of the Citadel will give us an inventory of the vegetation. Norm could do these inventories himself; trouble is there are only twenty-four hours in a day, and he and Doug Clayton, an assistant warden, also collect aquatic insect samples and preserve the creepy-crawlies for later analysis. These bugs are also sensitive indicators of water quality.

In his spare time, Norm works with Doug, while the landscape and building architects pore over blueprints for the visitor center and boardwalk. Comes the hunting season, and Doug, a veteran deer hunter and wise in the ways of poachers, heads them off at the pass.

Since it will cost about $30,000 to build the boardwalk, Carlyle Blakeney put his promotional talents to work and persuaded the various chapters in his region and elsewhere to "buy a foot of boardwalk for $5." In addition to the thousands of mailings made by Carlyle, he and Norm have been barnstorming the region with microphone and slide projector extolling the beauties of the Beidler. They've been collectin' nothin' but money. We think they'll reach the $30,000 mark if their ever-lovin' wives don't get lonely too soon.

When it comes time to build the boardwalk, we're depending on Jerry Cutlip from Corkscrew Swamp in Florida to be able to spare the expert services of Charlie Grimes, Ed Carlson, David Weeks, and himself to help see that it gets done and done right. Work on the approach road and parking lot for the visitor center is already under way.

JULY 1977 Old Busy Brunswig outdid himself in recent months. The silence of the swamp was shattered by sounds of hammering and sawing as Norm, Steve Winton, Doug Clayton, and John Price mucked around midst the cottonmouths, mosquitoes, and cypress knees. Thus, the boardwalk, which will soon be carrying hundreds of people (we hope) to Goodson Lake and back to the visitor center, grew at a rate of about one hundred feet per day.

Corkscrew Swamp's champion boardwalk builder, Charlie Grimes, decided Margaret Sprunt, returning to her home in Charleston, should not make the trip alone, so he made like a chauffeur. From Charleston 'twas but a short run to the Four Hole Swamp wherein the last section of the boardwalk was taking shape on a late afternoon in May. Since Charlie was in on the start and finish of this project, the men decided this historic occasion should be celebrated in his honor. Charlie made a few appropriate remarks as all the hammering and sawing gave way to popping of corks. A moment of reverent silence was followed by wild cheering that was followed by a bit of a tea party.

There will be a second celebration on the boardwalk, somewhat less auspicious, when the formal dedication takes place along in late October or early November. By then the temperature and the mosquitoes should be on the decline and our attendance on the increase. President Stahr, members of the Beidler family, Carlyle Blakeney, members of local chapters that donated money to build the boardwalk, and other dignitaries will be on hand.

In the meantime, as soon as the carpenters, plumbers, and electricians finish the installation of the solar heating system, we will be open for visitors. Larry Thompson, southeast assistant regional representative, has written a folder giving information about the sanctuary. Norm, Steve, and Larry are collaborating on a self-guided boardwalk booklet, such as we use at Corkscrew, which should be ready before the dedication next fall. Black and white photos by Larry, Norm, and Steve will also be used in the booklet to show visitors the difference between a loblolly pine and a spruce pine, a cottonmouth and a brown watersnake, a river and a swamp.

Because the wood storks set up housekeeping in the winter months and the Yankee snowbirds flock to Corkscrew at the same time, Jerry Cutlip and his staff can wait until summer to catch up on maintenance work. In contrast, the Four Hole Swamp may be busy all year round. Therefore, we will be closed one day per week—probably Monday—for repairs to buildings, boardwalk, and jangled nerves.

JULY 1978 Stahr cut the ribbon officially opening the boardwalk and visitor center last October, whereupon Norman Brunswig, Beverly Riley, Steve Winton, and Doug Clayton had to absorb the slings and arrows of a number of visitors who thought four dollars for nonmembers should include a six-pack of Schlitz as well as a peek at a prothonotary. But according to our mail, there were just as many who thought a stomp through the swamp was worth the price of admission plus the cost of getting there and back.

To Norm it seemed an interminable wait before the boardwalk guidebook was in the hands of visitors. Norm, Steve, and Larry Thompson did the writing and provided most of the photos. The final product was edited by Connie Stallings, of *Audubon* magazine staff in New York. It has only one fault. It is so beautiful that everyone keeps a copy instead of letting us use it over again. Francis Beidler III, who contributed generously to printing costs, is well-pleased with the product. So are we.

The Ware Brothers own a gravel pit or two along our eastern boundary. As with most strip mine operations, the environmental impact is not confined to the mine. Last February, Ware Brothers released a flood of sand, silt, and clay in solution into Santee Branch and into Four Hole Swamp. Norm and Steve have been monitoring the effects on water quality from the Horse Range Swamp, upstream from us, for some years, a sad but enriching experience. When this new pollution threat to the sanctuary occurred, they called upon this experience and stayed on it until they could document what our neighbor's carelessness had cost us.

The productivity of a mile of streambed in bugs, bass, and bream is difficult to measure in dollars. But as pollution from strip mining, stream channelization, agriculture, and industry continue, someone has to blow the whistle. We now have a commitment from the Department of Health and Environmental Control, which requires Ware Brothers to meet certain specifications before a permit is issued for continuing their operations. Our lawyer says this is a landmark victory that should hasten the day when stream pollution will no longer be accepted as the price of "progress" in South Carolina.

MARCH 1979 After a rather slow start, our visitor program is now in full flower. Every canoe trip through the swamp is a sellout. The same is true of the night walks on the boardwalk. Norm Brunswig plays a recording of a barred owl, and he says the barred owl may not be horned, but one of them sure is horny, since he practically lands on Norm's head to the great amusement and amazement of our visitors. Norm is especially pleased that most of these are local folks because this indicates they no longer consider us a bunch of damnyankees. Nice going, Norm, Steve, Bill, and Barbara.

MAY 1979 Busy is the word for Beidler. Norm Brunswig says help and high water were the best and the highest in his six years as manager. Barbara Thomas, for example, not only plays the typewriter, calculator, telephone, and reception desk, but has learned to separate out those burrowers, clingers, creepers, and hiders that are found on the bottom of the stream in Four Hole Swamp. Counting and classifying these wiggly critters is a time-consuming job shared by all hands. On the other hand, these benthos samples are the most sensitive indicators of quality and quantity of the swamp waters, so it's time well spent. Thus we can document the effect of stream channelization by the so-called Soil Conservation Service.

Bill Hussey's special interest is environmental education, so you are apt to find him in a school classroom giving a preview of what they'll see on the boardwalk, which is an outdoor classroom, conducting a field trip concentrating on medicinal herbs, or leading a nightwalk after 8:00 P.M. or a bird walk before 6:00 A.M. Bill and Larry Thompson compare notes and make joint plans for a long-term educational program with regional school classes. They hope to work with the same classes at least every other year, gradually increasing the complexity of the subject matter. He's also involved with teaching the teachers this summer, now that he and Steve Winton have our new storage barn built and wired, a new road built, exhibits prepared, and other projects too numerous to mention.

Steve Winton has done a photographic essay of the yellow-crowned night herons nesting in Beidler and made aerial photos of the entire sanctuary. His breeding bird population studies in cutover and virgin timber will be continued for several years, using standardized techniques that are also in use on some of our other sanctuaries. The Beidler is probably the outstanding prothonotary warbler area in the United States, and Steve says they "sell" the sanctuary to groups on the boardwalk and canoe trails with the greatest of ease. When not engaged in research, interpretive work, chasing poachers, or driving tractor, Steve makes like a carpenter, electrician, or museum director. But, alas! As with Susan Fitch at the

Miles, graduate school is calling both Steve and his wife, Heidi. So we will lose them come next August.

Our visitor center now has a display on soils and hydrology of the area, plus a unique display of the tools and process for making cypress shingles. It is not too hard to find the working parts of a whiskey still around our swamp, and there is considerable interest in assembling same. This might, however, detract from the interest shown in our new sound and color automatic slide show. This wouldn't be very diplomatic, since the money for the Sho-Corder was donated by three garden clubs plus a close friend of the Beidler Forest. Barbara can now show unscheduled groups a sanctuary slide show and operate the desk and other machines at the same time. We doubt, however, if she would have time to put out much sour mash bourbon.

February 17 was a historic occasion—the first night walk at Beidler. Bill had planned it in advance. On that day a damnyankee storm moved into sunny South Carolina. As the sleet and snow did fall, the telephone did ring. The callers all had one question, "We're still going, aren't we?" And go they did. 'Twas a sellout, in fact, with six from Columbia, six from Charleston, and eight in the local-folk category. Since then, every night walk has been a sellout, and the same is true of scheduled canoe trips and early-morning bird walks.

If you schedule a bird walk at 5:45 A.M on Saturday and Sunday, those who show are there to appreciate the swamp and its wildlife. But if you schedule a canoe trip on a weekend, the participants are apt to be more interested in outdoor recreation than in the cottonmouths and cuckoos. So, for the time being, canoe trips are scheduled for Tuesdays and Thursdays and are sold out ahead of time.

What with copperheads, cottonmouth moccasins, pygmy rattlers, poison ivy, and a good chance of getting lost, most visitors are either kept on the boardwalk or given a conducted tour.

Speaking of visitors, Francis Beidler III and his cousin and family from France came by last July. On March 12, a chap named Roger Tory Peterson went canoeing and boardwalking with Norm. Norm says Peterson knows his birds fairly well, but for some reason didn't add many species to his life list. Mike Link and party from the Northwoods Audubon Center in Minnesota were down in April. The visitors' list includes familiar names and faces such as Dr. and Mrs. Carl W. Buchheister, president emeritus of NAS, and Marie Aull, donor of Aullwood Sanctuary and Nature Center near Dayton, Ohio.

In spite of competition from such as the above, the weatherman shows up in Norm's warden reports more often than anyone else. In late February, some three inches of rain, added to the melting snow and sleet, brought the swamp up to record heights. As the water rose, huge cypress logs that usually lie quietly beneath the boardwalk began to float. Norm's report for February 27 says, "As the logs floated up, they began to lift the boardwalk. With cables, hand winch, and cold appendages, we were able to remove them."

George Porter, NAS controller and author of *The World of the Frog and the Toad,* please note: on March 3, 1979, Steve catches an upland chorus frog after hunting for two years.

Bob Arbib, editor of *American Birds,* please note: on March 14, 1979, a mist net catches an orange-crowned warbler, "life new" for Norm, Steve, Bill, and visiting ornithologist Paul Hamel.

MAY 1980 If variety is the spice of life, Norm Brunswig and staff can live on spice alone. On August 30, the gauge at Mellards Lake read twelve inches below normal, and six days later it stood at twenty-three inches above. In between, Hurricane David had come and gone. Whenever you go from drought to flood in six days, you expect to be the Legé brothers in Louisiana, but it can happen here.

Although wind damage was limited to broken rails because of falling limbs on September 4, it rained steadily for more than two days. The sudden rise of Four Hole Swamp to record height put the boardwalk to a real test. By September 9, the entire walk was under water. The day before David, Norm had purchased a mechanical hand winch and pulled most of the large logs from under the walk, so they wouldn't float up and lift the walk.

About 25 of the 560 sections of walk were raised by water, and Norm suspected that walking on them while inundated caused vibrations that broke them loose from the soil. So he issued himself a cease and desist order until after the water receded.

His report says, "When the water did recede, many sections that had floated did not drop back into place, so they were like a roller-coaster. We rented a high-pressure gasoline water pump, adapted the outflow to a three-fourths-inch garden hose, attached a five-foot section of one-inch PVC to the end, and used this apparatus to jet the pilings back down to their original depth. This worked very well. It was important to jet the areas on highest ground first while the swamp water was still available for the intake. In two days all of the leveling was done."

Class field trip on a guided walk through Beidler Forest.
(Photo: Beidler Staff)

When they weren't ducking hurricanes, Norm, Barbara Thomas, Bill Hussey, and Ken Strom were busy conducting classes on the walk and in schools, giving programs about Audubon and the sanctuary all around the state, spreading crushed limestone and scraping and packing the roads, repairing buildings, conducting breeding-bird surveys on a twenty-five-acre plot in cutover timber for comparison with a replica in virgin timber, and carrying on as busily as Art Gingert and Company up at the Miles in Connecticut.

For example, on October 29, 220 members of the American Forestry Association descended upon our stalwart staff and showed great interest in the goings-on. On October 6, Norm gave a lecture on the birds of Beidler for a joint meeting of the Carolina Bird Club and the Georgia Ornithological Society, held at Jekyll Island.

On June 2, Bill Hussey led twenty-five people through the swamp, identifying various herbs and medicinal plants, describing their real and supposed values and giving the history of "root doctoring." On October 13, his first night walk was a sellout, limited to twenty-two brave souls. Another night walk on February 2, with the temperature in the low teens, was short on wildlife sounds and sights, but long on spectacular bright moonrise through towering cypress, reflecting on virgin swamp waters.

Nobody wanted to leave, and Norm had to practically run 'em out in the middle of the night.

The entry for May 3, 1980, reads, "Bill and I led the first Swamp Stomp at Beidler—fifteen stompers and us. People who had never been in a swamp got neck deep in Moccasin Lake. It was a smashing success. We stayed open until 7:00 P.M. We are doing this every weekend in May to test the interest."

Old Dad wonders if the men are testing interest or insanity on the part of visitors. Imagine wading around in a place called Moccasin Lake with mosquitoes, alligators, and the critters for which the lake was named, plus two crazy biologists!

Frank Bellrose, of the Illinois Natural History Survey, is the nation's foremost authority on wood ducks. But Frank does not know how often woodies use pileated woodpecker cavities, the diameter of the entrance, or the depth of the cavity carved by the pileated, nor does anyone else. To gather data on same, he calls on the Beidler staff. Finding feeding cavities is easy, but nesting cavities are something else. Then there's the matter of shinnying up forty feet or so and taking exact measurements.

The men also have a good study going on the yellow-crowned night heron, measuring productivity, average nest height, species of tree used, and basic ecology. In contrast with the extensive literature on other sharp-faced fowl, surprisingly little is known about yellow-crowns, perhaps because they tend to nest in small colonies or singly.

The botanists are every bit as enthusiastic about the Beidler as are birders and snake hunters. The South Carolina Orchid Society, the North Carolina Botanical Society, various garden clubs, college profs and students, farmers, foresters, and housewives all expect the staff to know every plant in the sanctuary, where it grows, and when it blooms. The swamp has excellent variety, and some of the rarest orchids in the state.

MAY 1981 Judging from the letters we receive (frequently accompanied by a check) from visitors to the Beidler, Norm Brunswig, Barbara Thomas, Ken Strom, and Mike Dawson must be doing something right. Every program for visitors is sold out well ahead of time. These include canoe trips, night walks, birding trips, wildflower walks, tree walks, orchid walks, and old-fashioned ain't-nature-grand walks. The groups range from grad students from Antioch University in New Hampshire and the University of Georgia, to local grade schoolers, from nineteen executives of Southern Railroad and their wives, to the Senior Citizens Club, from a long list of garden clubs, from a class of gifted students, and the Retarded

Citizens Association, to the Audubon board of directors. In any event, Norm and his crew seem to take it all in stride, and the customers come back for more.

Some credit must also go to the furred, feathered, and scaly friends. Mama hooded merganser set a new sanctuary record by hatching a brood on Goodson Lake and parading the little saw-bills past the boardwalk for the benefit of the visitors. There are two or three records for northern South Carolina but none for this part of the state.

Norm says clear-cutting of swamp forests may be of dubious value from the standpoint of good forestry, but the alligators in our cutover swamp are increasing—probably due to more sunlight on some favorite loafing spots.

The forest tent caterpillars are a nuisance every spring, but every twenty years or so they hit disastrous numbers. On April 4, 1981, Ken Strom noted the first caterpillars. On April 13, Norm's report read, "A trip around the boardwalk was like walking through one giant continuous cobweb because of the web strands from descending caterpillars, which inevitably landed on anyone walking there. The caterpillars carpet the handrails of the boardwalk, and their droppings (frass) sound like rain."

The fuzzy worms first completely stripped the tupelos, then sweet-gums, then oaks, hickories, and fruit trees, but avoided most shrubs. There was no keeping them out of buildings, and constant vacuuming couldn't keep up with them. It was an unforgettable experience for staff and visitors.

A couple of days before the board of directors visited the swamp, the population declined to tolerable levels. On April 26–27, the population crashed. Norm says, "A naturally occurring and virulent fungus, bacteria, or viral disease probably built up in the insect population and devastated the caterpillars." And this without a drop of malathion!

According to Cap'n Wimby's Bird Atlas, only yellow-billed cuckoos feed on fuzzy tent caterpiggles, which is why they say, "Gowlp! Gowlp!" But the Beidler Foresters report Carolina wrens, prothonotary warblers, crested flycatchers, and tufted titmice, plus anoles, skinks, and a reduvid bug joining in with great zest.

Ken and Norm spent an entire day with a couple of lost souls from The Nature Conservancy who are struggling to develop a management program for their preserves. On February 5, Norm took a day off to hunt quail with the famous Charles Banks Belt, who is a potential good supporter of Beidler. It was hardship duty, but duty is duty.

A writer-photographer for *Southern Living* magazine spent a full day at Beidler. In July 1980, this magazine had a fine article on Tim Williams and the Buckley Sanctuary in Kentucky. We hated to see Bill Hussey go back to graduate school, but the torch was passed to Mike Dawson without a hitch on June 2, 1980. The county superintendent of schools has already written Old Dad extolling Mike's abilities as a teacher of woodsy lore.

In the research department, Norm, Mike, and Ken continued their study of wood duck–pileated woodpecker relationships. Ken continued his turtle home range study, and the spring breeding survey was completed and forwarded to Bob Arbib for *American Birds*. On May 8, 1981, Ken and Norm recorded nine yellow-crowned night heron nests. One week later, eight were broken up. Because the nests are quite widespread, and egg loss is almost complete, the researchers do not believe coons or snakes are the culprits. They suspect that after complete defoliation of tupelos and ashes by caterpillars, nothing was left to conceal the nests from crows. The clever Corvids probably learned what to look for and found every nest. If there be such a thing as reincarnation, very few humans are smart enough to come back as crows.

MAY 1982 The year 1981 had its share of adversities. In April the forest tent caterpillars chomped up the woods; in August an unusual number of electrical storms made lightning rods out of the tallest trees; in September the swamp went bone dry, which canceled our popular (and profitable) canoe trips; in October, Mellards Lake was at a record low; and in November, after two years of bad drought, *Hypoxylon* fungus infected and killed many water oaks. The fungus is normally not a problem for healthy trees, but our water oaks were a wee bit weary. And the crows ate up all the yellow-crowned night heron eggs.

On the other hand, sweet are the uses of adversity. On August 14, Ken Strom and Marie Lavoie were married in the sanctuary on the edge of Mellards Lake. After a nice reception at headquarters, off they went to West-by-god-Virginia on their honeymoon.

In October, Norm investigated a sixty-five-pound buck that he determined had enriched the life of a very big bobcat. The size of the scratches reminded him that there are valid reports of panthers up in North Carolina. If he'd had the benefit of Jack Daniel's, he might have read them as the first panther sign in the Four Hole Swamp in modern times. But being a sober man and true, he goes on checking the lives and times of deer and pussycats, hoping for a new record.

In November, Beidler bird seed sales returned a profit of about $350. Norm made a couple trips to Hilton Head Island to help The Nature Conservancy with some management problems on one of their preserves. On September 18–19, the swamp was full of redstarts heading south. On September 20 and again on 29, the swampers saw five wood storks around Mellards Lake, a brand new record for the Beidler.

In advance of Mike Duever's research crew in December, Norm and Company staked out the primary plant sampling transect. When the Ecosystems Research Unit arrived, they shot elevations every twenty-five feet across the swamp, placing a "nail-in-tree" benchmark every one hundred meters, did a series of soil borings across the swamp, and installed five wells for the long-term study of ground water. By drilling the wells deep enough to reach water during a severe drought, they assured that the wells never go dry in the future.

Comes January 10, 1982, and the temperature drops to seven degrees, a record low for this country. While the Beidler Foresters are repairing the plumbing, they wonder if 1982 is going to be another one of those years. As it turns out, the next five months in the cypress-tupelo swamp are tolerable, to say the least.

So far, the spring of 1982 has been delightfully wet and canoe trips are once again in order. In cooperation with the State Department of Health and Environmental Control, we have begun a study of possible exchange between Four Hole Swamp water and the deep aquifer beneath it. In our Mellards Lake field, three wells are installed. If it turns out that Four Hole does recharge the aquifer that supplies drinking and industrial water, then the value of our sanctuary, which protects that water, becomes obvious.

In March, William Mescher, president of the South Carolina Public Service Authority (local power company) met with Norm to discuss routing of a new transmission line across Four Hole Swamp. The most direct route would have been widening their existing right-of-way across the Beidler. Instead, the company agreed to a longer route that avoids the sanctuary. Mescher is a life-long birder, and Norm says there is nothing like having a prothonotary warbler do your negotiating for you. Be that as it may, this example of industrial cooperation is deeply appreciated by the thousands of people who visit the Beidler.

In April we found a colony of fifteen yellow-crowned night herons. By the end of May, they had forty nests under surveillance on their transect, with twenty-seven nests about to fledge.

Apparently the yellow-crowned squawks are making up for 1981. In

March, Ken Strom checked the seventeen newly erected bluebird boxes once a week. He found half of them occupied, and most of the winsome critters went on to raise two broods. Art Gingert wishes Connecticut bluebirds could be so prolific. Speaking of prolific, there are 350 nests of cattle egrets, 50 great egrets, 3 anhingas, and 8 little blues in a new rookery on our neighbor's property. At last count, cattle egrets were still building.

MARCH 1983 In spring, when it's daylight in the swamp, Norm Brunswig, Ken Strom, and Mike Dawson are out listening to the birdies sing. They call this work. Regardless of what you call it, the 1982 breeding-bird survey for *American Birds* says something about the value of Beidler Forest and the Four Hole Swamp.

On a twenty-two-acre plot in the virgin hardwood swamp forest, the lads found the following nesting pairs defending territories.

Species	Territories
Blue-gray gnatcatchers	29.5
Parula warblers	21
Red-eyed vireos	13
Great crested flycatchers	12
Tufted titmice	10
Acadian flycatchers	8
Carolina wrens	7
Prothonotary warblers	6.5
Hooded warblers	6.5
Red-bellied woodpeckers	6
Yellow-throated warblers	6
Downy woodpeckers	5.5
Carolina chickadees	5
White-eyed vireos	4.5
White-breasted nuthatches	3
Summer tanagers	3

Yellow-bellied cuckoos	2
Pileated woodpeckers	2
Hairy woodpeckers	2
Wood ducks	1
Red-shouldered hawks	1
Chimney swifts	1
Wood thrushes	1
Cardinals	0.5
Total: 24	167

Borderline cases, in which a singing male spends half his time within the study area and half across the line, are counted as half-territories. These data indicate a density of 714 pairs per one hundred acres, which happens to be the highest density in the eastern United States! Being very familiar with it, Norm believes this density prevails throughout the entire swamp. This prompts him to write in his warden's report, "Let's buy some more of Four Hole Swamp!"

Of 214 census areas across the continent, only 4 could equal or slightly exceed the Beidler. One was a transitional mixed forest-field in Ontario; one, a floodplain cottonwood forest in Colorado; one, a riparian woodland–live oak–juniper plot in Arizona; and one, a farmstead out in Jim Rod's old stomping grounds in Iowa. From a standpoint of breeding birds, this study firmly establishes the importance of eastern bottomland forests. Since we have been in the business of saving and managing wildlife habitat for eighty years, it is only natural that our Beidler Forest staff should covet the additional one thousand five hundred acres or so that would give us control of the swamp from bank to bank and keep summer cottages out of summer tanager range.

In addition to the nesters, the yellow-crowned night herons, white ibises, mourning doves, barred owls, ruby-throated hummingbirds, blue jays, common crows, common grackles, and brown-headed cowbirds showed up on the study plot.

As you know, the Beidler birders do their census in the virgin forest one year and in the cutover forest the next. They have three years of data for each. Although the total number of breeding pairs is about the same, certain species are consistently more abundant in the cutover than in the virgin forest and vice versa. As you might expect, crested flycatchers and yellow-throated warblers are much more abundant in the virgin forest, while the brush lovers, such as cardinals and white-eyed vireos, prefer the cutover.

During the last three nesting seasons, huge outbreaks of forest tent caterpillars have occurred. This may account for the 35 percent increase in total pairs compared to 1980. But the only bird that has declined steadily since 1979 is the yellow-billed cuckoo, a heavy consumer of caterpillars. Could be a bird with a belly full of fuzzy tent caterpiggles doesn't have the proper attitude toward propagation.

During the spring of 1983, three wild turkeys make a new record for the sanctuary. At last report, the yellow-crowned night heron colony was still inactive. At the Beidler, yellow-crowns feed almost exclusively on crawfish. Since the rains in March were enough to arouse Noah's interest, wading around the cypress knees in quest of mudbugs was probably so discouraging that the yellow-crowns postponed their colonial capers until the waters receded.

South Carolina's famous ornithologist-artist-photographer, John Henry Dick, recently visited the Beidler. Norm has been hunting and hoping for Bachman's warblers in the Beidler for several years. So far he has hunted in vain, and John Henry says he believes it may be too late, but if a Bachman's warbler can be found anywhere, Beidler Forest would be the place to look.

NOVEMBER 1984 Although Miss Nancy named him "Busy Butt" about ten years ago, Norm Brunswig says as far as accomplishments are concerned, Barbara Thomas and Mike Dawson make him appear to be standing still. Be that as it may, the Beidler is affecting the lives and times of a lot of folks.

Mike lectured in forty-three school classes, reaching 1,283 students. In twenty-nine canoe trips, the giant cypress trees, hootie owls, and cotton-mouths scared hell out of 213 people who keep coming back for more. Mike and Norm led seventeen walks that focused on special interests such as flowers, birds, or miscellaneous natural history, sometimes at night, sometimes wading deep in the black waters of Four Hole Swamp. In these, 314 people participated. Eight Saturday morning boardwalk tours attracted 104. By giving forty slide talks round and about the southeast, they entertained 2,131 people. As a result of such carryings-on, 4,045 people are now thinking about the effect of Beidler Forest and the Audubon Society on their air, water, and food supply and how these in turn affect that most sensitive organ, the pocketbook.

Barbara, Norm, and Mike agree that the success of 1984 was given a big boost by Carol Weeks and Michelle MacKenzie, the first spring interns we ever had at Beidler. Without their help, the Four Hole Swampers would have been swamped by the visitor load.

While our work with visitors at Beidler is very important and conspicuous, Norm is quick to point out that our first concern is for the swamp, itself. Without adequate management, protection, and research, the prothonotary warblers, orchids, bobcats, and alligators would disappear along with the big cypress, and our interpretive program would consist of a recitation of what-used-to-be and what-might-have-been. Threats to wild plants and animals of Beidler are revealed by Norm's manager's reports. They range from a preacher who bent the rules a bit while in pursuit of protein, to the largest illegal dredge-and-fill project along the East Coast, which threatened the very existence of the sanctuary by shutting off an important tributary. And when a coon hound fails to come home and his master strongly suspects "a gator et him plumb up," and the master shows up in gator habitat (Mellards Lake) with his caliber .30 in hand, it requires diplomacy and a lot of faith in Audubon's insurance policy.

Combating monstrous water projects, such as the Black River conversion and the damming of Goodby's Swamp, requires letters of protest to the Corps of Engineers, cooperation with the USFWS, and political pressure. It also requires a backlog of facts to properly evaluate the impact of such insults to the ecosystem.

Democrats, Republicans, and engineers have long been recognized as very serious threats to wildlife, and last March the Army Corps of Engineers, responding to a request by some Democrats and Republicans, proved the point. A supposedly low impact channel-clearing project by the Corps on a tributary to Four Hole didn't turn out that way. Simply clearing out logs and other obstructions to stream flow is one thing; clearcutting a two-hundred-foot strip of timber along one side of the creek is quite another. Even the Corps admits that what it actually did bears no resemblance to the plans they submitted to Beidler Sanctuary and to various state agencies. Norm, along with others, pointed this out by written report. Nowadays the Corps consults Norm and Mike and Barbara before playing in the streams.

Some threats to the sanctuary do not directly involve human-type critters. Alligator weed (*Alternanthera philoxercides*) has invaded Mellards Lake, and keeping it from covering the lake is a problem. It was probably brought in by someone's boat or trailer. Pine bark beetles invaded some slash pine on the Georgia Pacific tract. Norm plans to log and sell the slash pine and replant long-leaf pine that could benefit red-cockaded woodpeckers in the future.

Meanwhile, monitoring the quality and quantity of the stream flows through the swamp continues as Norm runs the chemistry and Barb identifies the invertebrates in the water samples.

An unusual request comes from International Paper to study the status of black bears on land owned by IP near Myrtle Beach. This is the last bear population in the state, but apparently no conservation organization—either state or private—wants to tangle with developers on this issue. Would-be saviors of Bachman's warblers are plentiful; bear lovers are scarce. Maybe because bears don't sing; they bite. So suburbia doesn't like bears, and neither do politicians.

Ecologists generally consider the extremes of weather more important than the means in its effect on plants and animals. If so, Norm Brunswig says the weather last year was very important in the cypress-tupelo swamp. Our normally wet spring was extremely dry, with 7.9 inches less rain than the ten-year average, forcing cancellation of all canoe trips. Then comes our normally dry fall, with 13.1 inches more than the ten-year average. But rainfall for the entire year was within 3 inches of normal. On January 20, 1985, the mercury dipped to three degrees above zero, the coldest ever recorded in the Low Country. For the first time in history, the surface of Mellards Lake was suitable for skating or high-ball mixing. But the rest of the year was generally warmer than usual. Office manager Barbara Thomas figures the federal government must have been put in charge of South Carolina weather.

In early March, Craig Olsen and John Corcoran began their spring internship. Monitoring use of our twenty-two wood duck and twenty-nine bluebird boxes, plus making new ones, was among their first assignments. But according to assistant Mike Dawson and Norm, it was in our on-sanctuary education work that Craig and John made the greatest contribution. Says Mike, "They not only improve the quantity of special walks, but the quality."

Several changes were made in the visitor center display room, including revamping and improving the graphics of several interpretive displays, making six new displays, converting the slide show room into a combination slide show and display room. A shingle riving display with antique tools found in the woods attracts much attention. The Beidler team presented twenty-seven slide lectures to 1,332 people, including school classes, garden clubs, civic clubs, NAS chapters, and others.

Mike was elected cochairman of the Heritage Education forum, a consortium of Charleston area museums, nature centers, historic sites, and so forth, in an effort to enhance the educational programs of the tri-county schools.

Aiding and abetting our interns and full-time staff were Bob and Lenore Rose, who arrived in July for a year of volunteer work. Mike's comment about Bob: "He's made improvement in things automotive, things electrical, things mechanical, things of wood, and things of metal." Lenore's middle name should be Versatility because she can do anything from running the office to leading fifth graders on the boardwalk and to identifying the wiggly, crawly critters in a stream-bottom sample, as part of our long-term monitoring of water quality.

The news from Beidler is not confined to the human type. Wild turkeys first appeared in 1983 and are now established as nesting. Our first beaver in Mellards Lake was not considered an unmixed blessing because young cypress and tupelo are high on the beaver's bill of fare. Fortunately, this adventuresome rodent apparently appeared on a gator's bill of fare. Protecting our virgin forest from the chainsaw is trouble enough without worrying about flat-tailed varmints.

Our spring breeding-bird survey of the cutover portion of the sanctuary will be in the January–February 1986 issue of *American Birds*. The total number, 143.5 pairs per hectare, was exactly the same as in 1983. There was a slight shift in species composition but not in total numbers. It should again be about the highest count in the country and shows the value of the sanctuary to wildlife. (We need the rest of the swamp!)

Mike Duever's dendrochronology (aging by tree rings) work and knowledge of Beidler Forest attracted a couple of scientists from the University of Arkansas. We thought our cypress trees were five hundred to seven hundred years old, but some are over one thousand. Those are probably some of the oldest on the East Coast.

And all the time ol' "Busy Butt" Brunswig is out there nosing around to see whether money grows on trees. Carole MacNamara (controller's office in New York) is not sure of the origin, but she says Norm keeps sending in checks from folks who have seen the Beidler and figure we oughta buy more cypress and tupelo. Jane Pelson (from NAS Development Department) came by in May to provide ideas and help plan certain fundraising events. (They paid off.)

Our colonies of dwarf trilliums are the only known population in South Carolina. Norm and a couple of botany profs from the Citadel are discussing possible management plans.

On October 6, 1985, our attorney from Abbeville, Louisiana, Silas Cooper, and his wife, Carolyn, came by to compare the flora, fauna, and congeniality of Four Hole Swamp with that of Acadiana. The comparison was reportedly very favorable. In their spare time, Norm and Mike help our neighbor, Tom Mim's widow, get some of her poorer land planted to trees.

JANUARY 1987 According to the old saw, money does not grow on trees. But Norm Brunswig says a virgin swamp forest of cypress and tupelo gum can sure raise a lot of it. He says the trees were ably assisted by Jane Pelson, Ivy Kuspit, and Lynne Poteau of NAS Development Department, plus a board member or two, and NAS president Peter Berle.

The $700,000 grant from the Goodhill Foundation had to be matched in three years. Ol' Busy Butt was busier than ever shaking the bushes from Carolina to California. Consequently, slightly before the deadline, his collection of the long green amounts to $1.4 million.

On November 18, 1986, we purchased two tracts of much needed buffer land, totaling 439 acres. Norm expects to have closed the deal on another 514 acres by the end of March 1987 and to make an offer on another 830. He cruised the timber on the latter to see how many trees, what kind, how big, and how valuable they were. He won't buy a forest in a fog. Our goal is to save what's left of the virgin timber, plus second growth, so we can keep the chainsaws and condos out of the entire swamp.

Superimposed on all that hustle and bustle, our interpretive program, under the able direction of Mike Dawson, reached out and touched a lot of folks. About 7,000 strolled quietly through the outdoor cathedral known as the Beidler boardwalk. About 3,000 others took part in seventy-four naturalist-led walks, and 764 took part in one of fifty special walks or tours. The disciples of John James Audubon presented thirty-nine slide lectures to 2,325 people, including sixteen slide and puppet shows presented to 1,100 schoolchildren.

It has been said that free help can be the most expensive kind. The exact opposite was the case with Bob and Lenore Rose, who volunteered their time and talents for a year. Their tour of duty ended last June, when Old Dad was on hand for a wee ceremony commending the lack of past regrets and future fears and bestowing Audubon life memberships on Lenore and Bob. Norm is highly pleased to announce they are coming back this summer for another year.

Last fall we had a sanctuary management and maintenance intern for the first time. That could be a scary title for a lass fresh out of Cornell, but Laura Mattei took to monitoring the creepy-crawlies, maintaining buildings, machines, and wildlife management projects like an otter takes to water. She also worked on a project involving interpretation and mapping of infrared aerial photography of Four Hole Swamp. Her color-coded forest-type map is mighty useful in assessing the nature and value of anticipated land acquisitions, as well as the analysis of existing properties.

The Natural Areas Association is probably more in tune with our brand of wildlife management than most so-called conservation organizations. So they invited Norm, Jeff Froke (Starr Ranch in California), Ken Strom (former assistant at Beidler, now manager of the Lillian Annette Rowe in Nebraska), Mike Duever (NAS Research Department), and Old Dad to tell 'em how Audubon does it and to compare notes on how to make eyes, ears, and taste buds worth having. Norm and Old Dad were officially on the program. So many area managers wanted to know so much about Beidler Forest that the session chairman had to ask them to catch Norm Brunswig later.

In the category of man-made environmental insults, an illegal canal was discovered in the swamp near our property. The u.s. Fish and Wildlife Service and the Army Corps of Engineers are considering appropriate wrist slapping due to the violation of their own regulations. Also, the nearby Giant Cement Company has plans for burning hazardous materials in their kiln. This will require much time, research, and probably testimony from a staff that has no extra time to fight such battles.

MARCH 1989 Norm Brunswig closed the deal on the Williams to Rudd parcel on March 30, 1987. This is 514 acres of beautiful swamp and one mile of bluff. It had an excellent access road and a very substantial pipe gate that can be locked. Another tract, acquired in December 1987 from Georgia Pacific, contains 821 acres and presented some problems in surveying. It has a turkey food plot that will be maintained as a place where gobblers and hens can dine and socialize. We hired a site prepara-tion contractor to disk the tract prior to planting improved longleaf pine seedlings.

Mike and Norm were involved in an Environmental Protection Agency short course aimed at teaching wetland scientists new techniques for evaluating wetlands. On July 28, the group spent all day testing the meth-odology at Beidler Forest.

Norm gave two programs at the National Audubon Convention in Washington, D.C. Some years ago, CBS called Old Dad, said they were planning a show called *Sunday Morning* and wanted to end each show with movies made on a wildlife sanctuary. Since then, Charles Kuralt's photographer, C. Lewis Bailey, has been to Beidler, Corkscrew, Sydnes Island, and several national refuges and parks. And a few million folks have seen beautiful areas filled with wood storks, alligators, egrets, cy-press, tupelo, and many other treats on our sanctuaries.

Very gratifying was a letter from the Robert W. Woodruff Foundation (Coca-Cola) about their decision to maintain Ichauway Plantation as a managed natural area dedicated solely to educational, scientific, and con-servation purposes. This is a milestone for conservation in Georgia. Cooter Connelly (Silver Bluff Plantation), Norm, and Old Dad had vis-ited the plantation a few times and urged the foundation to continue to operate it as a quail-hunting, forestry, agriculture, research, and demon-stration area. Says vice president McTier, "We will keep you posted on our progress as we need your continuing advice and support in our efforts to utilize Ichauway Plantation in the most meaningful way possible."

On February 9, 1987, Barbara Thomas brought forth upon this conti-nent a new Carolinian by name of Benjamin Murray Thomas. In addi-tion, she learns how to play computers, handles the paying customers, assembles information comparing Rowe Sanctuary on the Platte River with Beidler for a feasibility study of a visitor center at Rowe, attends the Governor's Conference on tourism at Greenville where she got ideas for expanding attendance at Beidler, and keeps Norm, Mike, and interns on the job.

OCTOBER 1990 The world will little note nor long remember what the Beidler Forest crew said on September 21, 1989. But it can never forget what Hurricane Hugo did there. Packing winds above 175 miles per hour, the storm slammed into the South Carolina coast and proceeded several hundred miles inland before playing out. In the days that followed, ac-

Boardwalk through Beidler Forest before Hurricane Hugo.

(Photo: Beidler Staff)

cording to Norm Brunswig's report, ". . . half of our mile-long entry road was an impenetrable tangle of downed trees; the boardwalk had 1,000– 1,200 feet totally smashed, with another 1,500 feet of minor damages. Amazingly, the visitor center and land were unhurt."

After the storm, Dan "Cooter" Connelly and Paul Koehler came over from Silver Bluff Sanctuary (near Aiken) to help Mike Dawson, Norm, Barb Thomas, Kathie Bradley, Jo Ann Dawson, and Susan Abrendson spend two entire days with four chainsaws and a tractor clearing the driveway just wide enough to get one vehicle in to the visitor center.

Norm, Mike, Dan, and Paul "started out onto the boardwalk, but balked at the immensity of the clearing and decided to back off temporarily to regroup and assess damage."

Mike decided a bird's eye view of the remains—from a soaring-type bird—would provide a better assessment. Norm also took to the air to assess the possibility of airlifting the downed hardwoods by helicopter. This type of logging is fairly common in South Carolina, but the lumber from regional swamps soon swamped the mills.

Boardwalk through Beidler Forest after Hurricane Hugo.
(Photo: Beidler Staff)

Later on, Mike literally crawled around the boardwalk to assess the damage more objectively, take photos, and make plans for rebuilding.

By the end of October, the crew had repaired over five hundred feet. They opened the visitor center in early October, but because of the lack of boardwalk on which to walk, they didn't charge admission.

The picture of the swamp in October was not pretty; it was ugly. And the cottonmouths and copperheads were as venomous as ever. But those magnificent old cypress trees that had seen hurricanes come and go for nearly one thousand years had many friends and admirers.

Papa Joe Edmondson arrived November 15. Norm's report says, "Mike, Katie, Joe, Dan Broughton, Carol Morse, and John Crosby began the full-fledged blitz of boardwalk repair. The lumber arrived, and by month's end the crew had repaired the entire first part of the walk and a small portion of the return loop! Amazingly, very few four-by-four posts were damaged, and very little boardwalk rerouting was necessary. Repairs consisted mostly of clearing the walk right-of-way, leveling and jacking up of four-by-fours, rebuilding cross-arms, stringers, decking, and hand and midrails."

A top priority was clearing the firelanes around the visitor center before the torn up brush became tinder dry. November was very mild and dry, which was fine for boardwalk rebuilding but very bad for sitting atop all that firewood.

Mike hired Carol Morse, John Crosby, and Dan Broughton through the State Job Training Partnership Act, which means we pay them but get reimbursed. The Federal Emergency Management Administration also offered to compensate for boardwalk repair. From the budget standpoint, this was a big help, albeit the many hours spent filling out forms was another story.

The crew kept busy, busy, busy and finished reconstruction by December 27, in time for a New Year's celebration. December weather reduced the fire hazard to zero, adding what amounts to a blizzard in South Carolina—four inches of snow on December 23. It was the first white Christmas at Beidler Forest in forty-eight years.

There is life after death of trees. In fact, before and after Hugo, monitoring the limnology of the streams, leading field trips, doing programs in schools, service clubs, and such went on as usual. Norm and Mike decided they had a unique opportunity to learn what forest species were affected by Hugo, how they were affected, and how the forest recovers. They called in Mike Duever and Jeanne McCollum, from our Research Department, to help set up study plots.

Of special interest will be the annual breeding-bird surveys of cutover and uncut forest to see what Hugo did to the dickey birds.

MAY 1992 During 1990 and most of 1991, Hurricane Hugo was gone but not forgotten. Every now and then a dead branch would come crashing down across the boardwalk, fortunately not on top of visitors.

Tourism in nearby Charleston was significantly lower than normal, and Barb Thomas says the same was true at Beidler. In September 1990, Barb prepared a news release discussing the forest one year after Hugo. Apparently it had the desired effect: visitation began to approach the good old days, and by March 1991, it was back to normal.

Guided canoe trips are so popular that we had to add Friday trips to the regular weekends. By early April, all trips were booked through May. Using six canoes, and making nineteen trips, 186 visitors were accommodated in the spring of 1991.

For several years, we've been censusing breeding birds on a plot of virgin forest and a cutover plot. Mike says after Hugo tore up the virgin forest, he and Norm had an interesting time trying to locate the area. Says he, "What used to take two hours now takes three and one-half due to scrambling over, under, through, and around downed trees. The waist-deep water didn't help!"

The *Charleston News and Courier* does an occasional "High Profile" on various characters, telling what the individual does to what and to whom. The Beidler and Norm caught their eye, and Mike reports, "This excellent article came out at the end of January 1991 and was very well received. It even proved to be good publicity for us; many visitors have mentioned the article inspired them to come."

In April 1991, Evy Chace, Peter and Patty Manigault, John Henry Dick, Norm, and other birders conducted a Birdathon to the tune of 145 species. There's just something about that old swamp!

OCTOBER 1993 In September 1992, Mike Dawson allowed as how the water was so deep that a tall man could stand up to drink in almost any hole in Four Hole Swamp. But by September of this year, the ever-popular canoe trips, being fresh out of flotation, had to be canceled.

In contrast, we had to close the boardwalk for four days in January because parts of it were under water. Mellards Lake level peaked at plus forty-four inches, the highest level since Hurricane David with a high of plus seventy-one inches in 1980. Plant ecologists say the effect of extremes of weather are more important than the means. The same rule seems applicable to people.

Visit any National Audubon Sanctuary and you will see priceless, often irreplaceable, wildlife habitat. When we created the Beidler Forest Sanctuary in the late 1960s, we saved the world's largest remaining stand of virgin cypress–tupelo gum. At one time there were hundreds of thousands of similar swampland acres in the southeast. Sad to say, precious little remains untouched.

As Mike Dawson says in our newsletter, *From the Heart of the Swamp,* "If trees had brows instead of boughs, they would be wiping off the cold sweat at having narrowly escaped the proverbial axe. One year later and the Audubon Society could not have preserved this forest, as it, too, was scheduled to be logged."

Although the thousand-year-old cypress trees cannot be replaced, much of the habitat that produced them can be restored. Recently Norm has been busier than usual meeting with executives of big timber companies that have lands for sale; the Environmental Protection Agency, which is interested in seeing us acquire such land; the Army Corps of Engineers; the U.S. Fish and Wildlife Service; and other interested agencies. Norm thinks a huge bioreserve containing over twelve thousand acres is well beyond the idle dream stage.

In addition, neighbors upstream and downstream from the sanctuary are coming around seeking advice on how to preserve their own forests for posterity. Norm and Mike explain the possibilities of conservation easements and other means. It is gratifying to see landowners wanting to treat their land as we treat ours.

In fiscal 1992–1993, Beidler Forest had 10,000 visitors. To date, 1993 has been a great year, including 1,500 schoolchildren and the most successful canoe trip season— 449 people on forty-four trips. All this in spite of high water, low water, and South Carolina summer weather.

We know that many visitors do not take the time to read the boardwalk guidebook. They come back to the visitor center asking questions that were answered in it. Perhaps this is to be expected in view of the percentage of people who do their "reading" in front of the television screen. How, then, do we get our message across about the value of wetlands, old growth forest, and biodiversity?

Norm, Mike, and Barbara are planning a series of state-of-the-art interpretive panels to be installed along the boardwalk. With great graphics and minimal text, each panel will blend in with the landscape. Core ideas that we want all visitors to understand have been chosen for the panels.

The first panel is already installed along the walk; the second has been produced; and we've raised the money for seven more from individuals and local industries.

Unfortunately, National Audubon Sanctuary management is not applied to all forests in North America nor to the tropical forests of South America. Consequently, in our annual spring breeding-bird census, we continue to monitor a decline in some neotropical migrants. In 1979 the northern parula warbler was our most abundant species. They've declined steadily until this year, when there were no parulas on our study plot!

Among the big surprises of 1993, the biggest of all was a surprise party on September 4 commemorating Norm Brunswig's twentieth year as manager of Beidler Forest. No one but Barbara Thomas could have brought in all those former employees and friends, including Old Dad and Miss Nancy, and kept it all a secret from "Busy Butt"! It was a grand success.

DECEMBER 1994 Because a swamp cannot exist as an island, Barbara Thomas, Mike Dawson, and Norm Brunswig spend much time with neighboring landowners, plus state, federal, and private agencies that own and manage land. Their aim is to keep regional wetlands wet.

In November 1993, Norm closed the deal on 10.1 acres along the edge of the swamp and the bluff that borders it. In June 1994, a 33-acre parcel became part of the sanctuary as a result of mitigation for wetlands destruction at the Blue Circle Cement Plant in Harleyville; in October 1994, another tract of 64.5 acres was added. In November 1994, a strategically located 5-acre inholding came up for sale. Its purchase removed a major source of disturbance from the Mellards Lake area and added a nice log cabin to Beidler Forest.

Acquiring all of the priceless wetlands, however, is out of the question. The next best approach is through education, demonstration, and cooperation with landowners who control thousands of acres.

We envision an eventual bioreserve of over twenty thousand acres with Beidler as its core, which will be managed on a sustainable basis. Landowner cooperators can continue to harvest timber; hunters can continue to harvest surplus deer; and forest-breeding songbirds can continue to entertain birders. Cooter Connelly and Paul Koehler have demonstrated at our Silver Bluff Sanctuary that a timber and wildlife management program can pay for itself indefinitely.

In the long run, however, without widespread public support, the tide of land-hungry humans led by real estate developers will overpower the dedicated resource managers and protectors. Fortunately, due to Mike Dawson's unique mix of entertainment and education, the understanding of environmental factors that enable plants, wild animals, and people to survive in and around a swamp forest is absorbed by preschoolers, retirees, and in-betweens. When the chips are down twenty years from now, cypress-tupelo may mean a lot to lot of voters.

For some four hundred years, *swamp* has been a dirty word on the American political scene. A gradual change seems to be taking place.

❧ 15 ❧

TAMPA BAY

SANCTUARIES

Tampa, Florida

When the Spaniards discovered Tampa Bay in 1528, the colorful wading birds, terns, and gulls were far too numerous to count. The natural barrier islands and protected mangrove keys, plus the bay waters teeming with fish, provided ideal habitat for colonial waterbirds.

Birdlife was plentiful until about 1850, when egret plumes were literally worth their weight in gold. Plume hunters were followed by egg collectors and gourmets whose mouths watered at the thought of tasty young ibises. Only remnant populations survived until 1930.

Then came Herbert Mills of Florida, who wrote in 1933 of his first visit to Green Key in Tampa Bay: "At that time I found gun shells scattered around the ground, young birds dead and alive on the ground, empty nests, and other signs indicating that birds had been killed and carried out by the sackful."

Fred Schultz, hired by Mills in 1934, was our first warden for Tampa Bay. With support from the National Audubon Society, Mills skillfully dealt with the state of Florida, local landowners, and a local phosphate-processing company and screened leases on islands supporting colonial bird colonies.

Under the watchful eye of Fred Schultz, Tampa Bay's bird populations recovered. By 1939, after only six years of protection, Green Key showed a 3,000 percent increase in nesting birds. The National Audubon Society now owns or leases nine important islands in the Tampa Bay area.

Green Key   Located fifteen miles south of Tampa, Green Key is a natural island covered with mangroves. It formed the nucleus of the bay sanctuaries. Wide stretches of mud flats and shallow bay bottom surround it, providing a good food source. Until the mid-1960s, thousands of herons, ibises, pelicans, and cormorants nested there. Probably because of extensive dredge-and-fill operations nearby, the birds still roost there, but don't nest. Being fairly close to the mainland, it is visited by raccoons, which is not conducive to nesting success.

Whiskey Stump   Fred Schultz, a carpenter by trade, built a cabin on this key in the early 1930s. The rumor does persist that during the "noble experiment," bootleggers left their merchandise on a stump on this island in return for just compensation. Be that as it may, the island provided a convenient base of operations for warden Schultz, and its shoreline still provides a good feeding area.

Alafia Banks   These two spoil bank islands total thirty-five acres, which the Gardinier Phosphoric Company leases for one dollar a year. Located in the mouth of the Alafia River, they provide excellent nesting habitat for about 15,000 pairs of at least fifteen species. In 1974 and 1975, reddish egrets nested here; in 1975 15 pairs of roseate spoonbills nested. Those were the first such records since the turn of the century.

Nina G. Washburn Sanctuary   This sanctuary on Bird Island was deeded by Mrs. Washburn to the society in 1970. Thirty-five miles south of Tampa, this thickly vegetative island lies in Terra Ceia Bay. Approximately 10,000 pairs of wading birds and pelicans nest here, and magnificent frigate birds roost on the sanctuary.

JULY 1974   Dusty Dunstan, otherwise known as Frank, joined the Tampa Bay sanctuary staff in March 1973. Jack Pulsipher, who has been a commercial fisherman and Audubon seasonal warden in Tampa Bay since way before day before yesterday, got Dusty off to a good start. Between the two, the brown pelicans, herons, egrets, gulls, terns, cormorants, white ibises, and anhingas did likewise.

Dusty and Jack are excited over the discovery of a reddish egret nest on Washburn Island, one of several islands that make up our Tampa Bay Sanctuaries. Reddish egret nests are old stuff to you Texas wardens, but they ain't been seen in these parts since 1910.

While the reddish egrets were very welcome, the red tide in March was not. Hundreds of tons of fish were killed, and the tourists, fishermen, and motel keepers were as unhappy as the biologists. Dusty counted 508 dead lesser scaup in 1.7 miles of shoreline in Hillsborough Bay. No other seabirds were killed, and there is no proof that the red tide did the ducks in. In fact, pathologists are still puzzled by the deaths.

Shell dredgers are up to their old tricks in Tampa Bay. Some of our sanctuary islands lie within the sixty-two-square-mile permit application. The state is beginning to take steps to regulate the dredgers, requiring the industry to pay for research on the effects of dredging through a $225,000 contract with the University of South Florida. We lack enough scientific data to win in court should we try to stop dredging at this point. We can, however, keep the pressure on the state for regulations that will keep the damages down.

Dusty has a good study of the spoil-bank islands under way and is doing some other research that keeps him out of mischief. He keeps in close touch with Sandy Sprunt and the Research Department on all such matters. His paper on "The Utilization of Spoil Islands by Breeding and Nonbreeding Avian Species in Tampa Bay," given at a workshop in North Carolina on the management of dredge islands, was well received. We recently won a favorable ruling from the Tampa Port Authority that required a developer near Whiskey Stump to modify his operations to prevent damage to our island.

JULY 1979 The various islands in Dusty Dunstan's saltwater domain were the scene of historic goings-on this year. To quote from the *Tampa Tribune* of June 1, 1975, "For the first time in sixty-three years, roseate spoonbill chicks are alive and well in the backwaters of Tampa Bay." In 1912 a man named P. J. Pacetti counted eighty-five spoonbills nesting on Alafia Banks, which was the last recorded nesting until Dusty and Joe Harris discovered about twenty pairs in April. Helen Cruickshank and her trusty camera documented the performance for posterity.

Last year Dusty and Jack Pulsipher found a reddish egret's nest on Washburn Island, the first since 1910. This year the reddish egrets fledged about ten young. That wouldn't make Friday Fluman on Green Island, Texas, very excited, but it's big news around Tampa Bay.

The endangered brown pelican, which met with disaster for the second time in Louisiana this year, suffered no such fate in Tampa Bay. The men figure they have 450 pairs on Alafia Banks and 200 pairs on Washburn. The first chick hatched by the satchel-mouthed mullet-burners was on March 21.

The white ibises occupied all their previous habitat this year and did better than usual. The cormorants nested a little earlier (by February 23) and heavier than usual. The great blues, yellow-crowns, both egrets, and other wading birds had a good year. Dusty' s final figures are forwarded to the Research Department, as are data from all of our wading bird sanctuaries.

Not to be outdone by wading birds, another fish eater at the mouth of Bullfrog Creek, about two miles southeast of Alafia Banks, had a successful year. This one young bald eagle left the nest about mid-April.

Dusty's paper at the Coastal Vegetation Conference offered hope that past mistakes in Florida's estuaries can be corrected. It's nice when conservationists can be *for* something instead of agin' everything.

Dusty and Jack also squired a bunch of schoolteachers around Cockroach Bay on what the teachers called a workshop. Then, according to their warden's report, they took the Junior Women's League on a similar expedition on May 10. They call this "hardship duty" and want extra pay, but so far controller George Porter ain't buying that. He says he never saw a workshop without a workbench in it and that these guys better not be cruising around in any yachts.

In fact, Dusty should trade his two too-small boats with worn-out motors for one seaworthy craft and motor, but his budget is short $2,600. So what else is new!

JUNE 1976   In 1975 roseate spoonbills came back to Tampa Bay to nest for the first time in sixty-three years. In 1974, Dusty found the first reddish egret nest that had been seen there since 1910. This year, both those species are nesting in fair numbers. Dusty and Joe counted thirty-two roseates on March 11, a mixed population of birds of the year, subadults, and adults in full breeding plumage. By the end of March, about seventy of the big pink birds were coloring up the seascape.

Sandy Sprunt, director of research, allows as how Dusty and Joe could be a big help to him if the Army Corps of Engineers comes through with a contract to study their spoil-bank islands. Now that the Corps of Engineers has spent many decades and millions of dollars dredging channels and throwing up artificial islands, it appears that they want a better measure of what the effect is on the surrounding waters and the plants and animals that depend on them. Surprise?

A far more enjoyable emergency befell Dusty this spring. He is explaining to his wife, Susan, why it takes so much time to check on all the islands, keep the boats running, serve on the Hillsborough County Planning Commission Advisory Committee, work with the Corps of Engineers, and NAS Research Department, and get his report in to Old Dad, when he gets a phone call from NAS Tour Division. They need someone to lead a tour of Ecuador and the Galapagos Islands. Hardship duty, but what's a poor man gonna do?

Anyway, Joe tended the store in Dusty's absence; Susan was waiting and still speaking when he got back; and the picnickers, poachers, and fishermen had been held at bay in the Bay. So the pelicans, herons, egrets, cormorants, and ibises went on doing what they do on Audubon Sanctuaries.

Joe Harris is a glutton for punishment. After being bashed about in a shipwreck, he decides his appendix is a nuisance, and the surgeon agrees. So our inventory for Tampa Bay now shows two boats, one truck, one cabin, two wardens, and one appendix.

MAY 1977 While Dusty was helping the Coast Guard control oil spills and rescuing oil-soaked birds, he also kept an eye on our old environmentalist friends, the Corps of Engineers. The Corps was behaving normally in Tampa Bay last winter: working on a harbor deepening project, blithely ignoring state water quality laws, preparing environmental impact statements containing all fat and no meat. Meanwhile, they kept their dredges working, roiling the water in Tampa Bay, while doing the same in the courts that try to decide whether the Corps is obeying the law.

Several thousand herons, egrets, ibises, cormorants, brown pelicans, terns, and gulls nest on our sanctuaries in Tampa Bay. All those gaping beaks have got to be stoked with produce coming out of Tampa Bay. In addition to our feathered friends, there are all those human critters that like crabs, oysters, and fish. It's the old story of people and birds being short-changed in the grocery department in order to subsidize waterborne freight haulers.

Dusty says he would rather spend all his time studying the lives and times of his wading birds and pelicans and protecting them from picnickers, kids with .22s, and run-of-the-mill hellraisers. Unfortunately, although that would be easier and more enjoyable, it would not guarantee that Tampa Bay could support pelicans and people twenty years from now. Hence, he has to deal with attorneys and engineers part of the time and work with our chapters to get the job done.

Last year Jim Rodgers, on a small research grant from NAS, worked with Dusty now and then while he was studying the little blue heron on

Alafia Banks. Jim is back again this spring and summer, continuing his study and, at the same time, wardening the islands and helping us keep track of what's going on around the rookeries. Is this what you call a symbiotic relationship?

Federal game warden Chuck Kniffin betook himself to Tampa Bay last fall while the duck season was in progress. Agent Kniffin happens to believe that the mighty nimrods who shoot too many ducks, or the wrong kind, or use corn and rice for decoys, should feel the long arm of the law. He also has the unusual notion that the law applies exactly the same to rich folks, poor folks, and in-betweens. Since Dusty knows the ducks, duck hunters, and water of Tampa Bay like the back of his hand, 'tis small wonder these two found themselves cooperating in a very effective joint effort. After they spent several twenty-hour days in succession, the legitimate duck hunters and some not-so legitimate had a new respect for federal regulations. Dusty and Chuck had a new respect for each other.

MAY 1978 Jim Rodgers is another saltwater sanctuary type whose duties range from wildlife warden, research ornithologist, membership on the Advisory Committee of the Tampa Port Authority, ship's carpenter, lecturer, bird-watcher's guide, student, and teacher.

There are several islands in our sanctuaries in Tampa Bay, of which Alafia Banks has long been the outstanding producer of sharp-faced fowl. Last November after much, much negotiating between the Tampa Port Authority, National Audubon, and Florida Audubon, Dusty and Jim worked out an agreement concerning the harbor deepening project. They kept damage to the productivity of Tampa Bay to a minimum and got the engineers to rebuild Sunken Island on the west end of Alafia Banks. Since then Jim has managed this spoil bank (about fifteen acres) for gulls, terns, and skimmers.

On May 18, Old Dad receives a report from Jim that reads as follows: "Success is ours!!!! About 125 pairs of least terns and black skimmers are now nesting on the spoil extension of Alafia Banks. It appears that more skimmers are roosting and flying and probably will nest. There are about seven pairs of Caspian terns that are showing interest in the same area. I shall keep a record and at the end of the breeding season, I'll write up a summary with slides and send it to you." Which proves that even the Army Corps of Engineers can do something useful if our wardens are there to tell 'em how.

MAY 1979 A brand new Ph.D. with a posthole digger in his hands is a sight you seldom see. But then a lot of things go on in the Tampa Bay Sanctuaries that are seldom seen elsewhere. In 1977 Jim Rodgers put gentle persuasion to the Corps of Engineers, and they tacked a twelve-acre spoil island onto the western end of Alafia Banks. Jim figured that, if he could keep part of the island barren of vegetation, the least terns would have a new home. He did and they did. He had 225 pairs nesting there in 1978. As of May 26, 1979, the leasts had not yet started nesting, but he had 13 pairs of Caspians and 118 pairs of black skimmers. He's hoping royals and possibly Sandwich Forster's terns will eventually build in the new subdivision.

To keep the big sandpile bare for least terns, he locates an eight-horse engine, takes it down to Corkscrew, where Charlie Grimes mounts it on their old roto-tiller. Back to Tampa he goes and on Saturday, April 14, he is roto-tilling up a storm, trying to get the job done before the terns return. On April 15, his report says, "Patrolled Alafia Banks. Finished roto-tilling the spoil island extension. Felt like an old man, that machine kills you!"

To keep the new island from washing away and to furnish nesting habitat for Forster's terns, Jim undertakes the ambitious project of creating a salt marsh and planting wire grass (*Spartina patens*) that he transplants from existing marshes around Tampa Bay. This is quite a project. It involves digging up the Spartina plants, loading them in a boat, running back to Alafia Banks, and unloading and planting in the intertidal zone. This is where the posthole digger comes in. Just thinking about it makes Old Dad's back go out.

Jim enlisted the help of the Tampa Marine Institute, which is competing with Satan in order to find work for hands of certain teenagers. Obviously, Satan didn't stand a chance because between Jim and these youngsters; they planted over seven thousand Spartina plugs and set several aside, growing in cans until after the birds leave, when the transplanting will continue. Jim also hopes to eventually get mangroves started around the shoreline.

The Tampa Harbor Deepening Project has resulted in increased turbidity around our islands. Jim has worked with the Corps, the Port Authority, and various environmental groups, which has held down the damage considerably. Consequently, dredging occurs when the birds are not nesting; boats and equipment must stay more than five hundred feet from the islands; construction boats are limited to five miles per hour to reduce impact on wintering manatees in the Alafia River.

But Tampa is the eighth largest port in the United States, due mainly to the bulk loading of phosphate rock. When proper measures are not taken, phosphate dust falls into Tampa Bay, which hastens eutrophication. Thanks to Jim, the local Environmental Protection Commission is paying closer attention. Much of Hillsborough Bay bottom is now sterile due to flourides leaching from a nearby phosphoric plant. Last fall, a sixty thousand-gallon oil spill occurred in upper Hillsborough Bay, but fortunately winds carried most of it out through Tampa Bay and into the Gulf. In other words, all is not beer and skittles, but life in one of the country's greatest colonial bird shows does go on.

JULY 1980   According to St. Matthew, only fools and real estate developers build houses on the sand. But according to Jim Rodgers, you can build a Spartina marsh and a red mangrove swamp, and they will hold the sand in place. Then terns, skimmers, gulls, and wading birds can build on it. It requires about four thousand old tires, strapped down, anchored, and filled with sand, in which the grass is planted. Otherwise, the severe wave action would wash away the entire island as wind-drive waves produce cuts that undermine the plantings.

Jim and his crew of Young Adult Conservation Corps established two such erosion barriers, one 35 feet by 250 feet, on a ten-acre extension of Sunken Island, adjacent to our Alafia Banks.

Along the south shore of the extension, Jim and his crew planted over four acres of *Spartina alterniflora* and *S. patens* in rows about one yard apart. The grasses have since spread and created the largest man-made marsh in Florida. Jim saw a clapper rail, a new record for his new marsh, on May 10, 1980. The creation of the entire four acres cost less than $7,000, whereas the u.s. Council on Environmental Quality estimates the return on the marsh to be $85,000 per acre per year. Bringing tires, materials, grasses, and crew out to the island took many, many days of backbreaking work in the Florida sun. Jim Rodgers is no arm chair biologist!

Other wildlife management measures included planting sea oats in nearby areas. The intricate root system of this grass enables it to get adequate water in sandy soil and hold the sand in place while the aerial portions of the plant catch the drifting sand, building up the dune. He girdled Australian pines because other woody species provide better nesting platforms. He also planted about 120 red mangrove seedlings on a sandbar.

Students assisting in erosion control.
(Photo: Rich Paul)

When mature, these should provide more nesting sites for white ibises and brown pelicans. But the old satchel-mouths did not wait for the mangroves to get big enough to support a nest. They were seen tearing up the seedlings and carting them off to build this year's nests. St. Matthew tells how, ". . . the rain descended, and the floods came, and the winds blew, and beat upon that house; and it fell." He does not mention what pelicans do to potential housing when they get the urge to build.

One fine day, Norm Brunswig (manager, Beidler Forest in South Carolina) stops by to see how a sanctuary consisting of a bunch of islands compares with a swamp. He is much impressed by the least, Caspian, royal, and Sandwich terns, plus skimmers (all on Florida's threatened list) and by the hundreds of brown pelicans (on everybody's endangered list). But the thought of poor ol' Jim fightin' that Jimmy-crack-corn roto-tiller is more than Norm can bear. So he dashes off a long and persuasive letter, complete with photos of Jim playing in his sandpile with his home-made machine. Next thing we know, a brand new Troy-Bilt Roto-Tiller from Troy, New York, is on its way to Tampa Bay.

In his spare time, Jim manages to finish his Ph.D., to get a paper published on heron breeding behavior, to give about twenty lectures on Audubon and Tampa Bay, to lead a dozen field trips, and to serve as an advisor to the Tampa Port Authority and the Corps of Engineers. Because Cortez Island is heavily used by brown pelicans, he tracks down the owner, which turns out to be the state. We are now in the process of leasing Cortez Island and will protect its pelicans from the ever-increasing people pressure in Tampa Bay. Picnickers, driftwood collectors, campers, boaters, hunters, fishermen, vandals, and photographers insist on landing on the sanctuary islands. Were it not for the efforts of one Audubon warden, the entire production of threatened and endangered species in Tampa Bay would be lost.

JULY 1981   Although Jim Rodgers planned to join the research arm of the Florida Fish and Game Department as of August 1, 1980, he did not take the short-termer attitude in July. Instead he planted a record 819 Spartina clumps on July 1, and 584 on July 10. He led twenty-two college students on a tour of our Tampa Bay sanctuaries and gave Rich Paul a fine orientation course on managing them.

On August 1, 1980, Rich took over where Jim Rodgers left off, and the colonial waterbirds went right on colonizing the islands. Thirty pairs of brown pelicans occupied the newly built Sunken Island. On adjacent Extension Island, 7 pairs of oystercatchers, 320 pairs of royal terns, 8 pairs of Caspians, and 200 pairs of skimmers set up housekeeping. According to the new Book of Peterson, page 94, the Sandwich tern "Prefers company of royal terns." Accordingly, when the royal families reached 700 on Extension Island, a pair of Sandwich terns dutifully nested among them.

On October 6, Rich gave Glenn Paulson (vice president for science, NAS) a firsthand look at the Spartina marsh restoration project, the erosion control project, and tern habitat management.

The Tampa Port Authority, Hillsborough Community College, nearby chapters, and miscellaneous environmental groups all call on Rich for advice. This is encouraging, but it is even more so when four employees of International Minerals and Chemicals tour the sanctuary to learn how we restore marshes, mangroves, and bird colonies. They are involved in restoration of mined lands and want to learn how it is done from the folks that know.

Some of the more interesting wild critters include a manatee last November 10; 200 pairs of skimmers on Extension Island; and a peregrine falcon on October 20. Although his usual habitat (cypress swamps, rice fields, rivers, and wooded ponds) does not exist in Tampa Bay, an anhinga surprised Rich on May 18 over Bird Island. On May 24, 1981, our black-bearded warden heard two black-whiskered vireos singing on Green Key.

MAY 1982 Dusty Dunstan, now assistant director, Sanctuary Department, and Old Dad spent a couple of February days on Tampa Bay with Rich Paul and agreed he had his act together. And a complex, difficult act it is, albeit very familiar to all other wardens. One man or woman on a big sanctuary, near a big town, in the busiest seaport in the region must be combination researcher, enforcement agent, lecturer, field trip leader, goodwill ambassador, and "the voice of Audubon."

On March 4, 1982, the *Tampa Tribune* put it this way: "While developers salivate over blueprints to urbanize South Hillsborough County, Paul looks beyond those trappings to what he might call the darker side of growth and development—the disappearance of wetlands that support wild fowl. He speaks out at forums whenever construction threatens to erase those feeding grounds. . . ."

The two-page spread goes on to describe what we have accomplished here since we started in 1934. Although it does refer to the great white heron, instead of great egret as our mascot, the article is unusually accurate for a newspaper. The photos and description of Rich, the Spartina planting project, and various fish-eating birds are very well done.

On top of all this people management, Rich manages to keep various forms of outdoor recreation from taking place too near the brown pelicans, terns, and other colonies. For the terns and skimmers, he tries to keep about three acres from being taken over by vegetation. Rich has tested burning on one plot, and burning plus roto-tilling on another. He says, ". . . burning plus tilling provides the terns with acceptable nesting habitat. Burning alone is insufficient. However, even with tilling, the vegetation recovers rapidly during the summer and is thick by late August. All we do is give the terns a head start, but that seems to be enough."

On July 1981, a great white heron showed up on Cortez Island, our newest addition to the Tampa Bay Sanctuaries. Since this sharp-faced fowl is some 250 miles north of its main breeding range in Florida Bay, Rich is wondering whether his distinguished guest will head south come next breeding season. Comes September and great white is still there. In January 1982, the second freeze in two years occurred, a new record for the twentieth century. Great white hangs in there, all decked out in his courtin' clothes, and is still there in February. Rich wonders if there's a female great white to observe this display, or is it another case of male vanity going for naught. Meanwhile, young great blue herons are out of the nest and staggering around on the shore.

In his report for November, Rich says, "Three diamond-backs on Alafia this month helped my pulse considerably." But while he was keeping duck hunters from disturbing pelicans too much, dodging rattlesnakes, buying a new Chevy pickup, and holding the line on "progress," his report also says, "This has been an interesting month—one of finding out, suddenly, how to run some of the maze. To feel like I've helped make a difference in a few local issues has been exhilarating."

The great white heron? Stay tuned.

SEPTEMBER 1983 Although it didn't rate a name from the u.s. Weather Service, Rich Paul had his own name for the storm on July 18, 1982, with its sixty mile per hour winds and five-foot tides. We lost twenty out of twenty-seven signs, which was not as disturbing as loss of about 10 brown pelican nests out of 209 nests on Cortez Island. At Washburn and Alafia Banks, the mangroves offered better protection, and pelican losses were not severe. But most of the 195 pairs of black skimmers failed. Royal terns, although nesting right with the skimmers, came through unscathed, On Passage Key, 20,000 pairs of laughing gulls and 1,000 royal terns lost about 95 percent of their young. As Rich says, "Those terns shoulda stayed at Alafia." At Alafia, eight pairs of Sandwich terns nested, which is a new high.

In his spare time, Rich was instrumental in stopping an illegal drainage canal that would have damaged the mangroves, plus two or three other projects that engineers thought were feasible.

JANUARY 1986 Apparently the staff writer for the *St. Petersburg Evening Independent* was much impressed by the sanctuary. He wrote, "Shadowed by towering chimneys and nudging a massive pile of phosphate waste, Florida's biggest bird sanctuary rests like a serene swell of nature within the belching industrial gullet of eastern Tampa Bay." That's pretty heady stuff for a newspaper in a seaport town.

Besides all of his other various duties and obligations, Rich found time for making some interesting observations: immature parasitic jaeger on November 18, 1984, in Alafia River; eight endangered manatees on the twenty-fifth; on April 8 and 30, 1985, peregrine falcons were trolling for fish crows and ring-billed gulls; and the first downy young black vultures were seen on Washburn Island on the seventeenth.

In July 1985, the average pelican pair fledged 1.5 young, almost three

Brown pelican nestlings.
(Photo: Rich Paul)

times the average reported by Ted Below down at Rookery Bay. A Florida gallinule with a downy chick on September 15, 1984, was a new record for the sanctuary. In April 1985, the white ibises got off to a late start and for the first time in Rich's experience, the drooped-snoots did not occupy all available habitat. He suspects the severe drought may have been a factor.

MARCH 1987   Rich Paul says the time was when an Audubon warden could protect the colonial waterbirds in Tampa Bay fairly well by just patrolling and flashing a badge now and then. You could spend all your time around the island in the bay and get the job done. But the proposed marina in Little Cockroach Bay, for which a channel would be dredged across the bay, is but one example of modern threats to wildlife, far more serious than the guns and fish hooks of bygone days.

For a biologist with an outstanding knowledge of wading birds and estuaries, it is cruel and unusual punishment to have to spend hours and hours as an adviser to the Tampa Port Authority, the City-County Planning Commission, the nearby Gardinier Company that produces phosphate and a mountain of sulfur, Audubon chapters in nearby cities, the Florida Audubon Society, International Mineral and Chemical Company, the Environmental Protection Agency, U.S. Fish and Wildlife Service, and the Florida Game and Freshwater Fish Department.

Some of those hours were spent to modify the Hillborough county land use plan because, as Rich says, "Without incentives for conservation easements or other land set-aside measures, there is little chance that nonjurisdictional wetlands especially important to wading birds will be preserved."

His efforts paid off. The Department of Environmental Regulation denied a permit to dredge a channel across Little Cockroach Bay. Rich was instrumental in stopping an illegal fill in a brackish marsh. And in between he still finds time to protect the birds and other critters in the Tampa Bay Sanctuaries.

JULY 1991 Rich Paul may not be all things to all men, but to the developers on the shores of Tampa Bay he is like a wave of the sea. Which is one way of saying that environmental awareness has never been so high.

The Environmental Protection Agency tagged Tampa Electric for $155,000 just for dumping contaminated water forty-nine times in five years. In contrast, Gardinier, whence cometh our lease on Alafia Banks and much dinero for patrolling and protecting our ten islands, gets a favorable editorial from the *Tampa Tribune*.

A developer from Sarasota is the first in Florida history to get twenty days and a $10,000 fine for illegally cutting protected mangrove trees. According to the *Tribune,* when warned in 1989 that he had illegally cut two thousand trees, he replied, "Go ahead and fine me. It's the cost of doing business." So he kept on cutting. When released from the pokey, he was privileged to spend 250 hours of community service work for the county Parks and Recreation Department.

On September 25, 1990, the Power Plant Siting Task Force told Tampa Electric to locate its next coal-fired plant in mined-out phosphate beds in southwestern Polk county—not on the shore of Tampa Bay as previously proposed. According to Rich, this important advance in protecting the bay brings credit to both TECO and the task force members.

Suffice it to say things are moving, and we can guess the identity of one prime mover. From a plethora of additional evidence, we will cite just one more case. The USFWS and Coast Guard issued a permit and announced the world championship offshore power boat race, with boats making over one hundred miles per hour to be held in Hillsborough Bay in November—in the wintering grounds of the endangered manatee and feeding grounds of wading birds. Guess what? The race was moved off-shore, where it should have been in the first place. Prime mover?

MAY 1992 The U.S. Census Bureau reports that nearby Brandon grew by 61 percent during the 1980s to 111,000. At the same time, white ibis numbers at Alafia Banks declined by about 50 percent to 5,000 breeding pairs. This was despite improvements in federal, state, and local wetlands protection. The war is not over, albeit we win a lot of battles. The time was when we didn't win any.

A year-end tally of media contacts shows Tampa Bay staff and wildlife were included in nineteen long newspaper articles complete with maps and photos, two magazine articles, and ten television shows. Charles Kuralt's *Sunday Morning* showed excellent footage of satchel-mouthed mullet-burners, a.k.a. pelicans, plus the local sharp-faced fowl.

Rich says one very important reason for our success stories came in January 1991, when Marilyn Kershner, with her marketing and public TV background, volunteered for office duty. She left a job as vice president and counsel for real estate lending at NCNB Florida to devote more time to environmental issues and public interest law. Her influence in Tampa Bay is very evident in Rich's reports.

More cordgrass and mangroves were planted by fifty-two marine biology students from Chamberlain High School. For educational purposes, a photo of seven girls kneeling in the sand with mangrove seedlings in hand made the *Tribune*. Folks nowadays don't often hear much good about high school students, so this publicity made a big impression. Rich's caption was, "As you can see, it was a great day!"

A state biologist announced Tampa Bay contains the most important waterbird colonies in Florida. Mars Van Liefde of the Cayman Islands, who is gathering info on U.S. conservation to take back to the Caymans, visited the sanctuary in March 1991. She must have liked what she saw because she mentions her intentions, which include Audubon, in her will. Rich straightaway calls on Wayne Mones, our ace money raiser, to follow up. "It's eleemosinary, my dear Watson."

MAY 1993 Rich and assistant manager, Ann Schnapf, patrol ten islands in Tampa Bay with special attention to those to which the birds pay special attention, such as Alafia Banks, Washburn, Cortez, Three Rooker Bar, and give the state and feds a little help with their refuges and parks.

The effect of dogs, boats, coons, and people on island nesters is fairly easy to see. But as the 1992 nesting season progressed, a gradual decline in

Aerial view of Alafia Bank.
(Photo: Rich Paul)

numbers of pairs of pelicans, small herons, and white ibises had Rich and Ann puzzled. Pelican nests numbered about 100 at Cortez, and 600 at Alafia, less than half the expected populations! Nesting was very late; first broods of downy chicks were seen in mid to late April; and brood size appeared small. One fisherman noted a shortage of bait in the bay. The Game Commission intensified its scrutiny (mostly through the eyes of Rich and Ann) of pelican nesting. By the end of May, the total rainfall for the year was only 8.36 inches, 40 percent below normal. Not good news for wading birds.

Islands 2D and 3D are large spoil banks managed by the Tampa Port Authority with help and advice from Rich and Ann. The bare sand provides good nesting habitat for gulls, terns, skimmers, and a few oyster-catchers. We erect signs and try to patrol nesting colonies, which is not always easy. On Labor Day, the swarm of boaters and beachcombers was not too cooperative. Ann tried to talk to two people on 3D and was run off by two large Rottweilers. In spite of such adversities, the islands are quite productive.

On May 31, at Alafia, Ann counted 75 pairs and 126 young spoon-bills, our all time high! On May 19, 1992, at Passage Key National Wild-life Refuge, we counted 2,360 royal tern nests, 205 Sandwich terns, 7,000 laughing gulls, 35 black skimmers, and 4 oystercatchers. At Tarpon Key National Wildlife Refuge, 488 pelican nests and four very young spoonbills were counted for the first confirmed record here since 1912.

Pelican counts at all colonies, however, reveal continuing problems for them. Rich suspects shortage of food, but the cause is unknown. Drought? Overfishing by purse seines? By thousands of sport fishermen? But a dim glow flickers at the end of the tunnel. Rich keeps his fingers crossed while the chamber of commerce shows some signs of realizing that bad news for birds, manatees, and mullet eventually means a deteriorating human condition.

For example, a headline in the May 24, 1992, *Tampa Tribune:* "Birds Flocking to Rooftops from Crowded Florida Beaches." A subhead: "Beachgoers Claim Untamed Shores." The article describes a least tern colony on Florida Power and Light Company's gravel-topped roof. Rich is quoted at length. "This is a problem that's absolutely pervasive along the entire Florida coast. It's strictly a numbers game. The higher the human population, the greater the potential that nesting sites will either be developed or heavily used for recreation."

In addition to extensive quotes from Rich, the Florida Fish and Game Commission promises to fine people who disregard sanctuary signs. And the feds and state managers are offering more protection and promising enforcement of refuge boundaries. The list of municipal, county, state, and federal agencies that call on Rich and Ann for data and advice is endless: like Sheriff Charlie Flesher, who asked our assistance in posting several islands along the Intracoastal Waterway south of Clearwater.

A proposal to designate the white ibis as a threatened species in Florida because it has declined about 90 percent in the Everglades and 80 percent in Tampa Bay has the Florida Farm Bureau, the Florida Chamber of Commerce, and the Florida Association of Community Developers crying, "We will be losing our homes and farms to the birds."

And Deseret Ranch, owned by the Mormon Church, claims the restrictions on water use are nothing short of sacrilegious, even though saltwater intrusion in some areas advances at one foot per day. Says Rich, "Water wars, here we come. Our ibis populations, of course, have been predicting this for years."

MARCH 1994 Rich Paul says that 1993 was the best year for colonial waterbirds—not just in our sanctuary—but in the Tampa–Sarasota Bay region, in over ten years. A longer nesting season, lower rate of nesting failure, and increased brood size (1.3 young per nest) all contributed to successful brown pelican nesting.

Since the Army Corps of Engineers made south Florida and the Everglades safe for sugar beets and condominiums, the endangered wood stork has had to look elsewhere for a place to fledge more flintheads. For the first time on record, 140 pairs produced 310 young in the Tampa Bay system.

Beach nesters are very apt to be flooded by water, people, and dogs. But in 1993, Caspian, royal, Sandwich, and least terns, black skimmers, and American oystercatchers all had notable nesting success. In fact, over half of Florida's black skimmers (1,000 out of 1,800 pairs) nested in ten Tampa Bay colonies. Through direct and cooperative efforts, we helped to protect all ten colonies.

For the foreseeable future, the people pressure on the natural resources of Tampa Bay will no doubt continue. Thanks to Rich Paul, Ann Schnapf, and the Audubon sanctuary personnel who preceded them, the wild plants and animals and people who depend upon them have a better chance of survival.

CONCLUSION

As the twentieth century draws to a close, the sanctuary department, as I knew it, has done likewise. In 1995 incoming NAS president, John Flicker, announced a reorganization plan for the National Audubon Society. The society would no longer be administered from the New York office. Instead, a strong central office in each state would oversee sanctuaries and all other administrative functions.

In several states, such as Texas, Wisconsin, Michigan, and Ohio, a rather extensive system of sanctuaries administered by the respective state is already in place. In Texas, for example, I believe the State Audubon Society can manage the Sabal Palm Grove, Green Island, and other coastal island sanctuaries very well. The same can be said for many states, although the Audubon Society's strength and influence varies from state to state.

Most federal wildlife refuges were established to benefit wild ducks and geese. Benefits to other avian species are more or less incidental. State-owned wildlife management areas are usually established as public hunting areas.

In contrast, Audubon wildlife sanctuaries were often set aside to save an endangered bird such as egrets at Cuthbert Lake in Florida, snail kites in the Florida Everglades, wood storks at Corkscrew Swamp in Florida, puffins on Eastern Egg Rock in Maine, and reddish egrets on Green Island, Texas. An endangered ecosystem such as the virgin cypress swamp at Corkscrew, or the prairie along the Platte River in Nebraska, or the sabal palm grove in Texas are often too small for state and federal agencies to manage.

Audubon wildlife sanctuaries have played a significant role in the fast-growing outdoor sport of bird-watching. Scenic wonders such as the Yellowstone National Park and Yosemite were attracting visitors before the Audubon sanctuaries were established. The thriving industry known as ecotourism, however, owes its beginning and growth largely to birders visiting Audubon sanctuaries.

In September 1995, the Audubon Society met in Rockport, Texas, to commemorate the Connie Hagar Wildlife Sanctuary. In the broiling sun, none other than Roger Troy Peterson, the patron saint of bird-watchers and the Audubon Society, addressed the gathering. Also on the program was Andrew Sansom, director, Texas Parks and Wildlife. The size and enthusiasm of the crowd undoubtedly impressed Sansom, and may well have inspired the trail of "birding hot spots" along the Texas coast, now in place.

At the 1998 National Audubon Society Convention in Estes Park, Colorado, the sanctuary managers just happened to have their own get-together. The camaraderie among managers of priceless wildlife habitat seems to be contagious and here to stay.

May there always be places to hide and seek.

(Photo: Silas B. Cooper Jr.)

INDEX

Abrendson, Susan, 219
Adams, John, 124
Alafia Banks, 226, 230, 231
Alkali Lake Sanctuary, 179, 183, 185–
186, 189, 195. *See also* Edward
Brigham Alkali Lake Sanctuary
Allbrecht, Mark, 181
Allen, Bob, 134
Allen, Durward, 123, 181
Allen, Jocko, 35
Allen, Robert Porter, 60
alligator, 102, 135, 207; at Rainey, 2–3,
4, 5, 8, 9, 13–14, 18
alligator weed, 214
anaqua, 146, 148
Anderson, Connie, 80
Anderson, Jeanne, 77
Anderson, John M. "Frosty," x–xii.
See also Old Dad
Anderson, Mrs. John M. "Miss
Nancy," 11; at Miles, 69–71, 78,
79, 80, 92. *See also* Miss Nancy
Andrews, Ralph, xvi
andropogon, 181
Angelle, Burton, 18

anhinga, 210, 226, 234
Anstet, Beth, 91
anole, 207
ant, fire, 105
Arballo, Gary, 164
Arbib, Bob, 103, 117, 204, 208
Army Corps of Engineers. *See* U.S.
Army Corps of Engineers
Arrowwood National Wildlife Refuge,
180
Ashley, Rick, 181
Audubon Society. *See* National Audu-
bon Society
Aull, Marie, 42, 203
Aullwood Sanctuary and Nature Cen-
ter, 35, 42, 203
avocet, 194; American, 192

baboon, chacma, 80
badger, 162, 191
Bailey, C. Lewis, 218
Bailey, Rob, 99, 100, 103, 107
Bailey, Sue, 29, 95–107
Baker, John H., xv, 25
Barbour, Bruce, 171, 184–196

Barrows, Mike, 85
bat, lesser yellow, 147
Bauer, Erwin A. "Joe," 105
Beacon Sloop Club, 119
bear, black, 140
beaver, 180, 215; at Miles, 68, 69, 70, 78, 83–90 *passim*
Bedell, Brian, 181
Bednarik, Karl, xvi, 187
beetle: click, 150; pine bark, 214
Beidler, Francis, 197
Beidler, Francis, III, 203
Beidler Forest Sanctuary, xvii, 202, 212, 222, 223
Bellrose, Frank, 206
Below, Ted, 237
Belt, Charles Bank, 207
Bennett, Hank, 135, 136
Bent, A. C., 72
benthos, 202
Bergh, Chris, 140
Bergquist, John, 75, 77
Berle, Peter, 22, 124, 126, 129, 130, 216
Betancourt, Adalberto, 151–152
Beyea, Jan, 173
Bielert, Craig, 80
Binnewies, Bob, 113
bittern, least, 125
blackbird, red-winged, 83, 89, 91, 125
Blakeney, Carlyle, 2–3, 5, 9, 39, 199, 200
Blankinship, Dave, 9, 32, 34, 38, 43, 143; at Sabal Palm Grove, 146, 148; at Sydnes Island, 105; and Vingt-et-Une, 64
Bletsch, Lloyd, 146
Bloom, Pete, 160, 168, 172
bluebills. *See* scaup, lesser
bluebird: at Alkali Lake, 187, 189, 191; at Beidler Forest, 210; at Miles, 75, 80, 81, 86–90 *passim*, 92, 93; at Rowe, 41
bluebird boxes, 191
bluestem, big, 180

blue-wings (blue-winged teal), 181
bobcat, 162, 188; at Miles, 70, 75, 81, 82; at Sabal Palm Grove, 147, 148, 150
bobolink, 192
Bontrager, Dave, 168
Borck, Bill, 92
Borneman, John, 157
Borror, Donald J., 51
Boscobel, 133
Bouteloua, 181
Boyle, Bob, 115, 119, 120, 123
Bradford Fen, 93
Bradley, Guy, x, xiii–xiv, 143
Bradley, Kathie, 219
brant, eagle-headed, 6, 14, 19. *See also* goose: blue; snow, at Rainey
Brazilian pepper bush, 141
Breaux, John, 10
Brees, Bart, 60
Brickhouse, Ernest, 84
Brigham, Edward M., III, 112, 113, 116, 178, 186, 189
Brokaw, Howard, 187
Broughton, Dan, 220, 221
Broussard, Pideau, 11, 12. *See also* Broussard Brothers
Broussard Brothers, 19. *See also* Broussard, Pideau
Brunswig, Beverly, 198
Brunswig, Norman, 3, 121; at Beidler Forest, 198–224; at Ichuaway Plantation, 218; at Tampa Bay, 233
Buchheister, Carl W., xiv, xv, xvi, 1, 68, 203
Buchheister, Mrs. Carl W., 203
Bullfrog Creek, 228
bull whip, 21
bunting: indigo, 17; painted, 140; snow, 86, 187
BuRec. *See* US Bureau of Reclamation
burning, prescribed, 42, 182, 183, 190, 235
Butorides striatus, 22

---

butterfly, 130; alfalfa, 41
Buzzo, Joe, 85

Cabot, Mr. and Mrs. Frank, 128
Cade, Tom, 130
cadmium, 115, 126
Callison, Charles H., xv, xvi, 35, 38
Camp, R. D., 25
Canadian Wildlife Service, 53
canvasback, 149, 177, 181, 184, 185, 187
cardinal, northern, 87, 211, 212
Carlson, Ed, 82, 199; at Corkscrew
    Swamp, 134, 135, 137, 138–141
Carroll, J. J., 25
Carter, O. R., 22
Case, Marshall, 117
Caspers Park Wilderness Area, 153, 171
catbird, 91, 116
caterpillar, forest tent, 207, 208, 212
cattle, 181
CBS (Columbia Broadcasting Sys-
    tem), 123, 218
chachalaca, 147
Chace, Evy, 222
Chandlers, the, 164. *See also* entries for
    individuals
Chandler, Glenn, 144
Chandler, Louise, 22
Chandler, Marvin, 143–144
Chandler, Noel, 19, 22
Chandler, Roderick, xvii, 117, 144
Chapman, Karen, 151–152
Chase Lake National Wildlife Refuge,
    180
chestnut, Eurasian, 114–115, 120
chickadee, 92; black-capped, 191;
    Carolina, 210
chickee, 137
Chinese tallow tree, 96, 99
Choate, David, 170, 171
Clayton, Doug, 199–201
Cleveland National Forest, 153, 155
coastal sage scrub, 171
Cofer, Jennifer, 85, 86

Cohen, Robin, 90
Cohn, Roger, 81
Compton, Warren, 196
Connecticut River, 112
Connelly, Dan "Cooter," 65, 80, 218,
    219, 224
Connelly, Sally, 80
Cooper, Carolyn, 216
Cooper, Silas B., Jr., 4, 5, 20, 22, 216
coot, 149
copperhead, 220
coral bean, 148
Corcoran, John, 214
cordgrass, 239
Corkscrew Region Ecological Wet-
    lands (CREW), 141
Corkscrew Swamp Sanctuary, xvi,
    xvii, 134, 135, 137, 138, 141, 154, 155
cormorant, 21; at Sydnes Island, 96–
    102 *passim,* 104, 105; at Tampa Bay,
    226, 228, 229; at Vingt-et-Une,
    56–59 *passim,* 61, 62, 64; double-
    crested, 89; olivaceous, 97–100
    passim
Corps. *See* US Army Corps of
    Engineers
Cortez Island, 234, 235
corvid. *See* crow
cottonmouth snake, 97, 220
cottonwood tree, 175
cougar, 155, 157, 160, 168. *See also*
    mountain lion
cowbird, 87, 88; brown-headed, 211
Cox, Mary, 97
coyote: at Alkali Lake, 180, 187, 191; at
    Green Island, 31; at Miles, 81, 83, 86;
    at Starr Ranch, 161, 162
crab, blue, 107
crane, 45, 46; sandhill, xi, xvii, 34, 35–
    39 *passim,* 43–44, 49, 177; whoop-
    ing, xi, 34, 37, 41, 43, 49, 192
CREW (Corkscrew Region Ecological
    Wetlands), 142
Crosby, John, 220, 221

Cross, Theodore, 103
Croton Marsh, 126–127
crow, 208, 211; Mexican, 150
Cruger Island, 110
Cruickshank, Allan, 51
Cruickshank, Helen, 227
cuckoo, yellow-bellied, 211; yellow-
    billed, 207, 212
Cunningham, Jim, 19, 42, 149
Cutlip, Jerry, 164, 199, 200
cypress, virgin, 197, 215, 220, 222

dace, black-nosed, 128
Davis, Anna May, 148
Davis, Douglas, 148
Dawson, Jo Ann, 219
Dawson, Mike, 121; at Beidler Forest,
    206, 208, 210, 212–216, 218–224
DeCecco, Jennifer, 90
deer, 13, 162, 172, 208; at Alkali Lake,
    178, 181, 183, 187–188; at Constitu-
    tion Island Marsh, 122, 126, 128; at
    Miles, 65, 70, 75, 81, 83, 85; mule, at
    Starr Ranch, 155, 156, 160, 161, 169;
    whitetailed, 65, 85, 183
deer mouse, 90
DeLuca, Diane, 77
DeSimone, Pete, 44, 190; at Miles,
    72–77 passim, 79, 80, 82, 83–84, 86,
    89, 160, 172; and Rowe, 44; at Starr
    Ranch, 164, 166–174
DeSimone, Sandra "Sandy" Mervis:
    and Miles, 76, 77, 79, 85, 86; at Starr
    Ranch, 166–169, 173–174. See also
    Mervis, Sandra
Dick, John Henry, 212, 222
dickcissel, 192
dickey bird, 70, 92, 116. See also
    bluebird
Donohoe, Robert, xvi
Donovan, Terri, 85, 87
dove, 191; mourning, 18, 83, 211;
    white-tipped, 147
Dove Canyon, 168, 174

Dowell, Barbara, 76
duck, 14, 15, 17, 42, 68, 191, 192, 193;
    black, 69, 70, 71, 84, 88, 123, 125;
    black-bellied tree, 147, 150; fulvous
    tree, 10; goldeneye, 88; hybrid,
    125; mottled, 8, 9, 13, 18, 107, 149;
    ring-necked, 149; ruddy, 177, 178,
    187; wood, 149, 192, 195, 206, 208,
    211; wood, at Alkali Lake, 184, 185,
    191; wood, at Constitution Island,
    109, 123, 125; wood, at Miles, 70, 78,
    81, 84, 86, 88–92 passim; wood, and
    pileated woodpecker, 206, 208, 211
Ducks Unlimited (DU), 194, 195
Dudek, Jan, 83, 88, 89
Dudek, Mike, 78, 83–93, 127
Duebbert, Harold, 196
Duever, Mike, 120, 209, 215, 217, 221
Dunn, Bill, 46, 48, 50
Dunstan, Frank "Dusty," 19, 60, 73,
    80, 105, 114, 117, 120, 171; at Alkali
    Lake, 184; at Miles, 81, 82, 83; at
    Tampa Bay, 226–230, 235
Dunstan, Jack, 130
Dunstan, Susan, 228–229
Dutcher, William, xiii
dwarf trillium, 216

eagle, 123; bald, 43, 228; bald, at Alkali
    Lake, 180, 181, 187; bald, at Consti-
    tution Island Marsh, 120, 125, 126,
    128, 130; bald, at Miles, 75, 81, 88;
    golden, 75, 158, 168, 170
Eastern Egg Rock, 52
Ebbs, Stacy, 128
ebony tree, Texas, 146, 148
Edward Brigham Alkali Lake Sanctu-
    ary, 193, 194, 196. See also Alkali
    Lake Sanctuary
Edmondson, Char, 46, 127, 167
Edmondson, "Papa" Joe, 19, 72, 90,
    167, 186, 220; and Constitution Is-
    land Marsh, 127, 128; at Miles, 80,
    82, 83, 86, 87; at Rowe, 42, 46

egret, xiii, 8, 9, 61, 65; American, 59;
cattle, 31, 32, 210; cattle, at Sydnes
Island, 96, 99, 100, 104, 105, 106;
common, xiv, 57; great, 26, 27, 87,
126, 210; great, at Sydnes Island,
96–104 *passim*, 106; great, at Vingt-
et-Une, 61–66 *passim;* reddish, xi,
xiv, 63; reddish, at Green Island, 25,
26, 27, 29, 31, 32; reddish, at Tampa
Bay, 226, 227, 228; snowy, xiv, 13,
98, 106, 192; snowy, at Green Island, 26, 27, 29, 31, 32; snowy, at
Sydnes Island, 96, 97, 99, 100, 102–
104 *passim;* snowy, at Vingt-et-Une,
57, 59, 61, 63–66 *passim;* at Tampa
Bay, 226, 228, 229; at Vingt-et-Une,
57, 59, 62–66 *passim*
elderberry bush, 99
Emily Winthrop Miles Sanctuary, 68–
69, 94
Ensminger, Al, 14
Environmental Protection Agency
(EPA), 115, 123, 124, 128, 131–132,
145, 218, 223, 238
Eskow, Jessica, 90
Evarts, Bill, 119, 122
Everitt, Dave, 160
EXXON, 62, 124, 146

Faanes, Craig, 44
falcon, prairie, 165, 180
Farmer, Rose, 150–151
Fawcett, Ann, 127
Fawcett, Howard, 127
finch, house, 87, 90
Fitch, Susan "Sue," 72, 73, 79, 81, 202
flat-faced fowl, 6, 12, 45, 46, 69, 180.
See also duck; goose
Flesher, Charlie, 241
Flicker, John, 152, 243
Florida Audubon Society, xiii–xiv
Fluman, William J. "Friday," 26–32,
98, 101, 185, 227
flycatcher, 17; Acadian, 210; ash-

throated, 168; crested, 207, 212;
great crested, 210; olive-sided, 87;
scissor-tailed, 150
forbs, 182
Foundry Cove, 131, 132–133
Four Hole Swamp, 197, 200, 208, 212,
222. *See also* Francis Beidler Forest
Sanctuary
fox, 185; red, 178, 187
Francis Beidler Forest Sanctuary, xvii,
202, 212, 222, 223
Fraser, Pat, 171
Fraser, Tom, 171
Franson, John, 4, 57, 95
frigate bird, 226
frog: Mexican tree, 147; upland chorus, 204
Froke, Benjamin Bray, 160
Froke, Jeff, 157–167, 217
Froke, Martha, 158, 160–161, 163, 165–
167
fulgorid tree hopper, 150

gadwall, 11, 149, 181, 185
gallinule, common (common moorhen), 106, 149, 237
General Electric (GE), 109, 110, 116,
131
Germond, Florence, 76
Gingert, Art, 8, 44, 189, 198, 205, 210;
at Miles, 69–83, 85–90, 92–93, 160
Gingert, Daniel Ethan, 71
Gingert, Jacob Koenig, 75
Gingert, Susan, 70–71, 75, 76, 77, 79,
82–83
Glazebrook, Catriona, 152
globe-flower, spreading, 76, 85
Glowka, Art, 115
gnatcatcher: blue-gray, 210; California, 170
golden club, 110
gold-finch, 88
Gonzales, Roberto, 22
Goodall, William, xv

goose, 17, 42, 49; Atlantic snow, 84, 125; blue, 9–10, 14, 15, 17, 19, 21, 23 (*see also* brant, eagle-headed); Canada, 125, 187, 190, 191; Canada, at Miles, 69, 70, 72, 78, 83, 84, 90, 92; giant Canada, 184, 186–187, 191; lesser Canada, 184, 192; lesser snow, 17; long-neck, 19; at Miles, 68, 69, 84, 87, 88, 89, 91; snow, 18, 41, 49, 81; snow, at Alkali Lake, 183, 184, 187, 191, 192; snow, at Rainey, 10, 14, 18–19, 21, 23 (*see also* brant, eagle-headed); white-fronted, 15, 149, 187

goshawk, 70, 72, 73, 86, 160

grackle, 83; boat-tailed, 26, 31–32; common, 211

Graham, Frank, Jr., 97

Grantham, Jesse, 32

grassland, native, 37

grebe: horned, 130; least, 147, 148, 149; pied-billed, 149

Green Island Sanctuary, 25, 31, 32

Grimes, Charlie, 199, 200, 231

Grinnell, George Bird, xiii

Griscom, Ludlow, xiii

grosbeak, 20; evening, 77, 91; pine, 77; rose-breasted, 88

grouse, sharp-tailed, 179, 180, 187, 190, 191

gull, 53, 221, 229; laughing, 236, 241

Gurung, Chandra, 47

gyrfalcon, 88

hackberry tree, 148

Hall, David, 18

Hall, Russ, 199

Hamel, Paul, 204

Hamilton, Frank, 15

Hanson, Harold, 186

Harper, Jack, 198

harrier, northern, 192

Harris, Joe, 227, 228–229

hawk, 114, 116, 191; broadwing, 125, 147, 192; chicken, 160; Cooper's, 72,

73, 86, 160; duck, 125, 130, 149, 234, 236; ferruginous, 190; Harris, 22; red-shouldered, 72, 73, 82, 160, 211; red-tailed, 70, 89, 180, 190; rough-legged, 187; sharp-shinned, 18, 86, 187; short-tailed, 140; sparrow, 76, 90, 191; Swainson's, 147, 190; white-tailed, 180

Heffern, Dan, 150

Henderson, Dave, 159

heron, 9, 56, 65, 226, 229; great blue, 228; great blue, at Sydnes Island, 99, 100, 106, 107; great white, 235–236; green, 13, 57, 65, 66, 125, 140; little blue, 26, 27, 31, 32, 57, 59, 140, 210; little blue, at Sydnes Island, 96, 99, 100, 102, 104, 106; little green, 59, 61; Louisiana, 26, 27, 31, 32, 57, 59, 63–66 *passim,* 96, 97, 99, 100, 102–106 *passim;* tri-colored, 140; yellow-crowned night, 18, 140, 206, 208, 209, 211, 212, 228. *See also* heron, black-crowned night; heron, great blue

heron, black-crowned night: at Corkscrew Swamp, 140; at Green Island, 27, 31, 32; at Sydnes Island, 96, 97, 99, 100, 102–106 *passim,* 140; at Vingt-et-Une, 57, 59, 60, 62, 64

heron, great blue: at Corkscrew Swamp, 140; at Green Island, 26, 27, 28, 32, 33; at Miles, 84; at Tampa Bay, 236; at Vingt-et-Une, 57, 58–59, 61–66 *passim*

Heth, Scott, 80

Higginson, Jim, 75

Hoffman, Robert, xvi

Horton, Tom, 171

Hosea, 193

Housatonic Audubon Society, 74

Houston Audubon Society, 60, 67, 97

Hudson River Fishermen's Association: and Constitution Island

Marsh, 120, 122, 123; and pollution, 109, 110, 114, 116, 124, 126
Hudson River Foundation, 120, 123, 124
hummingbird, 128, 148; buff-bellied, 147; ruby-throated, 211
Hurricanes, 20, 65, 90, 204, 218, 221
Hussey, Bill, 202–206 *passim,* 208
hyacinth, water, 141
Hypoxylon fungus, 208

ibis, 12, 226, 229; dark, 12; glossy, 21–22, 29, 144; light, 12; white, 21, 27, 31, 32, 140, 241; white, at Sydnes, 97–100 *passim,* 103–106 *passim;* white, at Tampa Bay, 226, 228, 237, 239; white, at Vingt-et-Une, 57, 62, 65, 66; white-faced, 21–22, 29, 31, 32; white-faced, at Sydnes Island, 96, 99, 100, 101, 104, 106

Jack Smith Bird Walk, 158
jaeger, parasitic, 236
jaguarundi, 147
James, Gary, 103
jay: blue, 147; scrub, 168
Jaycox, Jesse, 127
Java plum, 141
Jensen, Paul, 178–181
Joanen, Ted, 2, 14
Johanssen, Krisa, 170
Johnson, Franny, 130
Johnson, Lowell, 130
junco, Oregon, 168, 170
Juneberry, 180

Kahl, Phil, 97
Karlsson, Sture, 43
Kelchin, Eric, 90
Keney, Peggy, 15
Kentucky bluegrass, 181
Kershner, Marilyn, 239
kestrel, 77, 90. *See also* hawk, sparrow
King, Kirke, 64

kingbird, 13, 17, 19; eastern, 17
kingfisher, 87, 88, 125; ringed, 147
Kirsch, Leo, 181–183, 186, 196
kiskadee, 147
kite: Everglade (snail kite), xi, 140, 143–145; swallow-tailed, 15, 140; white-tailed, 119, 155, 159, 160
Kiviat, Eric, 114
Klataske, Ron, 35, 36, 37, 41, 42, 48
Klemens, Mike, 75
Kniffin, Chuck, 230
Knoder, Gene, 10–11, 190
Knoop, Paul, 42
Koehler, Paul, 219, 224
Koerner, John, xvi
kop-kop (green heron), 19, 22, 61. *See also* heron, green
Kraft, Kathy, 191
Kress, Stephen W. "Steve," xvii, 51–55
Kuhl, Dave, 127, 141
Kuhl, Kay, 141
Kuspit, Ivy, 216

Laguna Hills Audubon Society, 167
Lapland longspur, 184
lark, horned, 86
Larson, John, 25
Lavoie, Marie, 208
Laycock, George, 11
leafy spurge, 182, 196
Legé, Barry "Chop," 144–145
Legé, Berton, 2–22, 46, 119, 135; mentioned, 74, 81, 90, 101, 118, 144
Legé, Lonnie, 1–23, 46, 119, 164; mentioned, 74, 81, 90, 101, 118, 144, 150, 189
Legé, Margaret, 13, 20
Legé, Patrick, 4
Legé, Pierre, 6
Legé, Ricky, 4
Legé, Terry, 4
Legé, Valla, 4, 20, 22, 23
Legé brothers, 164, 204. *See also* Legé, Berton; Legé, Lonnie

Legé Island, 3, 4, 46
LeMaire, Ray, 18
Leopold, Aldo, xvi, 74, 84, 175
Lillian Annette Rowe Sanctuary. See
    Rowe Sanctuary
limpkin, 140
Lind, Eric, 128, 129, 133
Linduska, Joe, 71, 123
Line, Les, 124
Line, Lois, 124
Line, Mike, 203
lizard, eastern fence, 128
Logan, Tom, 35, 37, 199
Ludwig, Shannon, 141
Lugo, Guillermo, 11
Luna Barbour, Carmen, 184–187, 189–
    192, 196
Lydia Ann Island, 25

MacKenzie, Michelle, 213
Mackie, Andrew, 140
MacNamara, Carole, 215
Madson, Dycie, 123
Madson, John, 123
Madson, Rich, 171, 176, 179, 181
magpie, 187; black-billed, 187
Majetich, Steve, 85
Malik, Mumatz, 45, 48
mallard, 185, 188, 189; at Alkali Lake,
    181, 184, 187, 192; and Constitution
    Island Marsh, 123, 125; at Miles, 69,
    70, 88, 90
manatee, 234, 236
mangrove, 236, 239; red, 232
Manigault, Patty, 222
Manigault, Peter, 222
margay cat, 147
Marion, Francis, 197
Marrs, Mrs. Kingsmill, xiv
Marshall, William "Bill," 115, 117
martin, 6; purple, 10, 191
Mattei, Laura, 217
Maurice, Kevin, 87–88

McCaull, John, 172
McCollum, Jeanne, 221
McCrimmon, Don, 114
McHenry, Steve, 127, 186
McIntosh, Beverly, 155
McIntosh, Michael, 124
McIntosh, Norm, 153–157, 160
McIntosh, Robert, 156
McKenzie, Carl, 164
Meadows, Don, 164
Medcalf, Ross, 46
Meeks, Robert L., xvi
melaleuca, 60, 141
Melazzo, Chris, 128
Mellards Lake, 208, 214, 222
Meng, Heinz, 77
menhaden, 21, 29, 61
merganser, hooded, 191, 195, 207; at
    Miles 70, 78, 81, 83, 84, 86, 89–92
    passim
Mervis, Sandra, 74. See also De-
    Simone, Sandra "Sandy" Mervis
Merwin, Amanda, 91
Mescher, William, 209
Midstate Reclamation Project, 34, 35,
    37, 48
Miles, Corey, 68
Miles, Emily Winthrop, 68, 78
milkberry, David's, 147
Mills, Herbert, 225
milo seed, 47
Mim, Mrs. Tom, 216
mink, 70, 88, 192
Miss Nancy, 152, 164; at Constitution
    Island Marsh, 112, 117; at Miles, 89;
    and Norm Brunswig, 212, 224. See
    also Anderson, Mrs. John M. "Miss
    Nancy"
Moeller, Bob, 70, 72
Mones, Wayne, 171, 239
Moore, Dan, 15
moorhen, common (common galli-
    nule), 149

Morrison, Mike, 98, 99, 100
Morse, Carol, 220, 221
Morton, Duryea, 178
mountain lion: at Starr Ranch, 155, 158, 161, 162, 166, 168, 170, 172. *See also* cougar
mouse: deer, 90; white-footed, 86, 90
Munroe, Kirk, xiv
Murray, Judi, 88, 89
muskrat: at Constitution Island Marsh, 123; at Rainey, 6, 14, 18, 19, 21
musk thistle, 40

Nagel, Hal, 41, 47
National Audubon Society, x, 36, 56, 114, 117, 223; aims of, xiv, xv; Development Department of, 147; Ecosystems Research Unit of, 209; El Dorado Chapter of, 155; Enpro Chapter of, 175, 178; intern program of, 82, 141–142; Jamestown Chapter of, 176; Research Department of, 26, 80, 143; sanctuaries of, 28, 34, 113, 130, 134, 146, 153, 197, 225, 244; sanctuary program of, 80, 112, 136, 243–244; Tour Division of, 229. *See also* Florida Audubon Society; Housatonic Audubon Society; Houston Audubon Society; Laguna Hills Audubon Society; Nebraska Audubon Society; Omaha Audubon Society; Pomona Audubon Society; Sabine Audubon Society; Sawmill River Audubon Society; Sea and Sage Audubon Society; South Coast Audubon Society; Whittier Audubon Society
Nebraska Audubon Society, 36, 49
Nina G. Washburn Sanctuary, 226
Northern Prairie Wildlife Research Station, 178, 184, 185
Northshield, "Shad," 104

nuthatcher: red-breasted, 77, 81, 91; white-breasted, 210
nutria, 14, 18, 19, 60

O'Brien, Donal, 123, 130
O'Brien, Kate, 130
O'Brien, Lois, 150
ocelot, 147
Ogden, John, 96, 161, 184
Ogden, Mary Ann, 161
Old Dad, 2, 5, 157; at Alkali Lake, 178, 181, 186; and Bailey, Susan, 97; and Bauer, Joe, 105; and Beidler Forest, 198, 206, 217; at Constitution Island Marsh, 112, 117; and Corkscrew Swamp, 137; and Fluman, Friday, 30, 32; and Froke, Jeff, 159; and Froke, Martha, 165; and Green Island, 26; at Ichuway Plantation, 218; and Kress, Steve, 52; and Legé, Lonnie, 7–8, 22; at Miles, 68–71, 75, 77, 80, 82, 84, 92, 166, 172; and Pearson, Gary, 176; and Rainey, 20; and Rod, Jim, 131; and Swenson, Myron, 176; at Sydnes Island, 103; at Tampa Bay, 235; mentioned, 16, 22, 35, 37, 120, 124, 147, 150, 152, 158, 217, 224, 229, 230, 231. *See also* Anderson, John M.
Olsen, Craig, 214
Omaha Audubon Society, 40
orchid, 206
oriole, Alta Mira, 147; Baltimore (northern), 140; orchard, 13, 19
Ortiz, Ernest, 32, 98, 146, 148, 149, 150, 164
Osburn, Hal, 97
osprey, 89; at Constitution Island Marsh, 109, 125, 130
otter, 122; at Miles, 68, 70, 81, 83, 85, 86, 88; at Vingt-et-Une, 61, 62, 63
ovenbird, 88, 91, 166
Owens, Phil, 135

owl, 75, 160; barn, 13, 20, 77, 160, 168;
barred, 72, 73, 135, 202, 211; great
horned, 28, 72, 77, 83, 149, 155,
160, 178; saw-whet, 86, 88, 89, 195;
screech, 78, 86, 88, 191; snowy, 125;
spotted, 159
oystercatcher, 65, 66, 234, 241, 242

Pacetti, P. J., 227
Palmer, Chris, 43
Palmer, Jim, 33
Palmer's bloodleaf, 147
Panicum, 181
panther, Florida, 140
parasitic jaeger, 236
parrot, 149
Partelow, Janet, 76
partridge, gray, 190, 191
Partridge, Karen, 101
pasque flower: at Alkali Lake, 175, 178,
180, 187
Paul, Rich, 3, 17, 29–30, 96, 234–242
Paul J. Rainey Sanctuary. *See* Rainey
Sanctuary, Paul J.
Paulson, Glen, 43, 48, 120, 234
Payne, Emily, 143
Pax, Jimmy, 33, 152
Pearson, Gary, 171, 176–177, 179–181
Pearson, T. Gilbert, xiii, xv, 158
pelican, 35; brown, xi, 226, 227, 229,
233–236 *passim*, 237, 241; white, 28,
29, 63, 106, 180
Pelson, Jane, 123, 216
Pembleton, Ed, 44
Pembleton, Sil, 42, 44
peregrine falcons (duck hawks), 125,
130, 149, 234, 236
Perry, Bubba, 19, 21, 22
Peterka, John, 179
Peterson, Lillian, 11
Peterson, Roger Tory, 51, 119, 174,
244; at Beidler Forest, 203; field
guides of, 126; at Sydnes Island, 99,
107

Peterson, Russell, 11
pewee: eastern wood, 91; wood, 88
pheasant, 191; ring-necked, 180, 190
phoebe, 84, 88; black, 161; Say's, 192
Picard, Cecil, 18
Pilz, Kevin, 172
pintail, 123, 149, 185, 188; at Alkali
Lake, 178, 181, 184
Piper, Lori, 141
Platte River, 35, 37, 39–43 *passim*, 45–
48 *passim*
plover: piping, 41, 43, 46; golden, 187
Plunkett, Dick, 42
Pomona Audubon Society, 167
Porter, George, 204, 228
Portnoy, John, 97
possum, 122
Postupulski, Pete, 171
Poteau, Lynne, 216
Price, John, 200
puffin: at Maine Coastal Islands, 51–55;
at Todd, 117
Pulsipher, Jack, 226, 227–228
Putnam, Emmet, 22

quail, California, 161

rabbit, 191
raccoon, 28, 30, 185, 226
racer, speckled, 147
rail: clapper, 107, 232; Virginia, 41, 125,
126; yellow, 17, 187
Rainey, Matt, 17
Rainey, Patty, 17
Rainey, Paul J., 1, 16
Rainey, Roy, 17
Rainey, Sam Plum, 17
Rainey Sanctuary, Paul J., xv, 16, 61,
137, 155, 183
Rainwater Basin, 46
rattlesnake, 70; canebrake, 198; dia-
mond-back, 236; timber, 70, 92
raven, 84, 88, 89; white-necked, 152
Rea, Bart, 23, 42

Rea, Liz, 23
Reader's Digest, 113, 123, 131; Foundation, 108
Redfish Reef, 62
redhead, 30, 177, 181, 184, 185
Redmond, Mike, 72
redpoll, 86, 88, 125
redstart, American, 91, 209
red tide, 226–227
reduvid bug, 207
Reed, Jay, 159
regal fritillary, 41, 43, 47, 49
Reid, Ogden, 109, 110
Reitherman, Bruce, 43
Research Ranch Sanctuary, 47, 167
Rhindress, Dick, 71
rigolet, 16
Riley, Beverly, 201
Riley, Bill, 43
ringtailed cat, 159
Riseborough, Bob, 163
Roach, Michael, 196
roadrunner, 168
robin, 83, 97
Robinson, Peter, 77
Rod, Dee, 122, 124
Rod, Doug, 111–112
Rod, Jim, 35, 198, 211; at Constitution Island Marsh, 111–112, 118–131, 133, 312; at Miles, 70
Rodgers, Jim, 9, 229–234
Rogers, Grace Rainey, 1
Root, Mike, 72, 73, 76, 79, 89, 160
Rose, Bob, 215, 217
Rose, Lenore, 215, 217
roseau cane, 105
Ross, Bill, 130
Ross, Nancy, 130
Rowe, Lillian Annette, 43, 48, 50
Rowe Sanctuary, Lillian Annette, xvii, 36, 37, 38, 39, 41, 47, 48–49
Ruane, Gene, 183
Rumsey, Warren, 84
Ruppert, Alan, 111

Russian olive, 40
Russian thistle (tumbleweed), 192

sabal palm, 146, 148
Sabal Palm Grove, 46, 146, 151, 152, 195
Sabine Audubon Society, 101, 103
Safina, Carl, 21, 77, 80, 87, 120, 173
salt cedar trees (tamarisk), 59, 60, 62, 65
salamander, 75; marbled, 128
Sanctuary Wardens Attack Team. *See* SWAT
sanderling, 41
sandpiper: least, 41; solitary, 87; stilt, 41; upland, 184, 186, 190, 191; white-rumped, 41
Sansom, Andrew, 244
sapsucker, 88; red-breasted, 168
Sawmill River Audubon Society, 119
scaup, lesser (bluebills), 149, 187, 227
Schafer, Edward T., 195
Schnapf, Ann, 239–242
Schultz, Fred, 225, 226
Schulze, Steve, 148–150
Schwartz, Terry, 186
Scotsman, the, 115. *See also* Seymour, David
SCS. *See* US Soil Conservation Service
Sea and Sage Audubon Society, 167, 170, 172, 173
sea oat, 232
seal, harbor, 130
Seitz, Jason, 140
Serrano, Reyes, 164
Setzer, Gene, 119, 122
Seymour, Anne, 111, 117
Seymour, David, 109–118, 119, 126, 131
sharp-faced fowl, 8, 64
Shelton, Agee, 155, 159
Shockey, Barbara, 75
shovler, 149
shrike, northern, 88
shrimp, 21, 62, 64

Silstoff, Greg, 32
Simeroth, Joyce, 75
siskin, pine, 77, 87, 88
Skaggs, Kent, 48, 49, 50
skimmer, 8, 233, 234, 235; black, 27, 28,
    98; black, at Tampa Bay, 230, 231,
    236, 241, 242; black, at Vingt-et-
    Une, 57, 59, 60, 63–67 passim
skink, 207
skunk, 78, 185
Slack, Douglas, 97
Smith, Gene, 22
Smolenski, Andrew Ivanov, 47
snail kite. See kite, Everglade
snake: cat-eyed, 147; coastal patch-
    nosed, 170; coral, 150; green, 41; in-
    digo, 147, 150. See also cottonmouth;
    rattlesnake; water moccasin
Snodgrass, Randy, 36, 91, 171, 172, 197,
    199, 202
Solometo, Lisa, 74
South Coast Audubon Society, 170, 172
sparrow, 60; chipping, 125; fox, 84, 90;
    grasshopper, 172; native, 191; olive,
    147; rufous-crowned, 172; sharp-
    tailed, 180; song, 87, 88, 89, 91;
    swamp, 84, 121
spartina, 231, 232, 234
spoonbill, roseate, xi, 140; at Green Is-
    land, 26, 27, 31, 32, 33; at Rainey, 8, 9,
    21; at Sydnes Island, 96–106 passim;
    at Tampa Bay, 226, 227, 228, 240,
    241; at Vingt-et-Une, 56–66 passim
Sprunt, Alexander, Jr., xv
Sprunt, Alexander, IV, 10, 39, 63, 71,
    106, 120, 184, 227; at Corkscrew
    Swamp, 134–135; at Rowe, 38; at Sa-
    bal Palm Grove, 147; and Tampa
    Bay, 228; at Vingt-et-Une, 57
Sprunt, Margaret, 200
squawks, yellow-crowned, 209
squirrel: gray, 86; ground, 185; thir-
    teen-lined ground, 192
Stackpole, Steve, 171

Stahr, Elvis, xvi, 35, 43, 119; at Beidler
    Forest, 198, 200, 201; and Constitu-
    tion Island Marsh, 111–112, 120, 122
Stallings, Connie, 201
starling, 60, 86
Starr, Eugene, 153
Starr Ranch Sanctuary, xvii, 154, 155,
    157–158, 162, 166, 167, 168, 171, 195;
    described, 153, 173
Stechert, Randy, 124
Steele, Janet, 88, 89
Sterling College, 93
stilt, black-necked, 17–18, 107
Stokes, Donald, 43
Stone, Ward, 114
stonefly, large, 120
stork, wood, xi, 57, 200, 209, 242; at
    Corkscrew Swamp, 134, 135, 138, 139,
    140
Strom, Ken, 205–208, 210, 217; and
    Rowe, 39–48, 50, 188
Strom, Marie, 39–44, 46, 184
Sunday Morning, 218, 239
swallow: bank, 185, 190; barn, 185; cliff,
    161, 165–166, 184; tree, 70, 81, 84, 90
swan, 184, 191; tundra, 187, 192; whis-
    tling, 180
SWAT (Sanctuary Wardens Attack
    Team), 19, 32, 82, 127, 135, 164, 186
Swenson, Charlotte, 177
Swenson, Myron "High Pockets,"
    176–178
Swift, Bryan, 125
swift, chimney, 211
Sydnes Island Sanctuary, 95, 96, 97,
    102
Szarkowski, Jim, 181

tamarisk. See salt cedar trees
Tampa Tribune, 227, 235, 241
tanager, 20; scarlet, 13, 88, 91; sum-
    mer, 13, 210
Taylor, Carol, 10
Taylor, Roy, 172

teal: blue-winged, 9, 149, 181, 185, 188; cinnamon, 149; green-winged, 123, 149, 181
Tebbel, Paul, 50
tern, 27, 28, 226, 229, 235; Caspian, 28, 230, 231, 233, 234, 242; common, 27, 28, 55; gull-billed, 8, 17; least, at Rainey, 3, 4, 7, 8, 10, 13, 17, 19, 23, 24, 47; least, at Rowe, 41, 43, 46; least, at Tampa Bay, 230, 231, 233, 241, 242; least, at Vingt-et-Une, 61, 62, 63, 64, 66, 67; little, 13, 15, 20; roseate, 55; royal, 27, 233, 234, 236, 240, 242; Sandwich, 27, 28, 233, 234, 236, 240, 242
Texas Parks and Wildlife Department, 29–30, 57, 95
Texas wild olive, 148
thistle: musk, 40; Russian, 192
Thomas, Barbara, 202, 203, 205, 206, 212, 214, 218, 219, 221, 223, 224
Thomas, Benjamin Murray, 218
Thompson, Carl, 119
Thompson, Larry, 200–202
three-cornered grass, 14, 18
thrush: hermit, 87; varied, 159, 165; wood, 88, 89, 91, 211
Tinkham, Peter, 84–85
titmouse, tufted, 207, 210
trout, brown, 128
Tupelo gum, 197, 215, 222
turkey, wild, 212, 215; at Miles, 75, 78, 84, 86, 88, 91
turtle: Blanding's, 114; snapping, 116, 122, 123, 124

Upton, Simon, 22
US Army Corps of Engineers, 58, 64, 102, 213, 217; mentioned, 24, 36, 124, 192, 196, 223; and Tampa Bay, 228, 229, 231, 242
US Bureau of Reclamation, 36, 44, 192, 195, 196; and Platte River, 34, 35, 40, 41

US Coast Guard, 106, 128, 238
US Fish and Wildlife Service (USFWS), 5, 39, 47, 53, 124, 176, 177, 195, 198, 217, 223, 238
US Soil Conservation Service, 192, 195, 196

Van Liefde, Mars, 239
veery, 89, 91, 116
Vermilion Bay, 14
Vincent, Timmy, 21
Vingt-et-Une Islands, 25; sanctuary at, 56–65, 67
vireo: Bell's, 163; black-whiskered, 235; red-eyed, 17, 88, 210; white-eyed, 17, 210, 212; yellow-throated, 17, 88, 91
vulture: black, 138, 236; turkey, 22, 83

warbler: bay-breasted, 13; black-and-white, 91; black-throated, 150; blue-winged, 125; Brewster's, 89; Canada, 87, 118–119; chestnut-sided, 87, 90, 91; fall, 17, 20 70; golden-crowned, 150; golden-winged, 85, 87; hooded, 119, 210; myrtle, 100, 101, 102; orange-crowned, 168, 204; parula, 210; prothonotary, 207, 210; Wilson's, 87; yellow, 91; yellow-throated, 210, 212
Ware Brothers, 201
Washburn Sanctuary, Nina G., 226
water hyacinth, 141
water lily leaf beetle, 120
Waterman Bird Club, Ralph T., 73, 74, 119
water moccasin, 101
waxwings, Bohemian, 187
weasel, long-tailed, 150
Weeks, Carol, 213
Weeks, David, 199
Wertheim, Rebecca, 85
Wesley, Dave, 44
West Point Military Academy, 120, 122, 128, 129

Whidden, Sam, 135
Whipple, Jeannette, 120
Whitaker, Heather, 47, 49
Whitbeck, Gordon, 72
White, Windsor T., xv–xvi
Whitehead, Bernice, 58, 67
Whitehead, Buddy, 8, 56, 101, 104
Whitehead, Dawn, 66
Whitehead, Joe, 57, 67, 70, 77
Whittier Audubon Society, 170
Wibbe, John Herman, 115
Wicht, Bob, 34–39, 48
Wicht, Janet, 37
Wicht, Jason, 37
wigeon, 11, 149, 178, 181
Williams, Tim, 181
Williamson, Charlotte, 171
Winton, Heidi, 203

Winton, Steve, 200
wire grass, 231, 232
woodcock, 48, 82
wood nymph, 41
woodpecker: downy, 92, 210; hairy,
    211; Lewis's, 172; pileated, 88, 91,
    211; red-bellied, 86, 88, 89, 210; red-
    headed, 81
woodrat, 162
wren: cactus, 172; Carolina, 207, 210;
    house, 125, 156, 191; long-billed
    marsh, 113; sedge, 44; short-billed,
    44; winter, 86

Young, Milton, 176

Zagata, Michael, 9
Zern, Ed, 123